Soul Sacrifice

The Santana Story

Simon Leng

FIRE FLY

PUBLISHING

First published in 2000 by Firefly Publishing
Firefly is an imprint of SAF Publishing Ltd. in association with Helter
Skelter Publishing Ltd.

SAF Publishing Ltd.
Unit 7, Shaftesbury Centre,
85 Barlby Road,
London.
W10 6BN

ENGLAND

ISBN 0 946719 29 2

A CIP catalogue record for this book is available from the British Library.

Printed in England by Cromwell Press, Trowbridge, Wiltshire.

For Susan

Acknowledgements

This book is also dedicated to Armando Peraza, one of the greatest musicians of the 20th century and a living example of the dignity and strength to overcome racism and bigotry. Most importantly, Armando Peraza lives like he knows that success is ephemeral but respect for other people is not.

First and foremost my love and thanks go to my wife, Susan, my mother Tina, brother Andy and cousin Mary for all their love and support over the years. "Un abrazo" goes to all my Baptista relatives... as the man says, "baila la portuguesa"! Special thanks to Edward, Margaret and all the Nugents in Ireland.

Many people have helped me in various ways with this book including: Laurie Fahy, Garry Clarke, Stuart Shields ("mi hermano de alma"), Steve Farrar, Frank & Sandra in Dublin, Armando & Josephine Peraza, Alex Pertout, Eddie Rodriguez, the Soul Brother, Jonathan Hill, Stewart Tray, Gaynor Clements, Tom Coster, Bob Greenfield, Mrs Olga Brown, David Brown, Leon Patillo, Jill Strohecker, Jules Broussard, Airto Moreira and Steve Smith. Thanks to you all.

I owe a debt of gratitude to Carlos Santana for the time I spent at his concerts, rehearsals and his home. I thank him for his personal kindness and generosity.

Sources

This book is the result of many years' research and my past involvement as editor of a Santana magazine. This has furnished me with interviews I have conducted or other source interviews with: Carlos Santana, Gregg Rolie, David Brown, Michael Shrieve, Armando Peraza, Tom Coster, Leon Patillo, Jules Broussard, Jorge Santana, Greg Walker, Raul Rekow, Karl Perazzo, Alex Ligertwood, Airto Moreira, Tony Lindsay, Billy Johnson, Myron Dove, Narada Michael Walden, Steve Smith and Chester Thompson. A number of these interviews were conducted specifically for this book.

Other than this, the main sources for details of Carlos Santana's early life in Autlán and Tijuana were "A Portrait Of The Artist" in *Billboard* magazine, published on 7th Dec 1996, the *Rolling Stone* article "The Resurrection of Carlos Santana", published 7th December 1972 and the chapter on Carlos Santana in the BBC Publications book *Guitar Greats*, published in 1982. Another source of information was the 1992 American radio documentary, "Carlos Santana - Music For Life".

Preface

Mexicans rarely buy concert tickets in advance. They turn up and pay. For once, they were to break the habit of generations as thousands of tickets for a special show were snapped up well before the day. It was 21st March 1992 and the border city of Tijuana, the place that Mother Teresa observed had more poverty than Calcutta, was preparing to welcome home its most famous son, Carlos Santana. He left there in 1963 for a new life in the USA when it was easy to cross the border. Now the border is a festering sore.

Tijuana's bullring is found by the sea, a stone's throw from the beautiful beaches which are an antidote to the harshness of the city streets. Now the place was packed with 17,000 people, some Americans from over the border, but mostly Mexicans out to celebrate being Mexican with the world's most famous Mexican.

When the skinny guitarist emerged into the cauldron of noise and colour that afternoon, even as a veteran of more than two and a half thousand concerts in every corner of the globe, he looked stunned by the sheer tumult that greeted him. The fans were everywhere, pressed in and very close, the noise bouncing around the circular bull-ring, creating a cacophony of sound.

The noise increased as the guitar man took the microphone and addressed the people in Spanish. He told them that he was honoured to be in *their* presence and suggested that as the wall had come down in Berlin, the same could happen in Tijuana. As the cheers momentarily subsided, he announced that there were angels amongst them, that they are surrounded by them, dancing in the flesh. This set off the driving funk rhythm of a song, "Spirits Dancing In The Flesh", which delivered Afro-Cuban percussion, jazz solos and Sly

Stone chants in five minutes of sensual ecstasy. It triggered wild dancing. Santana moved to the front of the stage to deliver his first solo and his passion welled up through the strings of the guitar. A woman in the crowd seemed to be hypnotised by the sensual-spiritual power of the guitar, an involuntary smile illuminated her face as her body shuddered in time with each note. The sound was enormous, propelled to supersonic proportions by three drummers, gospel-style Hammond organ and a thumping bass riff.

Three hours of passion later, the show is over and the people of Tijuana and California go their separate ways, to their separate lives. Rich and poor. Believers and cynics. One thing that is not in doubt is that the return of the kid who used to ply his trade on the Tijuana streets playing Mariachi violin for tourists, or R&B guitar behind strippers in cut-throat prostitute bars, was a celebration in itself.

Introduction

An American of Mexican descent might call himself a "Chicano". He'd probably talk about "La Raza", the race, the people, the tribe. He'd mean Mexicans. The "Calendario De La Raza" is produced by La Raza Studies Department at San Francisco State University. Amongst the calendar's many interesting images is one called "Last Supper of Chicano Heroes", a mural which can be found at Casa Zapata, Stanford University in Palo Alto, to the south of San Francisco. The figures portrayed on the mural include the patron Saint of Mexico, the Virgin of Guadelupe, and many well-known political figures such as Ché Guevara, Pancho Villa, Emilio Zapata, César Chavez, Martin Luther King and Rigoberta Menchú. Right in the middle of the second row, amongst all these freedom fighters, there's a long-haired figure holding a guitar; Carlos Santana. How does a mere musician find himself in such exalted company?

Soul Sacrifice aims to answer that question and to put the story of Santana, both the man and the band into some kind of perspective. Santana was a true band for only a few years before it became Carlos' musical tool, but in those few years the signature sound of the group was defined, through the magical chemistry of true group dynamics.

The Santana story starts in Mexico, comes to fruition in San Francisco and reaches maturity in the concert halls of the entire planet. Mexico is where Carlos Santana learnt violin the traditional way, then discovered the blues and learnt it first hand from black American musicians. San Francisco was where he met singer-organist Gregg Rolie in the midst of a musical revolution which was being stoked by a local promoter, Bill Graham. Graham's

7

shows included everything and rejected nothing, through a musical eclecticism that seemed to prophesy the arrival of Santana.

The "Santana Sound" was created by six very diverse musicians who fell together in May 1969: Carlos Santana, Gregg Rolie, Michael Shrieve, David Brown, José "Chepito" Areas and Michael Carabello. The signature sound was a soup of guitar, Hammond organ, Afro-Cuban percussion, pumping bass and rocking, jazz drumming. The music was an astonishing fusion of blues, rock, Latin, jazz and soul. The sound and the band shot to literally instant fame, fortune and inevitable ruin in a three year run that saw them record one true classic, *Abraxas*, and do more to popularise the art of Afro-Cuban ("Latin") music around the globe than anybody before or since.

The 1969 incarnation of Santana was a true band, but Carlos soon had other ideas. The "rock'n'roll life" almost finished him off as it had done so many others, but he was too proud for that. Instead he took control and led the band on a journey through John Coltrane and Miles Davis to a new form of Latin-Jazz. In this quest he was guided by drummer Shrieve and master musicians Tom Coster and Armando Peraza. Santana, the band, came to rival Weather Report and Return To Forever, whilst the guitarist was feted by many of the leading jazz stars of the day for his work on the classic albums, *Caravanserai*, *Welcome* and *Lotus*. It was an audacious triumph.

Since 1974 Santana has been a backing band for Carlos Santana who, despite the occasional commercial blind alley, has successfully taken the Santana sound around the globe. Along the way, he has expanded its musical language to encompass reggae, funk, gospel, African and Brazilian influences with his new musical partner, Chester Thompson.

The focus of the group has always been Santana's unique guitar sound which, through being a cross between Mexican and blues inflections, coupled with jazz and rock overtones, has a universal quality which sits well with almost any musical idiom. Very few musicians could play naturally and in perfect harmony with such diverse artists as Wayne Shorter, Metallica, John Lee Hooker, Prince, Tramaine Hawkins, Bobby Womack, Third World, Salif Keita and Lauryn Hill. Carlos Santana can.

The other side of harmony is contradiction and contradictions abound in Santana's story. For one thing the group has rarely, if ever, been fashionable or critically acclaimed, but has nevertheless sustained a world-wide following for three decades. Another contradiction is the mixture of spirituality and sensuality that appears to characterise the Santana sound and yet another is the juxtaposition of experimental jazz-inclined music with some truly banal pop music that Santana made in the late 1970s and through the 1980s.

Perhaps the greatest contradiction is that Santana has rarely been a rock band. A visitor to any major music shop will find Santana's recordings in the "rock" section and he is generally referred to as a "rock musician". If that same music shop visitor were to listen to a representative sample of Santana's music, they will discover that the majority has little in common with rock, aside from the volume it's played at! Indeed, even though Santana emerged from San Francisco in the late 1960s and appeared at Woodstock, they were never a "hippie" band and had more in common with Sly Stone than Jefferson Airplane.

But, it is the sense of the spiritual that has caused Santana most difficulties with the popular media. Carlos Santana is a spiritual man - hardly surprising for a Mexican. It is natural for him to portray his strong sense of the spiritual through his music and it's a characteristic that his music shares with most indigenous music around the globe. In the society that Carlos Santana was raised, spirituality was as much a part of daily life as eating, so, it is natural for him to express this through his music and is part of what makes him a unique musician and one respected around the world. Clearly, a man who adapted traditional Mexican violin technique to the guitar and developed from a blues player to a guitarist who rubs shoulders with jazz greats like Alice Coltrane, McCoy Tyner, Herbie Hancock and Wayne Shorter is an exceptional artist. But, above and beyond this, it is Carlos Santana's unique ability to communicate directly with an audience that has secured his survival in the fickle world of popular music.

Soul Sacrifice is about a great band, an extraordinary musician and one of music's great survivors. It is also about a genuine Third World hero, the Carlos Santana of the "Calendario De La Raza". He is a true positive role-model for Latin Americans, amongst whom he is widely respected and as well known as, say, Bob Dylan is in the USA. Even though Carlos Santana alone was not the architect of the Santana sound, he has taken the concept around the globe for the last thirty years, keeping it alive and celebrating it. So, it is appropriate that this history of Santana begins in the heart of Mexico.

Chapter 1

Mexico is a musical pin-cushion; it has been peppered by musical influences from around the globe, from Europe, Africa, Cuba and America. Aside from "La Bamba", little remains of the music of pre-Columbian times and Mexico is more of a receiver than giver of musical styles though uniquely adaptable and open to new music where it is often fused into new, local idioms. Music is everywhere in Mexico, ranging from the municipal bands that perform on civic occasions to military bands that play popular tunes as well as marches. There are semi-professional performers who play popular street music at weddings and baptisms whilst radio and television introduce new commercial sounds from the United States or other Latin American countries. In Mexico music is taken very seriously, it's a natural part of the rhythm of life.

The traditional music of Mexico originates from two sources, Europe and Cuba. The European tradition is found in the widespread popularity of waltzes, polkas and light orchestral music whilst the quintessential Cuban song form, the son, swept through Mexico giving birth to local variations.

The state of Jalisco in central Mexico is well known for its musical traditions. The *huapango* style originated here, a form of music that retained the last vestiges of indigenous Indian elements and which is known around the world through the aforementioned song "La Bamba"- a genuine piece of Mexican folklore.

However, the one form of music that reigns supreme in Jalisco is the son, where it became known as the *son Mariachi* because it was played at weddings. The Mexican son is dance music for flirting. It is uplifting music with a strong, driving rhythm - some set in a fast waltz tempo - embellished with dazzling instrumental passages played on the violin. Harmonically it is simple: the guitars resonating to chord patterns originating from flamenco traditions. On top of the rhythm two voices soar: the singer and the violin. Most *sones* are characterised by an introductory passage from the violin, stating the melody with a few tangential flourishes. Throughout the son the violin maintains a voice, seeming to add a musical commentary to the tales of love, loss and money. The son Mariachi violin player requires plenty of skill to find as much "duende" (soul) as possible in the sad melodies, he very seldom plays with great speed, the focus is on putting as much expression as possible into the note.

In the 1920s, in search of work, groups of Jalisco musicians arrived in Mexico City where they naturally became known as Mariachi bands. Relative calm had descended on Mexico after the previous ten years of civil war, which only ended after the peasant revolution was secured by the election of Alvaro Obregón in 1920. Life for rural peasants in the preceding forty years had been awful, their land and liberty had been appropriated by the State, circumstances which saw the emergence of revolutionary leaders like Pancho Villa, Pascual Orozco and Emiliano Zapata. It wasn't until the 1930s that land reform came about and the basic infrastructure was developed: education, irrigation and better wages. As comparative peace took hold in Mexico the musicians from Jalisco would gather in the capital city, congregating in the Plaza Garibaldi dressed in a distinctive cowboy costume called "charro", playing their sones for tourists. Some supplemented the basic two guitars and violin formation with a trumpet, others kept the tradition of the violin as the featured solo voice.

Travelling was a part of life for the Mexican street musician and it was a tradition that José Santana was born into on 18th January 1913 in the spa town of Cuautla in the state of Morelos. Cuautla lies directly south of Mexico City, some four hundred miles east of Autlán de Navarro in the state of Jalisco where José moved as a child. José's father, Antonino, was a musician too, he played French horn in the municipal band and taught José the violin, another of the orchestral instruments that reached Mexico as a part of the European cultural invasion. The boy made rapid progress and by the time he was in his teens he was playing in a local symphony orchestra which he eventually went on to lead; José was already an accomplished and respected musician when he married Josefina Barragan in 1940. The couple had seven children: Antonio, Laura, Irma, Carlos, Leticia, Jorge and Maria; their middle son, Carlos, was born on 20th July 1947.

In the late 1940s Autlán de Navarro was an agricultural community with few of the basic infrastructure comforts that people in Mexico City took for granted. The people there lived a simple, peasant lifestyle in tune with the rhythms of nature in the sub-tropical climate. As he approached his fiftieth birthday, Carlos Santana recalled a return visit he made to Autlán in 1983, "The village is still the same, there's no fences, no paved roads, no electric lights. There's a few places where they have electricity but it's still a place in another century. Simple and beautiful and unpolluted outland, kind of moun-tainous."[1]

José Santana was well known in the town. "My memories of there were that everyone loved my Dad," Carlos later recalled. "He was the darling of the town. Everybody wanted my Dad to play for their weddings, baptisms, whatever. My father supported my mom, my four sisters and two brothers in Mexico with his music."[2] The Santana family lived in various houses and, while they were by no means wealthy, Carlos remembers no real hardship other than the struggle for space. "Of the houses we lived in there, there was one that was pretty big. It was a brick house but it was pretty primitive still. It had a lot of rooms, but I didn't have my own room. Since there were seven of us I always had to share."[3] The young Carlos was very much aware of the music his father played and the natural place it had in the rhythm of life in the town. In Autlán, music was an essential accompaniment to life's events, birth, marriage and death. Rather than an entertainment product, it was one of the elements of life and the musician was as necessary as the farmer or the doctor. Music was a profession. The musician played to lift people's spirits and they paid him for doing that. Still, in spite of the cultural dominance of traditional music, it wasn't long before the radio brought Carlos musical influences from beyond his culture: "My father was a street musician and also played local bars and terraces as far as I can remember. It's funny but even though it was 1947 and way down in Mexico, where they play mainly full tempo Mexican music, I can remember hearing Django Reinhardt and things like that."[4]

José Santana found that playing sones was a better way of supporting his extended family than the limited work of the orchestra and he created a band known as Los Cardinales to perform the popular songs of the day, "El Jilguerillo", "El Triste", "El Son De La Negra" and "Cielito Lindo". He was the leader of the group and played the first violin with a rich tone drawing out long, full, fat notes that resonated like a human voice. José put every drop of emotion into every note he played - it was a trait that he was to pass on to his son.

The expressive aspect of the music was one side of a coin that was balanced by its absolute role as the family's means of survival. The struggle to support his family was always uppermost in José's mind. At the time, it was generally known that way to the north of the country, the border town of Tijuana was booming. Just twenty miles from San Diego, the place had become a major tourist centre in the 1920s when prohibition of alcohol in the USA had sent streams of thirsty Americans and Hollywood stars over the border to the sleazy town. At the time the city had barely one thousand inhabitants, but it did have "La Ballena" (The Whale), the longest bar in the world at 170 metres! By the 1950s it was a major tourist centre and plenty of money was to be made playing what was now termed Mariachi music for the "turistas". Josefina Santana was also interested in moving the family to Tijuana, she wanted to emigrate to the USA, having spent many hours watching the American films that would be shown in Autlán. The 1940s and 1950s saw the American film and music industry spread like an extremely effective form of cultural imperialism. All over the world, people saw images of an idealised American lifestyle and hankered after the freedom and material comforts that the films purported to reflect. Josefina had made only one miscalculation, she thought that Tijuana was in the USA.

José Santana took Los Cardinales to Tijuana in 1954 and Josefina followed with the seven children a year later. The move north was a part of a mass migration from rural Mexico to Tijuana which saw the border town's population explode from fewer than 17,000 in 1940 to nearly 60,000 in the 1950s. People got there however they could and it was no different for the Santana family. In order to pay for the 1,000 mile trip, Josefina took all the furniture she owned into the street and sold it. With the proceeds she managed to convince a reluctant taxi driver to take her and her seven children to Tijuana. This was a determination and self-reliance that the young Carlos was to inherit.

Tijuana is like a desert - dry and parched. You can drink ten Corona beers and still be thirsty. The city is filled with strays - people and animals. The local Mexicans look with scorn on the "cholos" who fill the streets with their scams and rip-offs - young Mexican-Americans who don't speak Spanish and live the gang life. People make a living however they can, there are guys who will find you a parking space for ten pesos or, better still, three dollars. For another few bucks, they will halt the traffic so you can reverse out onto the busy road after your visit to the shopping malls. There are fruit sellers, juice sellers, music sellers and, at night, body sellers. It's the kind of place you prefer to pass through rather than reside in. Mexican youngsters go there to work in bars and clubs but soon make tracks for the less seedy climes of Cancún or Puerto Vallarta. Tijuana is too poor, deprived, plagued by unemployment and stricken with corruption. Even the local police official's son could be a drug pusher. The poverty is grinding, inhumane and it generates that most Latin American of contradictions - fierce national pride, living side by side with an equally fierce desire to get to the USA.

The border at Tijuana is a scar, an open wound where people are flung back like pieces of trash from the hope of a better life; the main trunk road from San Diego ends with a slip-road indicated by a massive arrow depicting a "U-turn", the last chance to get back to the States. Carlos Santana made it over the border to the better life, but never forgot the brutality and degradation of the border post. Tijuana caters for tourists, over thirty million a year, many of whom are from the naval base over the border in San Diego. There are the usual shopping malls, duty free shops, cabaret shows, bars and cantinas, but there is also a seedier side to the city – drug smuggling and prostitution are the staples of the shadow economy which gives a menacing undercurrent to the party-time atmosphere of Tijuana at night. The cruel reality of human life is unavoidable in Tijuana. It's a dose of reality. Tijuana has been like this for years and it was the same when Josefina Santana arrived with her seven children, searching for her husband.

After the family had been reunited, they moved into the shanty town area where they tried to set up home for two months in a house that was being built around them. The only firm fixtures were walls and a half-finished roof, there were no doors, windows or furniture and, of course, running water or electricity were beyond expectation. This was to be the closest to real poverty that the Santana family ever experienced and, whilst the children made the best of it as a new adventure, it took a heavy toll on their mother whose determination to make it to the USA became stronger than ever. Eventually, the family moved into a slightly better house in a better part of town and settled down into the routine of life. Carlos continued his schooling and pictures of him as a child reveal a happy, smiling face. He was interested in sport and comics like all his peers, but there was never any doubt that Carlos would be anything other than a musician. It wasn't so much that he discovered music in a blinding revelation, more that it was all around him. José Santana was a sophisticated musician and in addition to the folk music he made his living from, he played the music of Agustín Lara, the legendary Mexican composer who was world-famous for his romantic boleros. He was well versed too in European classical music from his orchestral days and the Santana children were well used to hearing Mozart, Beethoven and Brahms. As the guitarist later put it, "I was brought up on a diet of European classical music but then, when we got to Tijuana, like most teenagers I got bored with that kind of music." He may have grown bored of it temporarily, but the strong melodic qualities of classical music were already imprinted on his musical outlook.

José Santana recognised his son's musical ear at an early age and enrolled him in a local music college which the youngster attended after normal school hours. The first instrument Carlos came into contact with was the clarinet, but there was no empathy between pupil and instrument and the nine-year-old soon rejected his teachers' urgings to practise. The next port of call was obvious, the violin. This worked much better. At school, Carlos followed the teaching method that millions of children around the globe have endured to learn the classical violin. He progressed quickly and as he improved he tackled the violin music of Beethoven and a piece called "The Poet and Peasant Overture". The work of Franz Von Suppé, the music has a folk-like quality introduced by a long passage for solo violin. The melody is touching in a simple way but the violinist must play with feeling, there are no great flourishes of speed or flashy technique, rather the emphasis is on a tender delivery of each note.

Meanwhile, at home, José was grooming his son to be his musical successor and the two would sit down together and study the sones, waltzes and polkas that were the stock in trade of a Mexican musician. In the earliest example of a pattern that was to occur constantly throughout his musical life, the young Carlos was learning music from two cultures on the same instrument. José taught his son the long, flowing melodies of Mexican music. These hours spent with his father were by no means a casual affair, José worked the youngster hard, instilling discipline into those young fingers; as soon as the young man was ready to relax having completed one lesson, his father was ready to get his focus on the next one. Frustrating at the time, it provided Carlos Santana with the tools he would need to survive as a professional musician. One of the pieces this father and son team played was "Jema" featuring a romantic melody played by José with a full tone that sounded like a human cry. José was an accomplished technician and could manipulate the bow so slowly over the strings that the note was drawn almost indefinitely.

The main purpose music served in the Santana household was to bring money into the family. The young Santana made quick progress on the violin, and, by the time he was ten years old, he was accompanying his father on the streets and bars, playing for tourists. At other times he would be out on the streets playing by himself, or with a couple of other youngsters. It was instant economic exchange. He played, the tourists paid. He had a fixed rate per song and his main route was up and down Revolution Avenue, the strip of Tijuana. He'd be out there dressed-up in the "charro", the Mexican Cowboy garb, hustling tourists with his refrain, "Song Mister? 50c a song?". He looked pretty cute and scored more hits than misses. They played what the American tourists wanted to hear, songs like "Las Mañanitas", "La Paloma", "Cielito Lindo", or even that masterpiece of cross-cultural exchange, "Mexicali Rose". In the game of survival on the street the youngster had to be sure that what he played grabbed the attention of the listener. Away from the street, he was also playing music in the church orchestra, where he found that he could gain the attention of young ladies in the congregation by adding a little improvised flourish, or by playing just a little differently from the main melody. It was a technique worth developing.

The bars, on the other hand, were bad news and what Carlos saw when playing in them with his father was not to his taste. Mexico, in the 1950s and 1960s, was not exactly a model of female emancipation and the macho lifestyle of hard-drinking and hard-fighting was the norm. Tijuana attracted party-minded Americans from over the border, and so magnified things a thousand times over. In his mind, the young Carlos came to associate his father's music with drunken violence and a disrespectful, aggressive attitude towards women. There was little respect in the local bars for the musician who was looked upon as a mere hired hand who would play whatever the payer wanted. Sometimes the punters would get José Santana to play the same song all night and he would do it for the money. He had to support his family. The "charro" routine was hardly dignified and the bar scenes of knives, fights and brawls were worse. It all increased Carlos' negative feelings towards his father's music, which were compounded by the lack of opportunity for free expression or improvisation in Mariachi playing - the violinist was meant to stick to the melody, play a few standard lead-in notes for the singer and that was about it. This added to the youthful musician's frustration, "I played simple waltzes and really simple changes. After a while I got tired of it because my father wouldn't let me improvise when I wanted. I would memorise a piece as well as I could and when I tried to play some different notes, my father would stop me."[5]

When he finally became sick of playing in dingy bars, the clash of personalities became inevitable and the time came for Carlos Santana to strike out on his own. So, he plainly told José that he wasn't going to play the Mariachi tunes anymore. Simple as that. He had rebelled. He didn't expect José to take this too well, but apart from a few scathing remarks, nothing more was said. So, Carlos was free, but despite his bravado, he would keep playing the old Mariachi music for the tourists, it never did to look a gift horse in the mouth and it helped to support the family. For all that, his exposure to the violin, which he played well into his late teens, provided him with one of the keys to his future guitar style. Many musical instruments are designed to sound like the human voice and in this endeavour the violin has one big advantage over many others and that's the bow. This device may look innocent enough but it gives the player the power to hold the same note for a long, long time, creating a wistful, crying tone which is used to great effect in Mexican music. The violin player could hold a note almost indefinitely and much longer than if they just plucked it once and let it fade away. In electric guitar terms, the violin has an in-built sustain pedal!

Still, Carlos Santana was a long, long way from amplifiers and sustained notes by the time he became so bored with the violin that he even hated the smell and feel of the instrument. He was far more interested in the sounds of American music that were everywhere in Tijuana. The first defining moment in his musical life came when his mother took him to the main square in Tijuana, La Plaza, to see a young band called The TJs who played this new American music. Carlos' mother's fascination with the USA, which she probably saw as an escape route from the stifling confines of Mexican society, made her aware of this new music coming from over the border. Santana's father termed it "pachuco music". Pachuco, you see, was a barely polite word for a flashy, sharp dresser and American rhythm and blues was definitely pachuco music. Javier Batiz, leader of the TJs, looked every inch the pachuco with his Little Richard hair, leather jacket and drainpipe jeans. Every Sunday at noon this sixteen year old guitar player could be found at La Plaza playing covers of the latest hits of Chuck Berry, Little Richard, Bo Diddley, Freddy and B.B. King, songs like "Watch Your Step", "Rock Me Baby", "Johnny B. Goode", "Who Do You Love" and "Havana Moon".

Javier Batiz was a good guitarist who played basic rock'n'roll licks in a dramatic style, mixing bent blues notes with a Mexican accent. Carlos Santana was enthralled by the sound and power of the electric guitar and the newness of the music, it seemed exciting and a million miles away from his father's boring melodies. He quickly became a dedicated follower of the TJs, watching them whenever they played in the park or at the Club Latino-American where there was a "battle of the bands" most Friday nights. He was completely captivated by the music, the guitar playing and the electricity it generated and he decided that this was what he wanted to do with his life.

Chapter 2

After a few years of stability, the Santana family was on the move again.
Carlos' parents finally made the application for American citizenship and,
when they were successful, the first to go was José. In the early 1960s, he
headed for San Francisco, where there was already a significant Mexican
community clustered around Mission Street and Van Ness. Here was a good
market for him to continue his career as a professional musician and he soon
got started, forming a new group he led at the Latin American Club. Plans
were laid for the rest of the family to follow once José had established himself and soon messages were reaching him that his young violin protégé had
a fascination with electric guitars. His son may have lost interest in the violin
but any musical enthusiasm was worth supporting. So, one day, the young
Carlos Santana awoke to find a large package awaiting him containing a hol-
low-bodied Gibson L5 electric guitar; he was delighted, excited and desperate to get started. There were only minor technical problems to be overcome,
he didn't know that he needed an amplifier, which was just as well as he put
nylon strings on it, instead of the more magnetic metal variety ! As he took
up the guitar, Carlos discovered that his violin training had given him a head
start in mastering the new instrument. He already knew how to hold down
the string and put expression into the note and the frets of the guitar were a
useful guide to playing the right note which the violin did not have. It
seemed easy.

The Santana household constantly resounded to the sounds of music as
Carlos' younger brother Jorge Santana recalled, "Music has always been my
dad's profession, that's how he made his income and that's how he provided

for everybody. Carlos liked the music and then having our size of family with four girls and three boys we always played music, so in that sense no more different than any other family where the kids listen to music but just the fact that we had musicians in the household, we were more exposed to music."

The radio was always on and it picked up the hits of the day which were a mixture of Mexican and American records. The main guitar music of the period was instrumentals played by groups like The Shadows and Santo and Johnny. These were simple tunes that anyone with an ear for music could copy on their own guitar. This is how Carlos started and when the Twist "phenomenon" hit Mexico from the States he had no problems copying the elementary guitar part of "Peppermint Twist", the master-work of Joey Dee and the Starlighters. Likewise the Shadows who, before The Beatles and The Stones, were the guitar band par excellence. They had a massive 1960 hit in Britain with "Apache", which in the US was a hit for a Danish guitar wizard, Jorgen Ingmann. Either way Carlos Santana picked out the tune on the guitar just from hearing it on the radio. It was easy.

Carlos' head was a musical sponge. Already he knew traditional Mexican melodies and the basics of European classical music and, in a house filled with seven children, the radio showered him with the Mexican and Latin American pop music of the day. Soon, he took in the way the guitar was played on these tunes. Some of this was a blatant imitation of the latest trends from the US or England, but the majority were traditional style ballads sung by vocal groups, mostly of two or three male vocalists who had names like Trio Los Panchos. They were accompanied by acoustic guitar played with a very Spanish inflection. One of the most famous was "Sin Ti", a gorgeous, sentimental melody which has a constant commentary from Spanish guitar as a background to the vocalists. A staccato guitar run introduces each section, a picking technique that Carlos Santana would adapt to his own blues style for later use. Another was a later piece, "Y Volveré" from Latin pop crooners Los Angeles Negros, which was based around some sophisticated jazz chords and a dramatic melody which would find a close echo some years later in an equally emotional song, "Europa". The two key features of these songs that left an indelible imprint on Carlos Santana were the rich, romantic melodies, layered with lush vocal harmonies to enhance the effect and the lyrical Spanish guitar flourishes that accompanied many of them.

Of all the music he heard on the radio, Carlos was taken the most by the blues and he tracked new releases by B.B. King, Freddie King, Jimmy Reed,

Bobby Bland, Chuck Berry and Ray Charles, as well as becoming acquainted with the classics of earlier, earthier blues from John Lee Hooker and Lightnin' Hopkins. This was the music of survival, of overcoming terrible adversity while retaining some dignity. Its subject matter was basically the same as that of the Mexican music he grew up with: love, money and drinking.

The attraction of the blues for a guitar player was that it was very easy to master, once the basic chord pattern had been understood, it could be applied in myriad ways. Another attraction was the use of the guitar to annotate the singer's melody with passionate flourishes that sounded like another human voice. As time went by the young Santana would become entranced by the supplicating guitar of B.B. King and the flashy power of Buddy Guy. Carlos had to work out most of the new licks from these records for himself. When he went to see The TJs, the guitar player would turn away from the young Santana's gaze so he wouldn't pick up too many ideas! As the young guitarist got to grips with the blues he discovered another of its hidden secrets – most blues guitar passages are based around a simple five-note scale. The trick was that this scale could be moved up and down the neck depending on the basic key of the song. Most blues and rock guitarists play their whole lives within this blues scale but Santana had something to add to it; he had the scales he'd learnt from his father on the violin and the Spanish guitar scales of Mexican pop songs. It became his signature Mexican-Blues style.

Carlos Santana listened intently to the blues albums he could find in Tijuana, the TJs having suggested to him that he should check out the originals rather than their second-hand interpretations. Here was music that was entirely his own; he wasn't told to listen to it by his parents or his teachers, it was all his. Quickly, he understood the blues players' language – both musically and emotionally. He didn't just hear the music with his ears, he felt it with his heart. It helped form his vision of what music should be.

Things started moving fast for the young Carlos and he was soon a very good guitar player. It wasn't long before his skills were ready to be tested in a band. His first home was with a unit who were in competition with the TJs. They were The Strangers, a five-piece outfit, heavy with no fewer than three guitarists, all of whom were older than Santana, so he had to make do with playing bass on the R&B tunes they covered. They played dances and small gigs and wore a kind of uniform, black trousers with white shirts and a variety of "formal" neckwear! In the manner of most "garage" bands, guitars had to share the tiny amplifiers they could afford. Carlos was very much the junior partner in the band and could be found behind the main line of the three guitars, already holding the instrument high at an angle to his head. Playing the bass was no problem for Carlos, but his violin training had taught him to play quite a few notes, which wasn't really what was wanted from a bass player in those days – consequently, he only stayed a few months and was estranged by The Strangers.

Of course, Carlos wasn't the only young guy in Tijuana who played the blues, there was Javier Batiz too, his original guitar hero, who knew how to deliver a gut-punching blues tirade that turned his younger friend on to B.B. King. Now the younger guitarist was back and he'd mastered King's licks and had a few of his own too. The two musicians started to jam with other local players or the guys from the TJs. Santana already had experienced playing music in bars, so when the chance came to make a regular gig at a club called El Convoy he took it. El Convoy was on the main drag in Tijuana, Revolution Avenue, which they used to call the Broadway of Tijuana. It runs right through the centre of the city, a couple of blocks away from the cathedral of the Virgin of Guadalupe. It's lined with bars, clubs, cinemas and street traders hawking anything they think might sell. At night the bars and joints take on a more sinister feel; once the sun goes down it's the haunt of pimps, pushers and prostitutes. Some revellers would be heading for El Convoy, which was just another of the sleazy, steamy strip joints with a makeshift stage stuck haphazardly in the dimly lit room. Even today, the lucky visitor to one of these basement clubs is bombarded with offers of girls, dope, anything. This was the environment where the teenage Carlos Santana first cut his teeth as a professional musician, knowing that if his playing wasn't hard enough he might end up with a knife across his throat or a bullet in his back. Tijuana was that kind of town.

Carlos came to admire the dignity of the prostitutes who gathered there, knowing full-well that nobody would do *that* for a living unless they were desperate. The musicians played in between the strippers' "performances", one hour on, one hour off starting at four in the afternoon and playing through the night to six in the morning. The young guitar player learnt how to play in sympathy with the pseudo-erotic moves of the strippers and the sexual under-current of the club soon found its way into his playing too. It was during these long sessions that Carlos Santana learnt that the way he played the guitar could have a sensual impact on women, he appeared to undress them musically. It was astonishing and a technique he never forgot. Carlos earned about $9 a week playing at El Convoy. It was big money and much more than his father brought in.

Naturally, bands and line-ups were pretty fluid and Carlos was a part of various loose musical combinations, sometimes playing with the TJs, sometimes on his own. He could either be found at El Convoy or playing for parties and weddings, replicating the American music he loved. Most of it was blues or R&B: "Hully Gully", "Nadine", Ray Charles' legendary "Georgia On My Mind", a funky Freddie King guitar instrumental "Hide Away" and "Green Onions". One of his El Convoy bands also played more soulful pieces like Etta James' "Something's Got A Hold On Me" and the T-Bone Walker classic "Stormy Monday Blues" which they did in the style of singer Bobby Bland – one of the first true sex-symbols of the blues. Carlos particularly liked Bobby Bland whose gospel-power voice and sensual style was a startling mix of the spiritual and the sexual. In between churning out the hits, his time at the Convoy gave the adolescent Carlos a marvellous introduction to a wider spectrum of black music. The clientele of the club included black American musicians down from San Diego or Los Angeles for the weekend, in pursuit of the various temptations on offer in the sleazy town. The musicians would invariably run out of funds so they would make some money to get home by playing the latest blues and R&B hits in the clubs along the Strip. It was Carlos' first exposure to real black music and it was taught to him by real black musicians who liked what he was playing and were prepared to teach the young guy a few new songs and licks. As he recalled, "I used to play with some cats who came from LA to play blues and jazz, Bobby Bland and Ray Charles stuff."[6] This is how he expanded his repertoire of songs from the Freddy King and Jimmy Reed tunes to include more sophisticated music with jazz influences like "Misty", "Summertime" and "I Loves You Porgy". These happy memories, coupled with his fascination with black music, left an indelible imprint both musically and socially on him. From these early experiences in Tijuana he developed a close affinity with black Americans and their music. Even today his musical heroes are largely drawn from the black musicians who led the way in the fields of jazz, blues, R&B, gospel and soul.

By the summer of 1962, the young Santana was pretty happy with his life, he was making money, getting fed, watching strippers and hanging out with Javier Batiz and their girls on 4th Street, or playing in dances in hotels on Saturday nights. His contentment was about to be shattered as his family were ready to move north again and join José in the USA. Carlos Santana was not at all keen to get on the bus out of Tijuana and over the border, he was happy to stay where he was earning his own money through music and running his own life. In fact, he had no intention of going and disappeared from view, hiding from them for days and weeks. When they eventually persuaded him to go, he let his feelings be known in no uncertain terms and brooded for three months. In his short first spell in San Francisco, he naturally started hanging out with musicians his own age and his brother Tony put him on to a guy from a well off family who played music too. Tony had a job at a tortilla maker's known as La Palma and the owner's son had a drum set and a friend who played bass. The drummer was Danny Haro and the bass man Gus Rodrigues. The pair were impressed by the new arrival's guitar skills and went as far as to offer to buy him a new guitar and amplifier if he would hang around in San Francisco rather than go back to Tijuana. It sounded like a good offer, but Carlos wanted, above all, to be his own man, so even a gilt-edged overture like that wasn't enough to keep him in California. At the end of October he returned south with just the money his mother had given him for the bus fare in his pocket.

☯

The bus trip from San Francisco to Tijuana takes hours and hours. By the time the fifteen year old Carlos got back to the border town it was dark and he found himself with less than $20 in his pocket, nowhere to stay and only an ability to play the guitar to help him survive. He had two ports of call in mind to get through the night on the unforgiving Tijuana streets; the Cathedral of the Virgin of Guadalupe and El Convoy. The Virgin of Guadalupe is the patron of the Mexican people. The tradition is that in December 1531 a simple Indian boy, Juan Diego, had a vision of the Virgin Mary who had a message of support for the poor masses. Later, her image with the features of an Indian was found imprinted on the cloak of a Bishop who was sent to verify the story. Carlos was desperate for her help and so he entered the doors of the huge cathedral and made his way to the statue of the Virgin. When he got there he didn't so much pray as set out a requirement for assistance. Apart from an entreaty for his family's protection, he only asked for one thing – that he got a gig that night. Leaving the cathedral, he made his way back to Revolution Avenue and El Convoy. When he presented himself to the owner of the club the businessman was wary, he knew Santana's mother had moved to San Francisco and knew of her formidable reputation. He wasn't sure – the kid was under-age. Santana showed him the letter of permission his mother had sent with him and made his way to the tiny stage, taking over from his own stand-in who was on the way out.

The next problem was where to stay, but Carlos still had friends at the club, "First I stayed with the drummer at this funky hotel his aunt used to own; then we both got thrown out and I started staying with one of my mom's friends back in the old neighbourhood."[7] Not for the first time in his life Carlos Santana's survival was through music, but this was no artistic fancy, it was subsistence, the guitar as a cash crop and if ever there were a way of developing self-reliance, this was it. Nevertheless, he was very happy with his lot and saw no point in joining Javier Batiz who announced his intention of going to Mexico City to make it in the big city. Carlos didn't want to go, he had already made it in Tijuana. He had his own money, nobody told him what to do. Though, for all his grown-up lifestyle, Carlos was still basically a child and he spent his free time at the beautiful beaches around Tijuana, or reading *Mad* and hot-rod magazines as any other teenager would.

Carlos lived this way for over a year until his mother arrived back in Tijuana for one last try at persuading him to move north and took her eldest son Tony with her to add muscle. Carlos tried to hide from them but once they had found him, there was no way back and at the end of 1963, just before the assassination of John F. Kennedy, Carlos Santana found himself heading back to a new life in San Francisco.

Chapter 3

The Santana family finally reached the Mission District of San Francisco in the late summer of 1963 with their reluctant son in tow. Carlos was still in a rebellious mood, he thought of himself as a man of the world at sixteen and was now faced with the prospect of James Lick Junior High. He'd been an adolescent street survivor who played guitar for a living, made his own decisions and ran his life the way he wanted to. Now he was back at school with kids far younger than him and he didn't like it. "On the trip here he was mad," José Santana later recalled, "He did not say a single word during the whole trip. Since the day of his arrival, all he did was cry, cry and cry. He was also always mad. Then he locked himself in his room for a week. During this time he refused to eat."[8] Eventually, Santana's mother had her fill of the moody youngster and presented him with an ultimatum, she would give him the money to return to Tijuana, but this time, she would not be coming back to retrieve him. Carlos embarked on another return trip to Tijuana, but this time something in his head told him that this wasn't a good idea, he looked at the signs of great prosperity that were everywhere to be seen in San Francisco and turned around and went back to the Mission, for good.

Carlos' time in Tijuana had left him completely immersed in black music which was now more natural to him than Mexican songs. In addition to the blues and R&B he'd learnt first hand from visiting musicians and from studying records – sucking in every nuance until he'd claimed them for himself – he also had more than a passing interest in the developing soul scene. He enjoyed The Impressions and Junior Walker but his main man was James

Brown, the boss of soul, who was etching out a new dialect which would, in time, be called funk. In those days, they called it "boogaloo".

As soon as Carlos was back in the Mission, he hooked up again with Danny Haro and Gus Rodrigues reviving their garage jams; by now Santana had mellowed and was prepared to show them some of his authentic blues licks. They played parties, bar mitzvahs and weddings and naturally covered the new James Brown hits, "Papa's Got A Brand New Bag" and "Out Of Sight". Carlos was already able to adapt his style to play with most passing musicians and his years in Mexico had given him a talent way beyond his years, he was already a real musician and not just a college kid who played for fun.

Carlos' next step was to branch out into working on some of the pop-soul hits of the day; he liked female soul singers and hooked up with a vocalist from Sly Stone's hometown of Daly City, Joyce Dunn. The guitarist had no problems blending in with the singer's style, after all, soul had the same musical roots as R&B and he was an accomplished rhythm guitar player – his style heavily influenced by the vibrant, clean sound of the guitar on James Brown's early hits. He had the opportunity to work on his rhythm playing as he, Rodrigues and Haro backed Joyce Dunn on her repertoire of current chart songs. One of her best was "Heatwave", a big summer hit for Martha and the Vandellas, which cracked the charts the same year that Carlos returned to the US for good. She also covered "Steal Away", which had been a hit for Jimmy Hughes back in 1965. These were simple songs and easy to play but also easy to mess up. One false move and they became cabaret. The soul of a song like "Heatwave" would resound through Carlos' career, it had a rising, ecstatic chord pattern that came directly from black Church/Gospel music, a spirit Santana would recall in later tunes like "Right Now" and "Praise".

Even though he was still in high school, 1965 became an important year for Santana musically. A local radio station ran a "battle of the bands" competition and the Santana-Joyce Dunn combo entered and crashed through the early school gym rounds to reach the last three and the final. The deciding round was anything but a high school bash, it was held at San Francisco's massive concert venue, the Cow Palace; this was something to savour for the boy from Tijuana. Just getting there filled him with confidence that he was going to fulfil his destiny and make it. The musicians' spirits were high as they waited hours to go on – hours which they filled by taking liquid refreshment. When their time came they were certainly well refreshed, in fact too well and just a little bit below their best. They blew it. It didn't matter though, Carlos Santana would be back at the Cow Palace and he took great heart from this first exposure to what must have felt like the big time.

The alliance with Joyce Dunn didn't last much longer, but it gave the young guitarist first-hand exposure to the singing style and intonation of a lady soul singer – soon his fascination would extend to genuine soul stars like Aretha Franklin, Dionne Warwick and Patti Labelle. Short-lived as it was, working with Joyce Dunn helped him on the road to delivering on Charles Mingus' demand to "Git It In Your Soul" and, to all intents and purposes, Carlos Santana was a black musician.

As he got back into school life at Mission High, the young soul guitarist found himself in the middle of a unique musical revolution in San Francisco that would eventually send out ripples around the world. It was promoted largely by a Jewish immigrant from Germany, Bill Graham, whose real name was Wolfgang Grajonka. Graham was a survivor. As a young child during the Nazi holocaust he'd walked from Paris to Lisbon to board a boat to freedom in the USA and, after being raised in New York, eventually found himself in San Francisco. He got there in 1963, the same year as Carlos Santana and by a series of twists, turns and deals found himself promoting a left-field theatre group and eventually putting on concerts at an old music hall in the heart of the city called the Fillmore Auditorium. As he staged more and more shows at the Fillmore, Graham became the most powerful promoter in the area and the Auditorium was the home of the "San Francisco Sound". Bands like The Grateful Dead, Jefferson Airplane and Quicksilver Messenger Service made their names at the venue. Graham's special gift was in seeing no barriers to putting on culturally diverse acts on the same bill at the Fillmore. In April 1966 a San Francisco hipster could have seen Jefferson Airplane supported by blues master Lightnin' Hopkins, or in November been tripped out witnessing Buffalo Springfield, Country Joe and the Fish *and* the extraordinary Brazilian guitarist Bola Sete. It was a musical eclecticism that would soon entrance the young Carlos Santana.

By now Santana had long been enrolled at Mission High School but he was hardly the best pupil. Often, he would turn up when they took the register and then disappear. The only class he enjoyed was art – a subject he excelled at. Encouraged by his teacher Mr Knudson he even considered entering art school. At the same time as *not* being at school Santana was working: scrubbing floors, peeling potatoes and washing dishes at the Tic-Toc, a drive-in diner on Third Street. He'd started there in 1964 and the Santana frame of mind was clear and determined. When he was washing dishes he would be the best there was and do the work of two men.

Still, potatoes or no potatoes, Carlos Santana knew what he really wanted to do as he recently recalled, "Before I got out of high school, people would ask, 'What are you going to do when you leave school?' I'd say, 'I'm going to play with Michael Bloomfield and B.B. King.' They thought I was crazy."[9] Santana didn't hang out with the other Chicanos in the Mission, the race driven gangs didn't interest him and reminded him too much of the old machismo of Tijuana. He felt more sophisticated and found his identity in music, not his race. He preferred to hang around with hipsters who knew about Jimmy Reed and B.B. King, people who were tapping into the new openness of the San Francisco scene. Two who fitted this bill were Ron Estrada and Stan Marcum. Marcum's parents owned a clothing store on Mission Street which gave him a comfortable upbringing, but Stan wanted more. He was keen to make a difference through music rather than just conform to the same ordinary life as his friends.

Stan Marcum would be one of the critical figures in Santana's musical story, he was the first to introduce the young guitarist in full to the sounds bubbling up from the Fillmore. Carlos and Marcum went down to the Fillmore regularly in 1966 and the range of music they saw there was panoramic; in the six months from the turn of the year they could have seen Junior Wells, Jimmy Reed, Gabor Szabo, John Lee Hooker, Joe Henderson, Elvin Jones, Bola Sete, Manitas De Plata, Otis Redding and Roland Kirk. The musical influences that were racing into Carlos' consciousness were like rays of sunlight bursting into a room. He was particularly impressed by a collection of mostly white blues players from Chicago who were led by a gifted harp player, Paul Butterfield. The Butterfield Blues Band featured Mike Bloomfield, an extravagantly talented guitarist and they were the first American white blues band who didn't just ape black musicians, they had their own sound and were respected by black blues players. Santana loved this band and Bloomfield was a hero. The Butterfield Blues Band's first album, which emerged in 1965, included interpretations of old blues classics like "Shake Your Moneymaker", but it was the second album *East West* that really created a musical revolution. Bloomfield had a fascination with the sound of Indian music and the title track of the album was an extended guitar jam which virtually invented the vogue for long, jamming guitar solos that would be emulated by the Grateful Dead, Quicksilver Messenger Service, Cream and, of course, Santana.

Butterfield's was the first white American blues band to gain credibility, but across the Atlantic in England, a blues revival was well underway creating its own stream of guitar heroes. The kindergarten for English blues players in the mid-sixties was John Mayall's Bluesbreakers where two significant players first made their names, Eric Clapton and Peter Green. Clapton went on to take the extended jamming style of "East West" to its natural conclusion in Cream but it was the introspective Green who had the bigger impact on Santana, particularly his work "The Supernatural". This shimmering guitar instrumental featured Green's heavily overdriven Gibson Les Paul fashioning a thick, fat, warm tone to intense emotional effect. It sounded like it had its roots in B. B. King but was also taking the blues in a different, more harmonically complex direction as Green used the amplified guitar to sustain long notes. "When he played "The Supernatural" with John Mayall's Bluesbreakers I mean he redefined feedback," Carlos later recalled, "It was more pure than Jimi's, more passionate than Eric's and more celestial than all of these, so I really miss Peter Green. Peter was the one, to me it sounded more like a voice than all the others."[10] Many have suggested that this track is where Carlos Santana derived his guitar style but that doesn't stack up with the evidence, Santana already had the sustain concept, it was a part of his Mexican violin heritage. The Peter Green record helped put it into focus in a blues context.

Santana's love for the blues soon expanded to embrace jazz, as a result of his exposure to the music in the eclectic San Francisco scene. He soon came to hear and admire guitar great Wes Montgomery and bandleader Chico Hamilton, who provided real fuel for his imagination. In the mid-sixties Hamilton led a band that included a mesmerising Hungarian guitar player named Gabor Szabo and a fine conga drummer, Victor Pantoja. For Carlos, Hamilton's most significant piece was "Conquistadores" from an album called *El Chico*, which in retrospect sounds like a template for the Santana Band. It is a loose jam based around a simple but uplifting guitar riff, with a funky, syncopated rhythm propelled by conga (Pantoja) and timbales (Willie Bobo). Over this the guitarist holds court. Carlos was immediately entranced by the sound of Hamilton and Szabo's band and it had an indelible effect on his musical outlook, "The band had no piano player," he later explained. "It was just congas, timbales and drums with Gabor. It sounded unbelievable."[11] Clearly, it was the Hungarian gypsy guitarist, Gabor Szabo, who entranced Santana most. He created a hypnotic, esoteric sound that was clearly defined on his 1966 recording *The Spellbinder* – which included the congas of Victor Pantoja and "Gypsy Queen", a track where Szabo showed off his fast picking technique. He would 'trill' the notes up and down the fretboard, a reflection of his Eastern European roots, an effect that Santana would soon incorporate into his own style. Aside from the influence of Szabo's guitar, Santana played "Conquistadores" live from 1968 and Victor Pantoja would briefly flirt with the band during the troubled autumn of 1971.

Meanwhile, though awash with all the new music he was hearing at the Fillmore in Marcum's company, Carlos was still playing small shows with Haro and Rodrigues. However, he knew that he wouldn't be limited to playing with these two forever and he sensed that something was eventually bound to happen. It did. On October 16, 1966 Marcum and Santana were at the Fillmore to see the Butterfield musicians jamming with Jerry Garcia and Jack Casady. Butterfield didn't show up and all was not well with Bloomfield. He looked out of it, which, by the standards of the day, must have meant *really* out of it. This was Carlos Santana's chance to make his entrance proper into the San Francisco musical revolution and he was itching to get on that stage. However, initially he didn't make a move. Fortunately, Stan Marcum was less reserved and did it for him. He went straight up to Bill Graham, who had the reputation of a concrete eater. Marcum explained that he had a friend... from Tijuana... he loves the blues... 'Can he jam with Bloomfield?' Graham growled, 'Why ask me? Ask Bloomfield.' Within minutes Carlos Santana was stepping up to the stage of the Fillmore swapping licks with one of his heroes. His life was about to change forever.

Chapter 4

Bill Graham was impressed with what he saw of the young guitarist and wanted to know if Carlos had a band. What's more, the promoter wasn't the only person dazzled by the young Mexican's skills that October evening. Word went around the Bay Area that the Chicano had blown Bloomfield away. Another guitar player was in the Fillmore audience that night, a middle class hipster who already had a band. His name was Tom Frazier and he came from the wealthy suburbs to the south of San Francisco. He had a musician friend called Gregg Rolie. When Tom got back to Palo Alto, he told Gregg about the great new guitarist he had seen and set out to search for Santana with a view to getting him to join the band. Frazier started hunting for the young Chicano around the streets of the Mission area, until he eventually tracked his prey down to Tic-Tocs. Santana must have been taken aback by Frazier's enthusiastic greeting and his offer to drive Santana to Palo Alto to meet his friend who was a great singer and organ player, but the approach worked. Carlos was soon on his way through the city to the comfortable surroundings of Palo Alto, just the other side of the Stanford University campus. This meeting of a Chicano street kid and a suburban business student was the kind of unlikely event that only the melting pot of San Francisco in the 1960s could deliver. They were virtually from different worlds, but music was the device that brought them together and broke down the barriers. After the introductions they soon got down to some garage jamming that lasted into the night.

The thing that struck Carlos Santana about Gregg Rolie was that he was a keyboards player, he'd never played with one before and the greater harmonic opportunities that this offered him must have been a revelation. The thing that struck Gregg Rolie about Carlos Santana was that he could really play the guitar and jam in his own style, he wasn't just a copy-cat player, he was a real musician. The musical chemistry was instant but they had the misfortune to attract the attention of the local police, so Santana and Rolie completed their bonding by hiding in a nearby vegetable field.

Gregg Rolie was born just a month before Carlos Santana but his background couldn't have been more different. He was brought up in comfortable circumstances in Seattle, but the family moved to California when he was seven. Like Carlos he took formal music lessons as a child, in his case on the piano, but he was also a good singer, a combination of skills that he used in a number of high school bands. Later he gathered some experience by playing and recording in a Top 40 band, William Penn and his Pals, who found work easily in the Bay Area. It meant hamming it up in cabaret garb, cranking out versions of Top 40 hits, but it was experience and soon he was a fine keyboard player in possession of a strong, soulful voice. His main musical interest was in white rock and he listened to The Beatles, Spencer Davis and The Stones, it was just the kind of contrast that was needed to the Santana blues fixation. Nevertheless, Rolie's organ style was heavily influenced by jazz man Jimmy Smith, a bridge to Santana's black music fascination.

In fact, the idea to start a new band came from Tom Frazier as Rolie noted, "The rhythm guitarist actually formed the group, but he was kicked out for not being serious."[12] The process of getting a new band together started and when they came to decide on a name, it was obvious, it would have to be a homage to Butterfield and Bloomfield. The Santana Blues Band was duly christened. The first line up included Santana, Rolie, Frazier, Haro and Rodrigues and was soon supplemented with a street-smart conga drummer who Santana and Marcum knew from high school, Michael Carabello. Carabello had heard his grandmother play Latin music but he had picked up the urge to play congas just from seeing others perform and basically played for the fun of it.

The new band started rehearsing in a garage on Potrero Hill just past the Mission District with a view to making weekend dates over the bridge at the Ark in Sausalito and the Matrix in downtown San Francisco. Gregg Rolie would drive up from Palo Alto for the rehearsals, the others, who hailed from the less well-heeled Mission District, assumed he was super-rich because he had his own car. It was a truly odd mix of people and they were still a college band at heart, scratching around for gear and gigs. Carabello could only afford one conga drum, the drummer a modest kit.

Naturally, the music the band played was based around the blues and R&B regulars, like the Ray Charles hit "Mary Ann", Butterfield's version of "The Work Song" and B.B. King's "Woke Up This Morning". Carlos had been playing these for years but this band started fusing musical genres, an approach that was to characterise Santana's music for the next thirty years. For a start they played their own version of Bloomfield's "East West", the long jamming testing their skills as improvisers to the limit. The way the band really made their mark was by adding conga drums to popular songs from musicals, taking them away from the saccharine Broadway style and turning them into something altogether harder. The conga drum, literally "the Congolese drum", originated in Afro-Cuban cults after arriving in the Caribbean with slaves from the Congo. It first appeared in America in the 1940s with legendary band leader Machito and it was popularised by great names such as Chano Pozo, Mongo Santamaria and Armando Peraza. The conga is a very musical drum capable of rendering melodies, but it is fundamentally derived from African spiritual rituals where it was used rhythmically to induce a trance-like state. The Santana Blues Band worked to add conga parts to music like "A Taste of Honey" and, most adventurously, crafted the film song "Chim Chim Cheree" into something completely new. They played it the way jazz musicians Oliver Nelson and Wes Montgomery did with the 6/8 rhythmic pattern of African music. Aside from this, they were still covering current hits by the likes of The Doors ("Light My Fire") and The Rascals ("Good Lovin'" and "Beautiful Morning"). The young band had no fear of taking chances and displayed evidence of a musical imagination that rejected any limits that categorised music.

The turn of 1967 found the Santana Blues Band working at the weekends and doing regular jobs in the day time, but the 9 to 5 routine was soon to be a memory for Carlos Santana and Gregg Rolie. Every Sunday the Fillmore had an audition spot for local musicians who would get a chance to play for free in front of mums and kids who had paid just $1 to get in. The Santana Blues Band's opportunity came late in January when they secured a slot on a bill which included Paul Butterfield and saxophonist Charles Lloyd. They took their chance well and Bill Graham was impressed enough to invite them to audition for him. Soon afterwards he started using them as stand-ins whenever an act let him down. What often happened when the Santana band opened for headline acts like Sly Stone or Creedence Clearwater Revival was simple – they blew them away! At this stage they were still playing mostly blues and R&B and their devotion to Paul Butterfield was such that on one occasion, they played all his songs before he did when they stood in as his opening act!

Carlos knew he was on the edge of something big, he had put together a creditable working band, developed a close musical bond with Gregg Rolie and added Michael Carabello's congas to the sound. San Francisco was an amazing melting pot of music at this time and the city most likely to be open to new and adventurous sounds. It had already embraced and developed the long guitar jams started by Butterfield and Bloomfield and welcomed original blues stars as heroes. Many of the older bluesmen were receiving treatment at the Fillmore that they only experienced in Europe or within their own communities. One of these players was B.B. King, even then recognised as one of the founding fathers of modern blues and a living legend to boot. King played his first date at the Fillmore in 1967 shortly after the Santana Blues Band's debut. Carlos Santana was in the audience on 26th February when King first emerged into the spotlight with Lucille, his trademark Gibson guitar. It was to be an emotional night. Santana had been listening to B.B. King for years, pouring over his old Kent albums like they were precious gems, but he had never seen King play before. Before he had even got a note out of his band, King was overwhelmed by a standing ovation filled in equal measure with admiration and affection. The admiration was for a man who had grown up working in the cotton fields down south but overcome it all to become a great star. The blues guitarist was moved to tears by the reception he received and his first note was incredibly powerful. The potency of emotion King packed into that first note was something that Carlos Santana would never forget. B.B. King wasn't just playing music that night, he was playing his whole life through his guitar. Santana left the auditorium knowing that he had to play music in this way. He, too, had a real story to tell.

The guitarist was hungrier than ever to play music as his livelihood again, but he was still living with his parents in the Mission and still washing dishes at Tic-Tocs to help out with money. In contrast, the Grateful Dead were already stars leading the scene in San Francisco with Jefferson Airplane. Carlos used to check out the Dead's shows and had no trouble recognising them from a side window when they pulled up at Tic-Tocs one evening in a limousine to buy some radical burgers and fries. At the sight of the limo, all the frustrated ambition in the young musician's heart welled up inside him and he made a pact with himself to achieve what the Dead had achieved. He took off his apron, clocked out and never swept floors for a living again. On returning home, the guitar player announced his intention to move out of his parents' Mission apartment and went to pursue his ambition to match the success of the Grateful Dead. His parents weren't to see him again for two years as he moved in with Marcum and Estrada.

☯

Carlos and Stan Marcum were soon extremely tight. They were virtually penniless and spent what they had attending gigs at the Fillmore, eventually running out of money. The doorman at the Fillmore knew the pair so well that he had a deal with them. They would pay when they could, he would let them in for free when they couldn't.

At home the three men lived a communal lifestyle – pooling all their meagre resources. They played in the street or in the park, just guitar and congas, to get money to eat, just as the young Chicano had done in Tijuana. However, if ambition and determination were no barriers to him, health was, as he contracted tuberculosis and found himself bed-bound for three months. Michael Carabello tried to keep the guitarist amused with visits, bringing with him a reel-to-reel tape player on which Carlos listened to Gabor Szabo while he considered his future. Meanwhile, the band fell to pieces as Carabello reported, "I was just playing 'cause I enjoyed playing. I wasn't really serious. Carlos had TB or something we were all waiting for him to get out of the hospital, so I didn't want to go to practice or anything, so I got kicked out of the band."[13] Carlos could only take so long of being on a hospital ward, watching people die and being told what to do by nurses and doctors. When he'd had enough and felt better, he simply checked himself out and went back to the street and the band.

Further changes were afoot in the Blues Band. Frazier, Haro and Rodrigues had too many domestic, family and business ties to engender the do or die attitude Santana and Rolie wanted. Rod Harper was brought in to take up the drums and Steve De La Rosa took over on bass for a short time; names that would disappear from view as quickly as they appeared. Despite the changes, the unit managed to get back on course again and were all set to open for The Who and Loading Zone on June 16th. It was at this date that Carlos Santana realised that some of the band's members weren't yet ready to play their instruments with the total commitment that he demanded of himself. Music was his salvation, his way up and out of the barrio, all he had ever wanted to do in his life. As for the others, some of them were more interested in how they looked and claiming more conquests with the ladies. The result was that the Santana Blues Band was late for its first proper date at the Fillmore and, as was his wont, Bill Graham hit the roof. The band fell apart again and another major overhaul was called for.

Meanwhile Carlos remained extremely close to his two roommates and while Estrada was content to be the band's roadie, Marcum fancied himself as their manager and more or less fell into the role. His first job was to take the lead in finding new musicians for a new Santana Band, players who had less interest in hair and more in playing.

While Marcum sought out new musicians, the group would jam at a club on the corner of Grant and Green in the North Beach area of the city. A guy called Don Wehr was behind the drums when a strikingly handsome black bass player called David Brown dropped by to jam with them. Brown had backed touring bands like the Four Tops around the Bay Area and was refreshingly professional. He'd been playing in neighbourhood bands, but like Carlos Santana he did not fit into any perceived racial stereotype. He couldn't play James Brown and was more interested in the hippie scene, attracted by the music of The Beatles and Jimi Hendrix. He rode a Harley and hung out with bikers. He was perfect for Santana and the band quickly asked him to join.

North Beach is also where Aquatic Park is located, a peaceful refuge with soft sandy beaches away from the hustle and bustle of Fisherman's Wharf. A tradition had developed at the park for conga drummers to gather here and at Dolores Park in the Mission, smoke a little, drink a little and play a great deal. The Park was the first place that Santana, Rolie and Marcum heard conga drummers and the sound of the massed drums mixed in a unique way with the sound of the city in the distance. One of the drummers who played here was another black musician, Marcus Malone, a hard man from the Hunter's Point ghetto who joined the band at this point. He's a rarely celebrated figure in Santana's story, but played a critical role in the development of the band. Malone knew the roots of Afro-Cuban music, a unique art form, which reached the USA from Cuba in the 1940s through émigré musicians like Chano Pozo, Tito Puente, Mongo Santamaria, Armando Peraza and Carlos "Patato" Valdes. Malone introduced Santana and Rolie to the Afro-Cuban roots of percussion and added a more authentic style to the percussion. One of the first things Malone did after joining the band was to acquaint his new compañeros with *Drums Of Passion*, a record by Nigerian master drummer Babatunde Olatunji that comprised African drum and choir chants. One song in particular from that album had been long heard at Aquatic Park, "Jingo-Lo-Ba". But, Malone was no hippie and he mocked the others for their "scene" clothes and outlook, he was more into flashy style and a showbiz approach. He was never really a part of the gang.

The San Francisco scene at the time made it easy to find musicians, anyone could play with anyone else, there were no barriers and no managers to overcome to sit-in and jam. Someone would know someone who knew someone in the band – they would meet at jams and connections were made. This is how Stan Marcum found the new drummer for the Santana Blues Band, Bob "Doc" Livingston. Now the new line-up was completed, the group needed a new name so they simply dropped "The Blues Band" and became plain Santana.

As the new Santana Band were forming, a young black guitarist from Seattle was just about to make a concert appearance at the Monterey Pop Festival in California. His name was Jimi Hendrix and within a few months he had changed the face of guitar playing forever. Hendrix was the first black rock star – the first to remind the rock world that rock'n'roll was a black music form, he played the guitar as if every note were his frantic last breath, whilst being a fine songwriter and consummate showman. By the end of the year Hendrix had put out two classic albums, *Are You Experienced?* and *Axis: Bold As Love*. These albums entranced Carlos Santana as much as they did the rest of the world. Santana recognised that Hendrix's guitar style was rooted in the blues and Buddy Guy, but was also amazed by the use of feedback and effects that Hendrix mastered to create new vistas of sound through the guitar, his music was a leap of imagination. 1967 was the start of a musical love affair with Jimi Hendrix that Santana would never grow out of.

The new Santana line-up was completed in July 1967 and soon started gaining a strong following in the Bay Area cutting gigs at the Straight Theatre, Golden Gate Park and the Carousel. They joined a Peace and Freedom Party bus, marshalled by a left-field theatre group the San Francisco Mime Troupe, that took the band into neighbouring Orange County for the first time. Santana were very much a local San Francisco band and the audiences at the Fillmore and Avalon Ballroom felt a pride for the band, they were "one of their own". It was a time of small egos and little violence, people didn't put up barriers and innocent love of music seemed to be calling the shots. As the band moved out of the Bay Area to reach a wider audience they learnt the hard way that their status as local favourites meant nothing a few hundred miles out of San Francisco. Opening for better known acts like the Grateful Dead they often faced open hostility until they started playing. Audiences soon lost their hostility and even in these early days, everyone who heard Carlos Santana knew that he was different, his sound was unique and was unconsciously breaking the musical rules of the time.

The Santana group would go on to break every musical rule in the book and this included the remarkable racial mix in the band. Even though the Santana players were from radically different social and ethnic backgrounds, the music was the glue that held them together and diffused any race or class tensions. As David Brown put it, it was simply that, "everybody was there to play music and love music." As long as the focus was solely on music, the thing would work.

These were days of naiveté when it really seemed possible to dismantle capitalism and live a communal lifestyle free of money and jobs, fuelled by drugs and music. Above all, music was the key to the revolution, it was the flag of rebellion. By now David Brown had moved in with Carlos, Marcum and Estrada; it was a house with a no-nonsense reputation in the area. Some said these were guys who were not to be crossed. Lifestyle and music were inextricably linked, you couldn't play the music without living the life and the Santana musicians lived simple subsistence economics. They played music to eat. Like any troupe of young musicians, Santana had two main needs, somewhere to rehearse and food. Luckily for them, the bass player's mum was very accommodating and let them rehearse in the basement of her house in Daly City, but that wasn't all. She cooked for them too!

With their appetites taken care of, the band got down to the business of playing music and having fun. Increasingly, they were helped by the local impresario. Bill Graham had always been a Latin music nut and fondly remembered his time watching the Mambo Kings in New York years before. Graham had also developed an affection for blues, so, when he heard the new Santana, it was like a marriage made in heaven for him. Whatever else is said or written about Bill Graham one thing is clear, he took chances to promote music he believed in, even if this meant going against the grain. As 1967 became 1968 Graham gave the band the use of rehearsal facilities where they honed their set. They still played blues numbers like Albert King's "As The Years Go Passing By", but the sound of the band was changing and slowly moving away from the blues-based style. David Brown had worked out the pumping soul bass of James Brown's hits and they also had tunes of their own for the first time, which had come together in the course of long jams out of which they might pick one lick or one guitar riff to build into a new song. One of these was a Chico Hamilton tune, "Thoughts", which was from *The Dealer*, an album that had a seminal influence on Carlos Santana. The band took just one guitar lick from the tune, developed a piano riff around it and produced a ten minute jam. They also had jams of their own and one of them was based around an infectious conga drum pattern and a simple riff on the guitar, based around just two chords. Over this Santana and Rolie just blew. They called it "Soul Sacrifice". The Santana Band was gaining a formidable reputation around the Bay Area and by the summer, the band was ready to make its debut as the headline act at the Fillmore. The date was June 16, 1968.

Chapter 5

It wasn't long before the record companies came sniffing around to check out the latest San Francisco musical phenomenon. The area had provided very rich pickings over the last few years. The Grateful Dead, Jefferson Airplane, Creedence Clearwater Revival and Steve Miller had all proved excellent investments, so news of a new hotshot band was bound to generate more than passing interest. The battle to sign San Francisco bands wasn't left to minor local labels, it was the province of the big boys and soon the two really big boys, Atlantic and Columbia, were after Santana. The record industry men invited the band to endless meetings during which they presented a rosy picture of potential economic prosperity which meant nothing to the boys in the band. All they wanted to do was play music for the people.

Rolie, Santana and the others soon found themselves preparing to audition for Ahmet Ertegun, the head of Atlantic Records. However, Carlos Santana wanted to be on the Columbia roster with Miles Davis and Bob Dylan. The other members of Santana were about to find out for the first time that if Carlos didn't want to do something, he wouldn't do it, no matter what they thought. As he didn't want to sign with Atlantic, Carlos simply threw the audition – much to the ire of his colleagues – and Ertegun left the Bay Area wondering what all the fuss was about, they couldn't play and it certainly wouldn't sell. Fortunately for the gambler in Carlos Santana, the men from Columbia were interested in signing the band, they journeyed to Santa Clara to watch the unit open for the Grateful Dead and liked what they saw.

A Los Angeles-based staff producer, David Rubinson, another Latin music fan, encouraged his company to take an interest in the band and was assigned the job of working with the raw band. It might have been different. The deal with Columbia had been negotiated for the band by local attorney Brian Rohan who handled the legal work for most Bay Area acts, especially those linked to Bill Graham. Rohan planted the idea of Graham and Rubinson going into partnership to launch a record label and Santana were an obvious choice to sign, the pair were attracted by the concept but didn't move quickly enough and lost the group to Columbia.

Almost as soon as ink on the contract was dry, the Santana Band started on the road to ruin. They were used to playing music to survive without thinking of it as a business; now they were thrust head-first into the murky world of accountants, lawyers and music industry sharks. At the time they still believed in "the dream", that music and the counter-culture lifestyle would sweep away capitalism and replace it with communal bliss. Music was their subsistence, they needed to play to put food on the table. Also crucially, the Santana musicians needed each other, which is why they lived a communal lifestyle. If they did make it in the business, would they still need music to survive and would they still need each other?

As Santana continued to gig, supported by the cushion of an advance from Columbia, plans were laid to record the band when they headlined a series of shows at the Fillmore in December. However, this wasn't to be the recording debut of Carlos Santana, as the close knit world of the Fillmore gave Columbia the chance to showcase the guitar player ahead of the first Santana album. Michael Bloomfield was due to record a live album with Blood, Sweat and Tears singer-organist Al Kooper at the Fillmore across a number of nights in September, but didn't make it for one of the nights and so Carlos was drafted in. He took his Gibson and joined Kooper on stage for a blues-rock piece called "Sonny Boy Williamson". He played a short guitar passage, which moved between blues licks and some of his Mexican inflections, but he could and would do much better. The album appeared in February 1969, but importantly the Santana musicians had also seen a young drummer called Michael Shrieve during the Kooper-Bloomfield sessions and were impressed.

Santana worked on their live act as the December recording dates at the Fillmore loomed and it was David Rubinson himself who oversaw the equipment for the shows on 19, 20, 21 and 22 December. Writer Robert Greenfield gives us a glimpse of what San Francisco was like in the last days of the hippie revolution: "A good concert at the Family Dog or the Avalon would bring them out of their rabbit warrens where they had been holed up, high for days, watching that record go round, getting off on Love or the

Airplane or the Dead, so very high that it took a full day to get it together enough to actually venture out into the street where you had to deal with concrete realities like traffic lights and telephone poles."[14] Many of the musicians were in the same condition and such trivialities as being in tune were overlooked in the mayhem of mind-bending light shows and neurone-mashing chemicals.

Once they got onto the Fillmore's stage that December it seemed that a major leap forward in musical eclecticism had taken place. They were slowly moving away from a blues and R&B style and developing the signature "Santana sound". There was more of a real Afro-Cuban flavour as they covered material by Willie Bobo ("Fried Neckbones") and Olatunji ("Jingo") and they were showing, too, that they could handle jazz moods with their own "Treat" and Chico Hamilton's "Conquistadores". The eclecticism was really a function of the fact that blues, Afro-Cuban and jazz all have large elements of improvisation. By now they had their own pieces which were largely in the contemporary jamming style. Numbers like an early "Soul Sacrifice" and the huge "Freeway" had a tendency towards formless jams and drifted along with minimum precision. The latter was the usual set-closer, clocking in at over thirty minutes, including solos for every musician. It was based around the loosest of gospel-funk riffs and just went on endlessly. (Music from these Fillmore concerts was released in 1997 under the title *Live At The Fillmore '68*. The 2 CD-set is a fascinating document of the band's musical genesis).[15]

Santana were at a musical cross-roads, somewhere between being blues imitators and true innovators. The band had already developed a unique identity but they were not quite the finished article. There were holes in their armour, notably Livingston's one dimensional rock drumming which fell short of the unique blend with the conga that Santana needed. Also, the band's time keeping was hit and miss and the musicians didn't all end the song at the same time. Sometimes, Carlos' guitar could sound a little out of tune. At its worst, the whole thing had the air of a loose jam. Malone was no virtuoso conguero. He played in a raw, unsophisticated street style like Michael Carabello. He had plenty of showman's tricks, but his main value to the band was introducing them to true Afro-Cuban music. Santana in 1968 certainly had an unrefined power that made them stand out from some of the more vapid music that was part of the San Francisco scene, but there were errors to be ironed out and a need for a more direct, concentrated approach to the arrangements. David Rubinson was far from satisfied with the band's endeavours, there were too many mistakes. He was under pressure to get a product into the stores to benefit from the band's local popularity, so after Santana played a set at the Fillmore on New Year's Eve, they headed to Los Angeles for a ten day recording session when they would all try again. More problems loomed. Just before they set out for Los Angeles, there was an incident involving Marcus Malone and the estranged husband of his girlfriend. A knife was involved, Malone was arrested and weeks later the unwelcome visitor died in hospital. Eventually, the conguero was convicted of manslaughter and didn't return from jail until 1973.

So, the Santana dream was already on rocky ground when the band set-off for a head-on collision with the music industry in Los Angeles. Santana thought of themselves as "funky cats" from San Francisco, while Los Angeles, with its Hollywood glitz and glamour, was the exact opposite of funky. Moderately funky themselves, Columbia Records rented a mansion for the Santana players while the recording went on and so the band found themselves holed-up in luxury on Sunset Boulevard, the very epicentre of Hollywood. They were not happy and David Brown characterised the accommodation as, "real plastic, real phoney, real miserable." It did not bode well for the work in the studio. The band's aim was to capture their live sound on tape while David Rubinson's understandable aim was to replicate the success of acts like Moby Grape – two or three minute radio-friendly bites. It was going to be difficult to reconcile the Santana jamming style with that target. The working name for the album was *Freeway Jam*. This title said it all about the band's approach which was based around long jams which reflected the fluidity of time in the San Francisco scene. To an audience smacked out of their heads and spellbound by the light show, a three-hour guitar solo felt like a couple of minutes – after all the Grateful Dead played shows that lasted twelve hours! The chances of turning this approach into a product that would please Columbia Records were slim.

Another fundamental problem was that the band had never been in a recording studio before and knew nothing of how such a place actually worked. The result was disaster. With understatement Gregg Rolie said the album "wasn't very good," while David Brown was more forthright: "It was awful, the sound was tinny, it didn't sound anything like us." They tried all their stock tunes again but the absence of a live audience added to the band's hang-ups. Rubinson's patience was running out and though he was aware of his own possible failings – admitting that he might not have been "as sensitive to the insecurities of a new band going to record their first album as [he] could have been" – he was quite clear on the nature of the problems: "There were technical inefficiencies, the out-of-tuneness, dropping of time, the screwing up of charts."[16] He was particularly unhappy with Livingston and the continual uncertainty around just who would be at liberty to play the congas. Everyone sensed that changes were on their way.

Dejected, the band headed back to San Francisco and more rehearsals at Pacific Recorders in San Mateo, a small city directly south of San Francisco. It was left to Rolie to tell Doc Livingston that he was out of the band. Then fate played a hand. It just happened that at that precise moment Michael Shrieve was also at the Pacific facility trying to cop some free studio time for his band. Santana remembered Shrieve and suggested he join the band for a jam. Things went well and the session lasted long into the night. At the end, Santana and Rolie invited Shrieve to join the band and before long the young drummer was installed at the band's Mission District house.

Other percussion problems remained and Michael Carabello was the agent of change. Firstly, he regained his place in the band and secondly, he remembered a small conguero who had approached him to join in a street jam at the Playland At The Beach. This guy was definitely *not* a hippy, he came over more like a street hustler, he was confident and he was sharp. He was José "Chepito" Areas. His small stature had given him the nickname "Chepito" which meant "chipmunk" but he was also known as "El Nicoya", "The Nicaraguan". When he joined Santana, Chepito Areas was by far the most accomplished musician in the band. He was a percussive child prodigy in Nicaragua before he immigrated to the USA, eventually finding his way to the Bay Area where he played a version of Latin-Soul music with a unit known as The Aliens. He was a virtuoso of the timbales, the tight skinned drums made famous by Tito Puente that had a high-pitched, very musical tone. He could play conga and bongo *and* he was no mean flugelhorn player. As if this weren't enough he wrote music and was well versed in the background of Latin music. The addition of Chepito Areas, coupled with the excellent, sensitive drumming of Michael Shrieve provided the missing elements in the Santana jigsaw. They were both jazz players at heart.

Even before Areas arrived, Santana were beginning to work on a new, sharper sound with the lithe Shrieve behind the traps. By March they had a stock of new songs, "Waiting", "Savor" and "We Gotta Live Together", which eventually became "Shades of Time". By May 1969 the new Santana band was complete. It was a six man line up comprising Carlos Santana, Gregg Rolie, David Brown, Michael Carabello, Michael Shrieve and José Chepito Areas. The whole was now greater than the sum of the parts. Each of them brought their own sound and personalities to the unit and unconsciously created an entirely new musical sound. It was a balance of musical influences and personalities; namely Carlos Santana's unique singing guitar tone, Gregg Rolie's merging of rock styles with an earthy Jimmy Smith approach to the Hammond organ; Chepito Areas' genuine knowledge of Latin music and jazz. These were combined with David Brown's James Brown funky bass solidity; Michael Carabello's street conga sound and Michael Shrieve's mixture of jazz and rock drumming. But, this chemistry could only last as long as the mix of personalities held together. Over the next three years it was going to be fully tested, but for the moment, this unlikely melting pot of a Chicano, a Puerto Rican, a Nicaraguan, a black American and two white boys from the suburbs, ripped through the difficulties of the past and set about changing the face of popular music around the world.

Chapter 6

In May 1969, the new Santana band returned to the studio. As this was now the band's third attempt at recording an album, they were under a lot of pressure to get something reasonable down on tape. To make matters worse, they only had three weeks.

This time they chose not to stray too far from the Bay Area and checked in at the Pacific Recording Studios in San Mateo, where they sometimes rehearsed. Paul Curcio, the owner, was also a fan of the band. After the two experiences working with David Rubinson, the musicians decided to bring in their own choice to help them produce the album. Brent Dangerfield had never worked in a recording studio but was the sound man at the Straight Theatre where they often played. The band thought he did a good job there, so brought him in to help on the new recordings.

Even with a new producer who knew how to harness the Santana sound, there was still plenty of work to do. Two people were instrumental in getting the obviously talented band to focus their energy into a tighter format. Alberto Gianquinto was an accomplished pianist from the Bay Area who had spent a couple of years in Chicago playing with bluesman James Cotton. Santana brought Gianquinto in to help with the arrangements for the new album and having listened to the band the pianist immediately identified the problem. The solos were too long. Bill Graham also felt the same thing, he knew that if the band were going to reach the market beyond the San Francisco scene, they had to stop playing jams and start playing songs. It would help if the songs had discernible beginnings, middles and ends like "As The Years Go Passing By". The band were grateful for the advice, after all this was their third try at getting it right on a recording. Graham's influence was strong and, on one occasion, he summoned the band to his office at the Carousel Ballroom and played them a track by New York based Latin musician Willie Bobo, "Evil Ways" – an urban guitar groove that mixed latin with R&B. Graham liked this song and kept thinking of Santana when he heard it. He was sure it would get the band radio play and eventually convinced them to record it.

Taking in the new advice, the band worked quickly to rearrange their songs into shorter, snappier pieces. They worked hard in the studio, sometimes twelve or sixteen hours a day – Rolie getting to grips with recording lead vocals to a backing tape and Santana, stripped to the waist, punishing himself and his guitar, with Brown rocking behind him watching his moves.

When the band's debut album, named simply *Santana*, was released in October 1969, it revealed a stripped-down Santana sound where tight arrangements and concise solos realised the full potency of the music. Not all of it was earth-shattering or especially inventive, "Persuasion", "Shades Of Time" and "You Just Don't Care" were honest but unremarkable tunes, but most of the album astonished listeners with an entirely new sound. "Waiting", "Savor", "Jingo" and "Soul Sacrifice" showcased the new unit creating a pure melody of rhythms, over which a pleading guitar and stabbing Hammond held court.

The record starts with a masterstroke of arrangement. The introduction of "Waiting" has the conga and bass in tandem setting down a backbeat of the classic Afro-Cuban rhythmic pattern, the "guaguanco". Afro-Cuban had been fused with rock in an instant. The music is intensely rhythmic, reflected in the organ and guitar solos which reveal their players' interest in Jimmy Smith and Jimi Hendrix respectively. But, there had never been such a dirty sounding Hammond organ in rock before and the guitarist sounded like he was *squeezing* the notes from his instrument. The three drummers laced in and out of the rhythm, bouncing off each other in a melody of percussion, while David Brown kept up the thundering guaguanco on his bass. The energy and sweat were tangible as the band peaked with Santana's roaring solo. It was an incredible debut.

An earthy, urban mood was captured on "Evil Ways" and "Savor", which both climaxed in overtly sexual passages of rhythmic intensity, coloured by primal guitar or organ. "Savor" introduced the chattering timbales of Chepito Areas, which were an entirely new sound in rock, as was the Afro chanting on "Jingo" which found Santana's guitar soaring into the clouds with a gripping sustained note. The bass tracks Carabello's compelling conga drum pattern – a real innovation. No-one had heard anything like this before and many didn't know what to make of it at all, but it was pure Afro-Rock, all the instruments working to emphasise the rhythm more than any harmonic quality.

In fact, the Santana harmonic range was relatively limited on this LP. Five out of the nine tunes were based on a single two-chord pattern but that wasn't the point. In any case, the intellectual aspects of harmonic complexity would have bent out of shape an album that was so pure in expression.

This isn't to say that there was a lack of sophistication about the album. A brief encounter with "Treat" showed that Santana were already capable of handling a jazz-blues mood and showcases Rolie's fine piano and Santana's melodic guitar, which is equal parts jazz, blues and Mexican. It is a tight, accomplished performance, revealing a fine sense of dynamics. There was also energy to spare on the mesmerising "Soul Sacrifice" where double congas and trap drums introduce an adapted rhythmic pattern which finds its counterpoint in Brown's booming bass. Gregg Rolie's organ takes the place of the absent horn section, continuing a dialogue with the guitar, before rhythm takes over in compellingly brief conga and drum solos. Shrieve's drum solo here is a model for restraint. He doesn't stray far from the basic rhythm of the piece, but works around it masterfully adding colour and texture. By the time the piece moves into the second part, it's an invocation, a ritual to rhythm – an irresistible, elemental force.

Santana was an extraordinary recording debut, lashing the listener with a forceful pot-pourri of Afro-Cuban rhythms, blues and rock. The group had some forceful improvisers, Rolie's macho Hammond blew away the more vapid users of the instrument and Shrieve was an elegant, sensitive drummer. Chepito Areas was already a master percussionist and Santana's guitar, in particular, seemed to be bursting with the desire to succeed in its mix of blues and Mexican notes. "Shades Of Time" includes some trademark Mariachi violin flourishes that José Santana would have recognised. The whole band played with a stunning commitment, but it was inevitably the guitar player who received most attention, this was the guitar hero era after all.

With a great album in the can Santana continued to play plenty of shows around California – venturing as far south as San Diego – but they really needed to make themselves known outside the sunshine state. This was achieved through a tour of the midwest, supporting Crosby, Stills and Nash – dates which exposed the band to a large portion of the US record buying public. Meanwhile, Bill Graham was working furiously behind the scenes to get Santana included on the bill at a big rock festival that was planned for mid-August 1969 in the New York area. The festival was called Woodstock.

Graham wasn't directly involved in setting up the concert and the promoter Michael Lang had stepped on his toes by signing up many of the acts Graham was putting on at the Fillmore that summer. Ex-Graham employee John Morris was working for Lang on the show and wasn't sure about Graham's insistence that an unknown act called Santana be included on the bill. However, after he heard the band, Morris was sure he wanted Santana to appear. They were to be paid the sum of $2,500 – Jimi Hendrix earned $30,000. Still, the band enjoyed the Woodstock experience – before the shows they lived collectively in a house in the area and went down to the Pink Elephant Club nearby to jam with Mick Taylor, Buddy Miles and Hendrix. The gig itself was beyond anything they had experienced before.

Santana were due to play at eight o'clock on the Saturday night of the festival, by which time the concert grounds had been declared a disaster area; half a million people had overwhelmed the organisers who expected no more than 60,000. Santana were flown in by helicopter at lunchtime and they passed the time with the Grateful Dead. Carlos was a little worse for wear when the band were unexpectedly told to go on early, it was now or never.

The scene at Woodstock that greeted the San Francisco band was one of an enormous, open, wooden stage surrounded on all sides by a 360 degree sea of faces and bodies. The band take up their normal positions; Chepito and Carabello at the front of the stage hunched over two sets of congas, David Brown behind them in a trademark woollen tea cosy hat, Shrieve behind a small kit to his left. On the other side of the stage, Rolie rocks behind his organ and Santana is almost hidden from view, between Shrieve and Rolie, protected by the amplifiers. Their music starts as if it were a ritual – as bassman Brown leads the rhythmic clapping that soon reverberates to the edge of the horizon, the congueros lay down the rhythm of "Soul Sacrifice". Areas looks every inch the hustler while Carabello's muscle-bound arms give him the appearance of a street fighter as he pounds the drums. Carlos Santana seems in pain as he wrenches notes from his red Gibson, teeth grinding his bottom lip helping him overcome the physical pain of dredging the licks up from his gut. He looks as if someone's driving knives into his belly.

Carlos waits for Rolie to add the call and response chords from the Hammond. Rolie too is dripping in sweat, red faced, driving chords from the heart of the grinding Leslie speaker. The music reaches one shuddering climax after another in a rhythmic explosion of sheer, sexual power. Brown moves to the front of the stage, crouching in rhythmic harmony with the congueros, as Areas snaps sharp licks from the drum, flicking them like he were flashing a switch blade. Immediately, attention switches to the drummer who keeps the rhythm in tact, embellishing it with exhilarating snare drum rolls and rim shots. The others watch, Brown's head rocks up and down in sympathy with Shrieve who is lost in a world of his own, face down, firing volleys of sound from the modest drum set. It starts again, the menacing riff, the guitarist is straight for a stomach-churning tirade of angry intensity that threatens to shatter his body. The organist takes over, breathing heavily. He looks exhausted. He moves to a wild, gospel climax, before the mood comes down, but it's a short respite. The entire group drums its single being to another climax that bursts out with a potency leaving the gang physically drained. Listeners seemed to react to the sound in a sub-conscious, almost primitive sense as if this elemental fireball of sensual power was a sound that reached the very heart of their being. Rolie staggers from the stage into Bill Graham's grasp. Santana had given their complete body and soul.

☯

An extraordinary mythology has grown up around the Woodstock concerts, mostly fuelled by the speculations of people who weren't there, but who saw the film. The film gave the event a life of its own in the consciousness of cinema-goers the world over to whom it would mean whatever they chose to make it mean. The truth of the event was a side issue, Woodstock had become a media event, largely abstracted from its reality. To some, it epitomised the positive hippie ethic of peace and communal life, but to the music industry it revealed the real potential of this new "rock music". When the industry men saw that 400,000 people would suffer every kind of sanitary indignity to hear music (or in most cases not hear it), they knew that the potential sales were beyond their wildest dreams. Woodstock was seen by millions as the beginning of a "new world", when, in actuality, it changed the entire face of music promotion and the record industry. In that respect, Woodstock represented the death of music's age of innocence, though the real death knell came on December 6th 1969, when the Rolling Stones played a free show at the Altamont Racetrack in the North Bay near Novato. Unusually for a big show in the Bay Area, Bill Graham was not involved, but he knew the Stones and got Santana onto the bill. They probably wished they hadn't been so lucky, as the naiveté of the hippie era came crashing around its ears with the ludicrous idea of using Hells Angels to provide the security for the free show. Fights were breaking out while Santana played and the mayhem built towards a climax as the Stones took the stage. At the end of the day, one black teenager was dead, killed by the counter-culture's own security. Even aside from the personal tragedy, the concert was an utter disaster – entirely the result of simple-minded incompetence.

Still, by the time Santana had raced through "Conquistadores", "Jingo" and the rest at Altamont they were stars. The album was sitting at number four on *Billboard*, well on its way to selling a million copies – a massive figure for the time. Although Stan Marcum was ostensibly the band's manager, Bill Graham was scoring the biggest results for them. In October, he convinced the producers of the legendary Ed Sullivan show to beam Santana across the nation – giving unimaginable exposure to the band. They worked hard to capitalise on the success, playing almost constantly through the length and breadth of the States throughout August, September, October and November. After every show the standard temptations were on offer, be they physical or toxic. They were buying homes for their parents and being feted by peers like Jimi Hendrix. In fact, the story goes that Hendrix wanted more than to admire Santana from a spectator's vantage point, as Carlos recalled: "When I saw him last in Berkeley, California, he was talking about joining the band ! He loved the percussion. He was serious. What the hell was I gonna play?"[17] On another occasion, Santana was taken to watch Hendrix recording and what he saw frightened him, "The first time I was really with him was in the studio. He was overdubbing "Roomful Of Mirrors" and it was a real shocker to me. He started recording and it was incredible. But within fifteen or twenty seconds he just went out. All of a sudden he was freaking out like he was having a gigantic battle in the sky with somebody. The roadies looked at each other and the producer looked at him and they said, 'Go get him'. They separated him from the amplifier and the guitar and it was like he was having an epileptic fit."[18] Even a cautionary sight like this wasn't enough to stop the old "instant fame and money" LP hitting the turntable again. It was Santana's turn for the roller-coaster ride.

Chapter 7

1970 was the year that Santana really hit it big: the year of the *Woodstock* film and the year of their staggeringly successful second album, *Abraxas*. It began as it would go on, with the January release of "Evil Ways" as a single. The song stayed on the chart for thirteen weeks and peaked at number nine. Santana were well on their way to superstar status which they fomented with a national tour headlining over Country Joe MacDonald and Bread. *Santana* had sold well around the world, but the time was overdue for the band to cross the Atlantic and meet its European public for the first time in April as a part of a Columbia roadshow. They introduced some new material, "Toussaint L'Overture", "Se A Cabo" and a cover version of a song by British guitar hero Peter Green, called "Black Magic Woman". The band was tighter than ever before, there were fewer mistakes and European audiences were ecstatically won over by the irresistible power of the group.

However, the one big problem with having a big hit album is that as soon as it's been out for a few months, the pressure comes to better it. When Santana went into Wally Heider Studios in San Francisco on May 2nd to do some further work to a tune they had cut with Gianquinto for the last album, they knew they had to come up with something to surpass *Santana*. Nevertheless, success had its compensations and there was no need to complete the whole exercise in two or three weeks flat, so the group could pay greater attention to the process of committing music to tape. They weren't that happy with the sound of the first album, although its roughness had been one of its attractions. However, their studio skills were still in development and they looked for outside help again, this time enlisting Fred Catero, a consummate professional with a long track record that included another multi-instrument ensemble, Chicago. The band already had a few ideas for the album. For months, Gregg Rolie had been trying to interest his colleagues in recording "Black Magic Woman" and Carlos had initiated a soundcheck jam on "Gypsy Queen", a favourite from Gabor Szabo's *Spellbinder* album. He thought the two would sound good stuck together. They also had that instrumental left over from the first album, a jazzy mood known as "Incident At Neshabur" and Carlos had a guitar melody that had come to him after the first European trip. They started work on sessions that would last well into July.

The key member of the band at this time was Chepito Areas, who was in many ways responsible for the sound of *Abraxas*. In some senses Chepito was virtually the band's musical director around this time. He was an expert in the theory and practice of Latin music – which the others knew next to nothing about. Gregg Rolie had little or no interest in playing salsa chords and to Carlos Santana it conjured up images of Hollywood and Desi Arnaz. The first Santana album contained very little, if any, Latin music. "Evil Ways" was the closest and even that was more R&B than Latin. The rest of the material on *Santana* was made up of songs that had been in the band's live set for almost two years, so Areas had little chance to influence its direction. Whereas the majority of Santana's conga drum patterns had been inventive hybrids up to now, Areas introduced them to the real rhythms, the cha-cha-cha and the merengue and by the time of *Abraxas* the band had a clear Latin sound and direction, entirely down to Areas. The Nicaraguan taught David Brown how to play the bass in a Latin style (Areas could play the "bajo", the bass of Latin music) and he taught Carlos Santana and Gregg Rolie about Latin music phrasing as well as introducing a number of instrumental breaks and linking riffs that gave the band's music a more polished and professional sound. *Abraxas* would probably never have happened without Chepito Areas.

The mood of *Abraxas* is some distance removed from the raw, rock feel of the first album, indeed there is little on this album that could accurately be described as rock music. There is a far greater Latin feel to the music and a definite sense of jazz dynamics in the arrangements. The opening music, "Singing Winds, Crying Beasts", is an atmospheric overture, a shimmering collage of electric piano, psychedelic guitar and percussion held together by David Brown's simple but strong bass line. The piece is more of an atmosphere than a song, evoking a dreamy, hypnotic air – which is a clear indicator of where Santana would head after this band fell apart. Santana had already proved that they were a great cover versions band, a reputation that *Abraxas* fully enforces with three excellent reworkings of old material. In fact, the treatment they give to "Black Magic Woman", "Gypsy Queen" and "Oye Como Va" is so radical that they amount to almost complete rewrites that retained only the basic themes of the songs. The most radical change is affected on "Black Magic Woman", which is reborn as a Latin-Blues, floating on a sea of conga, bongo and a devilishly inventive organ introduction from Rolie. Carlos Santana sounds like a new guitarist in his opening solo – a restrained, passionate passage – whilst Rolie's smooth, breathy vocal delivers equal measures of languor and power. These qualities are also found on Santana's main solo which avoids blues clichés to take the guitarist's art into a more melodic vein. A clever instrumental segue leads into "Gypsy Queen" which lifts Gabor Szabo into the electric era as Santana sticks close to the Hungarian's licks. The main point of interest here is Chepito Areas' outstanding timbales and a general sense that rhythm is more potent than melody. The cleverness of the reworking of "Oye Como Va" can be overlooked in the sheer joy of what still works today as a party song. Rolie and Santana take what were many layered horn parts on the original and replicate them with new life and relish. There is much empathy between the musicians here, from the clever percussion fills, to Rolie's exhilarating organ break, they are all slaves to the irresistible rhythm, building to the climax of the closing guitar solo which sets forth from the horn charts with a flourish. They used Rico Reyes as a singer on this cut – Rico was a neighbourhood singer who the Santana guys knew just from hanging out. He was no heavyweight musician but he could sing in Spanish.

The album's highlight is the extraordinary "Incident At Neshabur", which remains one of the finest moments of Santana music. It's a breathtaking journey which careers through rock, jazz and "soul meets Mexico". There are many layers to the track, an opening section of riffs with the flavour of Horace Silver, coloured by devilish percussion, before it breaks into a 6/8 section over which Rolie delivers another fine Hammond solo and Santana evokes other worlds with an ethereal break. There are some difficult jazz chords to negotiate, before a romantic mood sets in over which the guitar player sets out his stall as a player of exquisite expressiveness, with a short passage that simultaneously contains the essence of Mexican romantic ballads, the soul of a Dionne Warwick vocal *and* the blues! Much of the more complex writing here is clearly the work of Alberto Gianquinto, whose piano is excellent throughout, but the sense of melodic drama it contains is all Carlos Santana. This is the first impressionistic piece that Santana committed to tape and it gives notice that this group of musicians were producing a new school of music, it wasn't exactly jazz, it wasn't exactly Latin and it definitely was not rock.

Side two begins with Chepito Areas introducing millions of listeners around the globe to the merengue, the rhythm of the Dominican Republic, on "Se A Cabo". Its merengue foundation fashions a party time feel, over an invigorating melange of multiple percussion and the standard Santana cocktail of roaring guitar and growling Hammond. There are enough simple riffs here to give the tune a rock feel and the driving percussion makes this one of the most likely candidates for the epithet "Latin-Rock". Gregg Rolie's talent as a crafter of catchy pop-rock tunes is found on two of the LP's tracks that rather stick out from the rest of it as "white rock" – "Mother's Daughter" and "Hope You're Feeling Better". Perhaps because they are both in the rock genre of the era, they sound more dated now than the rest of the album, but are notable for Rolie's strong vocals and a tempting Spencer Davis style riff on the generally spaced-out "Hope You're Feeling Better". This finds Carlos still caught up in his Hendrix-Cream fixation with heavy, wah-wah guitar. He would sculpt more of an identity for himself with the exceptional "Samba Pa Ti", a melody which some of the band members were none too keen to record, until strongman Rolie supported the guitarist's endeavours (he does it throughout the recording with his powerful Hammond statements).

"Samba Pa Ti" is a romantic melody that recalls Santana's Latin American musical heritage, infused with a blues syntax, which explains how quickly it entered the hearts of listeners the world over – in Latin America and Southern Europe in particular. Santana uses all that he learnt from his father about playing a melody, and what he experienced of B.B. King putting his whole life into one note, to set out in music a small part of himself. The guitar technique on display here is not about playing fast, it's about telling stories and he does this in a long flow of engaging melodies and counter melodies. The record closes with more folk music, "El Nicoya", being Chepito Areas' richly percussive and enjoyable tribute to himself !

Abraxas is one of the most important albums in the Santana canon, it forced those who had dismissed the first LP as "Latin-Rock" to reassess a group that was breathing new life into an Afro-Cuban favourite like "Oye Como Va" and conjuring some distinctly jazzy charts in "Singing Winds, Crying Beasts" and "Incident At Neshabur". The latter numbered Miles Davis amongst its champions. The recording of "Oye Como Va" in a notional rock context was extremely significant, bringing salsa music to a vast mass of music listeners. It is probably the one single event that helped to popularise Latin music around the planet. "Samba Pa Ti" introduced an entirely new style of guitar instrumental which called upon the melodic sensibilities of the old Mexican sones and romance ballads to produce a new Latin American folk anthem, a status it soon achieved. There was also a general sense of refinement on the album, the playing is far more controlled and focused than before. The arrangements too were exceptional: Santana's guitar and Rolie's organ mixed and matched horn parts with an ease that belied real ingenuity and there was a greater variety and clarity in the use of percussion, which was soon emulated by many other rock bands, as congueros became a "must-have" for everyone from Sly Stone, to The Rolling Stones, to Miles Davis.

Abraxas was the very peak of what the original Santana Band achieved and *could* achieve, it was a significant accomplishment, but one the band could never better. In fact, even with its very release the journey downhill had begun.

☯

The road to mega-stardom and ruin began in July 1970, with the release of the film of the Woodstock debacle, which helped to reinvent the happening in the minds of millions around the globe as a spectacular counter-culture victory. The cinema viewer of *Woodstock* had one significant advantage over the majority of the Woodstock crowd, an ability to actually hear the music ! The millions who saw the film fully expected to be overwhelmed by Jimi Hendrix's crazed performance, but they were less prepared for the raw power of Santana. By the time they left the theatre, having witnessed the astonishing performance of what looked like a multi-racial street gang, those who didn't already own the *Santana* album quickly rectified the situation, ensuring its amazing run on the *Billboard* album chart. The pictures of the wild organist, enraptured guitarist, funky bass player, baby-faced drummer and maniacally-driven congueros weren't easily forgotten and the Santana musicians, who attended the film's New York premiere, found themselves being recognised as celebrities when, a year earlier, they had been unknowns outside the Bay Area.

Once the image of Santana had been unleashed around the world through the film, viewers were free to form their own opinion of the group. Clearly the Santana musicians were just playing music, they had no pretension to change the world, but equally, had no control over what people read into them. The multi-racial nature of Santana had a major impact around the world and the fact that the guitar player was a Mexican resounded throughout Latin America. This was the height of the age of the guitar hero and Jimi

56

Hendrix, Eric Clapton and the rest were world superstars, so it was natural that a greater proportion of the media focus was turned on Carlos, even though Santana was a collective. Latin America had its first star of rock and his story of street survival added to the image of heroism. Chepito Areas instantly became a hero in his native Nicaragua and was soon voted the third most popular person in the country, after the president and Bianca Jagger! Santana appealed to nearly everyone, there was a face that most could relate to, be they black, white or Chicano. After the release of *Woodstock* on film, Santana became a symbol of racial integration and third world achievement, which goes some way to explaining the status the group has throughout Latin America, Asia and Africa.

In the midst of Woodstock fever, Santana's US tour in September and October was triumphant, climaxing with a triple header at Tanglewood, Massachusetts, in the company of Miles Davis and New York street soul band The Voices of East Harlem, who had a great bass player, Doug Rauch. Miles Davis admired Santana's music and, soon, percussion was a fixture in his band. Later, Davis could be found in the front row every night of a series of Santana dates at Bill Graham's Fillmore East auditorium in New York City. *Abraxas* had already caught the trumpeter's ear, particularly "Incident At Neshabur"'s combination of driving rock elements and delicacy. Davis was recording similar music and Carlos Santana found himself "hanging-out backstage" with one of the true greats of modern music. In retrospect, Santana's move towards a jazz-inflected approach in 1972 could have been predicted from *Abraxas,* especially as so many jazz musicians empathised with it.

The timing of the *Woodstock* film was a dream come true for Columbia Records, it paved the way for *Abraxas* in a free world-wide advertising campaign that was worth millions. When the album finally appeared in October, it made its way to the top of *Billboard* for six weeks and stayed on the chart for over a year and a half. The album was equally successful around the world and quickly sold millions. In some countries "Samba Pa Ti" was the single and in others it was "Black Magic Woman", which gave Santana its second highest ever chart placing on the *Billboard* singles chart, reaching number four.

After the tour the group took a much needed break and reflected on their phenomenal success and new found wealth. They could buy anything they wanted and all the clichés of the rock'n'roll lifestyle were lived out. But before long it appeared that the band's success would cause their downfall. Santana had lived communally for many years, something that had created the very tight bonds within the band, now that each of them had the money to buy their own properties, the group ethic was inevitably breaking. Nevertheless, they felt confident in their own abilities and this arrogance led them to a fatal mistake – shortly after the Tanglewood show, Stan Marcum called Bill Graham and told him that Santana no longer needed his help, they would handle their own affairs from now on. Obviously the band and Marcum still thought of themselves as a single organic unit, but the truth was that they were now becoming a group of individuals. So much so, that they were thinking about expanding the line-up to include a second guitar player and they already had someone in mind, a teenager from San Mateo called Neal Schon, who had hung around some of the *Abraxas* sessions. He was a "Grade A" Clapton and Hendrix freak and even added a second guitar solo to the end of "Hope You're Feeling Better", a debut which can be heard on the obscure quadraphonic version of the LP. Towards the end of November, the Santana Band and Neal Schon were rehearsing at Wally Heider's studio, while Eric Clapton was in town for shows at the Fillmore on the 18th and 19th with his new outfit Derek and The Dominoes. Bill Graham engineered a meeting between Clapton and Santana, which eventually found Clapton and his men heading to Wally Heider's for a jam session. Santana had a new song, "Everything's Coming Our Way", which Clapton embellished with a few of his slide guitar licks. But the lifestyle was ruining great encounters like this for Carlos Santana and he was getting tired of it, "The very first time we met was at Wally Heider's. I came in and Eric and Neal Schon were jamming. I felt really bad because I wanted to play, but I was too out of it. I'd just taken LSD. I used to take a lot of LSD in those days."[19] Clapton was impressed with Schon's precocious talent and Santana were quick to offer the fifteen year old a place in the band, to stop him being snatched off to England. Schon made his debut with Santana at a typically excessive New Years show in Hawaii. This was the start of what Carlos Santana called the worst year of his life.

☯

1971 started with some promise. In January the group used the ample studio time they were given at Columbia Studios in San Francisco, to cut a couple of tracks for the next record and a trip to Africa was on the horizon in March. Ghana had just secured independence from British colonial rule and a major concert of black American soul stars was planned in celebration. Carlos Santana was delighted at the prospect of being on the bill with Ike and Tina Turner, Roberta Flack, Wilson Pickett and the band's old friends from New York, The Voices of East Harlem. Before the trip, the first of many hammer blows that befell Santana in 1971 came when one day in February Chepito Areas didn't appear for a rehearsal. When the band got through the door of his house, they found him lying in a pool of blood. He'd had an aneurysm and nearly died, there was no way he could travel to Africa. The band was committed to go to Ghana, but to some it didn't feel right to go without Areas and tension grew. Santana was an unlikely combination of different backgrounds and the all-male environment allowed full reign to be given to the macho lifestyle. Bad feeling, fuelled by "rock life" excess, was never far below the surface. Michael Carabello was unhappy touring without Chepito, "We had a meeting, because Carlos was getting restless just sitting around waiting. He wanted a gig and I said 'I don't think we should gig, because Chepito's just as much a part of the band as anyone else. I don't think we should get another person to fill his place and go before an audience and say this is Santana, because we're not.' And I said if you're gonna get somebody else I myself would rather quit than play without Chepito."[20] For Carabello it was a case of gang loyalty, but for Carlos Santana music had always been far more important than being part of a gang.

Part of the problem was the incredible pressure they were under – the group were worked like dogs by their promoters and it is said that one of the main protagonists boasted that he could book Santana anywhere in the world at twenty-four hours' notice and frequently did. This kind of pressure added to the fragile nature of the unit. Still, for all the problems they made it to Ghana and played a reasonable set. In a little twist of history, they drafted in Willie Bobo as a last minute replacement for Chepito. Bobo was more used to the jazz setting of Cal Tjader than the double-guitar rock meltdown that Santana had started to favour and clearly was not the answer, even as a temporary substitute. By the time they reached Denmark for the start of another European tour, a new face had to be found. It came in the person of Michael "Coke" Escovedo, a very gifted timbalero who made his name playing with the very same Cal Tjader as Willie Bobo. Escovedo was known to be very charming and very strong-willed. The shows in Europe went well musically and Escovedo's influence was soon felt in the arrangements – they added a riff he had just been playing with Tjader as an opener to "Evil Ways". Some of the band would later say that Escovedo formed a clique with Carlos Santana, telling the guitarist that he was the real leader of the band and should get away from some of the negative forces in the group. Producer David Rubinson pinned the source of trouble directly to the new timbalero, "This bullshit started with Carlos and Coke being bosom buddies against someone else and this one was against that one and then finally it came back with they all had a meeting and Coke wanted to get rid of Marcum and then he got a couple of the guys on his side. Coke made too much trouble. I think he could have done whatever he wanted and taken over the band because he was a very strong force, a very strong person."[21] Escovedo himself remained unrepentant, "In a way I was responsible. But I'm glad. If I brought two good musicians out of a band of six bad ones, I'm glad."[22] Carlos Santana was already tiring of the rock'n'roll life and what he perceived as the arrogant attitude of certain band members, coupled with what he viewed as a disrespectful stance towards women. The others called him a humbug and a hypocrite. Such was Carlos' confused state of my mind at the time that he agreed with them, "I know they think I'm crazy because I used to contradict myself so much. I would demand this, I would say this and the next time I would be just like – worse than them."[23] Tension mounted yet higher and Michael Carabello seemed to be the focus of Santana's dissatisfaction, as the conguero recalled, "He like had this thing about me, I don't know, all the time, about what I did, the people I hung around with, how I ran my life."[24]

A certain amount of violence seemed to be surrounding Santana in 1971. The twin-guitar attack and pounding, elemental percussion gave rise to an excess of testosterone in some members of the band's audience. There were running battles between the police and audience at a Paris gig, a near riot in Milan and a more restrained, but unusually volatile reception in London. Things were getting out of control and as the band made it to Europe in April they were falling apart at the seams. There were factions and splits. Some members were in and some were left out with no-one to hang-out with. There were raging arguments, power games, high-stakes sulking and personality clashes of the first order. By the time they reached Montreux, Santana looked like a group of individuals appearing together rather than a band. After the concert Rolie told *New Musical Express*, "there's a lot of brotherly love in this band"[25], but there wasn't much in evidence by the shores of Lake Geneva. Carlos Santana was already thinking about going his own way musically and the reality was that Santana the band were on death row.

As soon as the band got back to San Francisco, they went straight back into the Columbia studios to try and fashion together a new album from the endless jams. Only two songs were in the can from the January session. One was another cover version, this time of jazz saxophonist Gene Ammons' tune "Jungle Strut". The other was a fine Latin original of Chepito and David Brown's called "Guajira". There were raging arguments in the studio, miles of wasted tape and general dissolution; a new song of Carabello and Rolie's, "No One To Depend On", seemed to be causing more problems than any other and there were rumours of money going missing. Coke Escovedo was still around, despite Chepito's reappearance and wasted no time in pointing out his perception of the inadequacies of the band's management.

Recording for the new album lasted well into June and, when it was finished, the band couldn't even think of a name for it, so it was called plain *Santana*, people added the *III* later. The music on this album is more manic than anything that Santana have recorded before or since, in some places it sounds as if it is about to explode out of the speakers in a massive elemental collision of percussion, guitars and organ. As a statement of pure macho power it exceeded anything the group had done before and sounded nothing like *Abraxas*. However, the new music seemed partly to rely on turning loose jams around guitar riffs into songs. Santana could make a song out of anything, any fragment of a tune, a couple of notes, anything. The opening track of the new album, "Batuka", emerged out of a jam the troupe did on a piece by renowned conductor Leonard Bernstein, which they had learnt for a television appearance with the Los Angeles Philharmonic. The track opens with driving conga, cowbell and drums supplemented by the artillery of a series of hefty bass and guitar riffs which builds to a two-guitar attack. Immediately, there is the heaviness of approach that characterises the album – this is underlined by Neal Schon's entry in a haze of wah-wah guitar that places the music firmly in the rock vein. "Batuka" gives way to the troublesome tune, "No One To Depend On", which itself had something in common with an old Willie Bobo effort ("Spanish Grease"). It's more of the same – heavy riffs, a menacing rhythm, blowing guitar and organ solos, it sounds like a formula but it radiates sheer thundering excitement. The two guitars send the thermometer up a notch or two as Santana overdrives his amplifier to the maximum point, while the precocious Schon favours a faster, flashier approach. His style also dominates "Taboo", where the teenager's closing solo threatens to melt the carpet.

As the well of song writing inspiration began to dry, the band turned again to cover versions and they start with an enjoyable remake of an old tune, "Karate", from an equally old band The Emperors. Santana gave it a new lyric, added thunderous percussion, another melting Schon solo, the Tower Of Power horn section and called it "Everybody's Everything". It was a great dance track, propelled by a dream of a percussion arrangement and Rolie's madly funky organ. It was the first time Santana had really committed any soul to tape, but it was becoming noticeable that Santana's best tracks tended to be covers. Another one was the old Tito Puente chart, "Para Los Rumberos", which really rocks Tito where their "Oye Como Va" had gently massaged him. Again, it's the spectacular percussion playing that stands out, as well as Luis Gasca's Mariachi trumpet. Yet another cover, "Jungle Strut", gave a fine airing to the two guitar set up, as they turned Gene Ammon's funky, soul-jazz number into something more like a speed-driven Funkadelic. Pure animal arousal is the product of the inescapable brew of bubbling percussion, duelling guitar solos and Rolie's untamed Hammond. A lighter mood is found on the first solo vocal composition that Carlos Santana contributed to a recording – the engaging ballad "Everything's Coming Our Way". It is replete with the guitarist's innate romantic melodicism and his own light lead vocals carry a lilting melody to a childlike chorus, coloured by a sympathetic solo from the organist. It was a small moment of optimism in an otherwise hard disc.

The two best tracks on the album were "Guajira" and "Toussaint L'Overture", both of which found the group adding something to their style, in contrast to the rather formulaic endeavours of the rest of the record. "Guajira" has an authentic Latin flavour thanks to fine piano from Maria Ochoa and a realistic Rico Reyes vocal delivering the infectious melody, but Chepito Areas is the main star here, starting with his bass introduction and climaxing with an outstanding flugelhorn solo. Santana plays his best Latin solos on the album, riding the melody, before flying off into the distance where the song had already become another Santana Latin anthem to go alongside "Oye Como Va". There's something honest and sincere about "Guajira" that makes it one of the real pleasures of a quite aggressive album. It introduced the music public at large to the classic Latin cha-cha-cha rhythm and the Spanish lyrics caused Hispanic people the globe over to iden-tify with the group even more. The Latin identity was stamped on "Toussaint L'Overture", which is probably the single best example of Santana's Latin-Rock style. Based on an old Spanish guitar chord pattern, the track is a series of shuddering climaxes, underpinned by towering percussion. The piece has an authentic Latin feel provided by the percussion, but it's easy to overlook the importance of Michael Shrieve's excellent drumming, which drives the opening section along by cymbal alone. He sits in a groove under the percus-sionists, not invading their territory, but underpinning the whole ensemble. In addition to the Spanish chords, the band use a traditional salsa bass line for the first time under the wild organ solo and a classic salsa hook as the piece moves into a tremendously exciting percussion-chant section. The music gains a nearly majestic quality as Santana's guitar starts the build-up to the finale which comprises a series of meltdown solos from Rolie, Schon and then Santana. Each one tries to take the intensity just a little higher and the result is a blow-out of maximum primitive passion. It's a Santana classic.

Santana III is an intensely exciting record and it was comforting that despite all the fighting, excess and bad feeling, they could still turn in a fine album, even if it was some distance from the classic *Abraxas*. Each of the tracks on the record is good fun, but mostly cast in the aggressively sexual mode. All the musicians play with great skill, but there was little doubt that, apart from "Toussaint L'Overture" and "Guajira", the well-spring of new songs that could be pulled out of the hat from the endless jamming was becoming one dimensional. Riffs, solos, percussion – repeat as required. The disc is a feast of great percussion and heady solos, but represented a retreat to a rock style after the adventurous arrangements of *Abraxas*. Always an enjoyable, stimulating album, it was clearly the end of the line for Santana's Latin-Rock. The Santana band was a collection of young men jostling for supremacy in a musical fight to the death conveyed in the aggressive mood of the record. Arguments would rage and profanities fly around the studio until the last second before the tapes rolled and the music started. When they were playing there was a channel for the aggression, when they weren't they only had each other. When gangs fall apart normally there is one who emerges from the pack to take over. It wouldn't be long now for Carlos Santana.

With the album completed, the band made one of its last appearances as a cohesive unit on the closing night of Bill Graham's Fillmore Auditorium on July 4th – the end of the Fillmore era neatly mirroring the disintegration of Santana. The entire band, augmented by Coke Escovedo, played a burning set of old favourites and new music, "Batuka", "Gumbo" and "Jungle Strut". Interestingly, they also included a cut down version of a tune from a Miles Davis album, "In A Silent Way". Miles' music was proto-jazz-rock, impressionistic, stark guitar chords from John McLaughlin giving way to minimalist solos over a pair of catchy but simplistic rock riffs. Santana cut it down to seven minutes and added percussion and power. Clearly, there were new influences coming into the heads of some of the Santana musicians. However, the mix of musical tastes within the band which had been so positive in the past was now beginning to be divisive, as Neal Schon reported in Denmark a few months earlier, "Everybody in the group likes different kinds of music. Carlos is way out there and he needs someone to pull him down to the ground. His stuff is really intricate."[26] Clearly, the guitar player had his own plans for the group and it was around this time that Shrieve and Santana had a conversation about the future of Santana, during which the guitarist set out his ideas. Shrieve was taken aback by Santana's approach, the band was a collective, there wasn't a leader, it wasn't the Mexican's band. The answer said it all. "Not yet."

With *Santana III* in the can at last and the Fillmore closed, the group could take time to relax before the start of the next US tour in September. The jazz influence was growing all the time and August saw most of Santana back at Columbia Studios to record *For Those Who Chant* with Latin trumpeter Luis Gasca, who had played on the new Santana album. This was a straight jazz date with accomplished players such as Joe Henderson, George Cables and Stanley Clarke; they also met other Bay Area players, pianist Richard Kermode, drummer Lenny White and conguero Victor Pantoja. The music was a form of Latin-Jazz with rock overtones as found on the "Oye Como Va" guitar riff that opens the admirable "Street Dude" – a series of improvisations suspended on a sea of percussion, it is a pointer towards work like "La Fuente Del Ritmo". Not much is heard from the Santana guitarists, but there is a notable passage of Afro-Cuban chants led by Victor Pantoja, highlighting an authenticity that Santana would move towards over the next few years. The other main piece, "Spanish Gypsy", was more free-form, held down by Stanley Clarke's bass and George Cables' oblique piano, a sound that Santana would later seek to replicate with Tom Coster and Richard Kermode who was on the session. Gasca's *For Those Who Chant* is a key bridge between the old Santana and the new and the timing is significant. In August 1971 *Santana III* was complete, but the cracks were there for all to see. Carlos Santana and Michael Shrieve were already developing musical interests wider than Sly Stone, The Beatles and the blues; they were investigating Miles Davis and John Coltrane. This must have seemed far more interesting music to Shrieve and Santana than *Santana III* and fired the guitarist's appetite for change. Another catalyst for change at the time was the day that Carlos chanced upon a philosophical work by the Indian spiritual teacher Paramahansa Yogananda in a Sausalito bookstore – it inspired him to investigate meditation and would change his life.

The good vibes of the Gasca sessions soon petered out as Santana's US tour loomed. The band hadn't seen much of Carlos Santana as they rehearsed for the tour and before they set off for the first date at the Spokane Coliseum on 16th September he presented the others with an ultimatum. Either Michael Carabello leaves or he leaves. This would be the real test, could Santana do it without the guitar player who gave the group its name? Was Santana a band or Carlos Santana? The group set off without the Mexican and managed until they reached New York for three dates at the Felt Forum, by which time Neal Schon had lost his nerve amidst repeated shouts for Carlos from the audience. Michael Carabello threw in the towel and left the tour. The guitarist was recalled from San Francisco, only to find that Stan Marcum had now quit and taken Carabello and Chepito Areas with him, there was no percussion left except for Michael Shrieve. The remainder of the band put the blame fairly and squarely at Carlos' door and the tour staggered on with worse feelings than ever. Santana, the band, was an utter shambles as they got through one of the New York shows with no percussionists. What would happen next? Before the next performance, a young conga drummer approached Santana road manager Herbie Herbert and offered to provide some percussion assistance, he knew the Santana set back to front he said. Furnished by Herbert with the few dollars he needed to get a taxi to his apartment and drum, James Mingo Lewis made the show and saved Santana's blushes for the time being. Michael Shrieve was torn between disapproval of Santana's action and a desire he shared with the guitar player to move on musically, "The reason I went on in New York was because we had commitments. I didn't feel it was particularly right on Carlos' part to do what he did, but if he felt he had to, he had to do it."[27]

Santana III was released to an expectant world in October, quickly moving to the number one slot on *Billboard* and beyond. There was no band promotion for the album expect for the short and ramshackle US tour, simply because there was no band to undertake any promotion. There is no little irony in the release of the album coming in the same month that the band was in total disarray, but worse was to come. A mere shambles turned to near disaster as a new line-up was hastily cobbled together to complete dates in Puerto Rico and Peru. David Brown was replaced by an old Music College contact of Shrieve's, the stand-up bass player Tom Rutley. The percussion duties were shared between Mingo Lewis, Victor Pantoja and that man Coke Escovedo, who also brought along his brother Pete to help out. The details of what actually happened to Santana in Lima, Peru that December 11th will probably never be known, what is clear is that there was a major outbreak of violence, either from "left-wing" students or the military. The band subsequently had $400,000 worth of equipment confiscated and were deported from the country. Some reports said this departure from Lima was at gunpoint. Months later, Herbie Herbert travelled to Peru to retrieve the equipment. Lima was Santana's Altamont, a dramatic kick in the *cojones* to wake up from their drug-induced stupor. The lunatic events of Lima left Carlos Santana deeply scarred and more determined than ever to bring the madness of Santana to an end.

Chapter 8

By the end of 1971 Carlos Santana felt that he was at a dead end, musically, spiritually and physically. The music was still there, but how much further could the Latin-rock concept go? As far as Carlos was concerned the answer was nowhere. It wasn't just Santana who were on the rocks in 1971, the whole of the rock world was in bad shape; Hendrix had died by choking on his own vomit, Janis Joplin was dead, Jim Morrison was dead, the Beatles were no more, it seemed that the "dream" was dead too.

As ever, Carlos' number one motivation was to survive and if that meant taking over the group, so be it. He had worked too hard to raise himself up from the Tijuana strip joints and had come too far to let the success he was now finally enjoying just disappear as a result of rock 'n roll excess. He had nothing else, it was his only means of survival and more than that, the only way he could support his entire family, which he took it upon himself to do. It might have been open to the business-minded Gregg Rolie to forget music for a year or two and open a restaurant, but music was all Santana knew. Just like a boxer from the ghetto it was his only way out and he was prepared to fight to keep it going. His innate pride and a new spirituality provided him with the framework around which to discipline his life. These were the keys to Carlos Santana not becoming the next acid casualty.

As far as the music business was concerned, Santana was still a potent name and by the end of 1971, despite the fact that he was in the midst of a personal and musical crisis, Carlos Santana was induced into forming a "supergroup" with Buddy Miles for a live jam at a music festival in Hawaii on New Year's Eve. Miles had just signed for Columbia and was well known for his work as a Hendrix sideman in the Band of Gypsies. A group of musicians were assembled at Miles' home for two or three days of rehearsal before the festival and the line-up was a mix of Miles' band, plus a few of Carlos' new musical friends like Gregg Errico (Sly Stone's drummer), Luis Gasca and Hadley Caliman. There was no Rolie, Shrieve, Carabello, Brown or Areas, just Santana and Schon. The Santana-Miles jam was kept a secret from the seventy thousand crowd assembled in the dormant volcano's crater, but despite the location there was little heat generated by the loose ensemble. The performance was set very much in the old Fillmore style, riffs and jamming solos of variable quality and the resulting album, *Carlos Santana and Buddy Miles! Live!,* is one that deservedly has few champions. It's really a very poor album, dominated by Miles' oppressively funky drumming and warbling vocals and notable for an almost complete absence of Santana's guitar. It is the far from shy Neal Schon who takes most of the solos in his customary meltdown style. A fairly formidable percussion section, comprising Coke Escovedo and Victor Pantoja, turn in a reasonable performance but the equally fine horn team of Luis Gasca and Hadley Caliman sound out of sorts. Still, the choice of material is quite interesting and reflects broadening horizons. There is John McLaughlin's "Marbles", from an album he cut with Miles, and a gospel inflected break, "Faith Interlude", which hinted at the spiritually evocative sound that Santana was about to embrace in 1972. The rest was diffuse: not least a sprawling jam that took up an entire side of vinyl, which had the accurate title, "Freeform Funkafide Filth". This one was so loose it almost failed to exist at all. In style it was vaguely similar to the free-jazz mood of Gasca's *For Those Who Chant* album, replete with wandering chord patterns, mono-chord riffs and solos of extremely changeable quality. For all its unfocussed sprawl, the piece did include a passage which quoted a tune from New York based jazz vocalist Leon Thomas ("Um, Um, Um"), indicating that Santana was already developing an interest in radical new jazz forms. Overall, the track and the album find the guitarist lacking direction, almost as if he were stuck between the old blues licks and the search for a new identity. The jamming format was too diffuse to sustain much interest, but it was a glimpse of how Santana went about writing music; there might have been a guitar riff or melody that they could turn into a modest five minute tune, but this was the raw material in all its amoeba-like nothingness. In the end it was just plain boring.

In spite of its basic lack of quality the record was a considerable success, achieving sales of more than a million, but the truth is that it was really a transition album, finding Santana mid-way between the later Latin rock of

Santana III and the Latin-jazz-fusion of *Caravanserai*. For all its artistic shortcomings, the Hawaii session with Buddy Miles was open heart therapy for both main protagonists. For Miles it was getting over the death of his friend Jimi Hendrix and for Santana it was coming to terms with the virtual demise of his group. As the guitarist went back to Mill Valley for a rest, one thing was certain, the Santana group temporarily didn't exist.

The guitarist headed back to San Francisco to further exorcise his musical and personal demons and work out his next steps. He was absorbing new musical influences with the same rapacity as he had consumed the blues as a teenager. This time however he wasn't alone in his quest. He had Michael Shrieve as a partner. After all, Shrieve was at heart a jazz drummer who played rock.

People assumed that the group was dead, but far from it, the two Santana men were getting tighter than brothers and forging a new musical identity for the band in their heads. Mike Shrieve and Carlos Santana spent days on end listening to jazz records, or visiting Bay Area music clubs to hear Gabor Szabo or Elvin Jones. On his trips around the San Francisco music scene Carlos got very lucky; he met his wife-to-be at a Loading Zone concert at Marin Civic Center. He also saw an impressive pianist, Tom Coster, playing with Szabo. At the same time he was keeping close tabs on the band that his brother Jorge was involved with, they were called Malo and also had a fine keyboard player named Richard Kermode who was expert at Latin piano stylings.

Carlos already had a taste for guitar jazz from his interest in Szabo and the Hungarian's Chico Hamilton stint, Shrieve broadened the picture, "When I was living on Army Street, Michael would bring me all kinds of records, Miles Davis and John Coltrane and I'd say 'Aw man, bring me some Albert King.' But when I heard *In A Silent Way* I thought it was interesting and when Michael brought me *Miles In The Sky* it was all over."[28] Shrieve was an intensely thoughtful drummer whose original heroes had been jazz masters, Max Roach and Roy Haynes.

His close musical friends included drummer Lenny White and jazz reeds man Hadley Caliman. He'd played in high school jazz bands, but took up rock drumming when he realised that there wasn't much else going down in San Francisco. Through the drummer, Carlos was introduced to the wider world of jazz beyond Szabo and Chico Hamilton and he embraced it with his usual total enthusiasm, which meant to the exclusion of everything else. Soon, he had a new set of musical heroes: John Coltrane, Miles Davis, Pharoah Sanders, Alice Coltrane, Archie Shepp, Leon Thomas, and Freddie

Hubbard. Davis and Coltrane were the two main forces of influence, Davis for the supreme aesthetic beauty of his playing and Coltrane for his intense spirituality. Coltrane's vision of a universal spirituality coloured both Shrieve and Santana's thinking, "In his vision of God he (Coltrane) saw a unity of all people and all things. All paths that led to the Absolute, ultimate reality, were equally valid. He believed that humanity, his music, the material world and God were all one and that feeling of unity governed his life. He believed that discovering this unity was man's best hope."[29] Coltrane's life was given over to expressing this vision and he released one astonishing album after another. Classics such as *A Love Supreme* and *Meditation* brought both the inner turmoil and ecstasy of Coltrane's direct relationship with God into the listener's home.

With their shared musical and spiritual vision, Santana and Shrieve set about reshaping the band, but it was a journey fraught with turmoil and might never have happened at all. At one time it seemed that the guitarist was going to go off on a collaboration with Gabor Szabo. The Hungarian stayed at his house and they spoke about doing something together, but it didn't materialise. Carlos realised he was tied to Santana. The group reformed in June for rehearsals and the new faces flowed in. David Brown and Michael Carabello were gone, having been replaced by Tom Rutley and Mingo Lewis respectively; but in time another bass face appeared, Doug Rauch, who they knew from the Ghana date with the Voices of East Harlem. Rauch moved to the Bay Area, lived with Shrieve for a time and got a gig with Loading Zone, along with the drummer's wife, Wendy Haas, and Tom Coster. Gregg Rolie was still around under sufferance and Wendy helped out on keyboards, but Shrieve and Santana were on the look out for a new face. They considered asking Larry Young, the left-field Hammond B3 player who shot delicate nerves to pieces in Tony Williams' Lifetime, but they didn't think he'd be interested in playing in a rock band. Next, they tried working with Boz Scaggs' keyboard player, Joachim Young. Young stayed for a while and they wrote some music together ("Castillos De Arena") but in the end, it "didn't work out". Santana were down to Rolie and Wendy Haas again.

The mood at Columbia Studios, where Santana still had ample rehearsal time, was intensely emotional, full of excitement, tension and musical exuberance. Sessions were held without Gregg Rolie, Chepito Areas or Neal Schon present and Rolie's reaction as new pianists appeared on the scene can only be imagined. He rightly considered Santana to be at least half *his* band and now it was being stripped away from him little by little. Santana and

Shrieve were living out their musical fantasies, finding time to jam for hours over a single funk riff conjured-up by Doug Rauch, experimenting by adding layer upon layer of percussion. By now Shrieve's drumming was sounding heavily like Coltrane's drummer Elvin Jones and the pair discussed with child-like enthusiasm the many-layered percussion sounds of the Brazilian master drummer Airto Moreira, who had just come to prominence. The euphoric mood of the two main protagonists could not be suppressed, the pair were high on music. They worked on ideas that were clearly inspired by Miles Davis' *Sketches of Spain* album, or riffs that would later take shape as "Give And Take" or "Spanish Rose". Doug Rauch was clearly a significant new face in the band, with his authentically funky chops which added a new flavour to the Santana musical drawing board.

Tension was high, maybe as high as on the *Santana III* sessions but of a different order, this time there were clear sides, as Neal Schon described, "Santana were breaking up left and right, David was gone, Carabello was gone, there were all kinds of new members and that's the way the sound started to change. It wasn't really Santana any longer and Carlos wanted to take a particular direction and direct it whereas everybody had different opinions about which way it should go. So as we didn't agree with him, we had to go. What happened was Michael Shrieve and Carlos really paired off and we were the enemy. It was like that .. Carlos and Michael wanted to produce the album, they didn't want anybody else to do it."[30] Everyone seemed to be setting out their musical stall, jockeying for position, finding out what they really wanted to do. The main architects were nervous and at one point Shrieve even quit the band briefly, "We were rehearsing. I felt that I had to get into a different kind of musical situation, where maybe I could play lighter because this band is loud." [31] The drummer returned, refreshed from a brief sabbatical playing club dates with Luis Gasca and at last the disintegrating Santana got down to some very hard work, working through until dawn for nights on end. The direction came from three men; Santana, Shrieve and Doug Rauch, who added a large dose of funk and a firm taste for the new hit of the year, The Mahavishnu Orchestra. Rauch also brought in an old New York friend of his, Doug Rodriguez, to add authentic funk guitar parts and Shrieve enlisted veteran sax-player Hadley Caliman. Even if their musical outlook had apparently changed the band's working method hadn't, it was still largely building music from jams on fragments of tunes or solos from LPs or tapes of live shows. On their musical travels Santana and Shrieve carried a tape recorder which they used to tape club dates they went to. Afterwards they'd listen to the tapes over and over to find ideas from one lick or fragment of melody. Shrieve was picking up rhythmic inspiration from the Russian composer Igor Stravinsky and the guitarist was immersed in Coltrane and classical Indian music. There was a sense of purpose to the pair, they were on a journey and the new music stepped beyond standard rock rhythms. They called the journey *Caravanserai* and picked up some more hitch-hikers on the way.

The music on *Caravanserai* reflects the tensions that were ripping through the musicians as they recorded it, it is a compelling mix of urgent, spiritually focused jazz fusion charts and some meaner, dirtier funk grooves. It is probably the finest and certainly the most emotionally complex and naked of all Santana recordings. The first side of the record is intended as a suite where each piece would melt into the next as a cohesive statement. The first sound is Hadley Caliman's phased saxophone which, by being recorded backwards, creates an appropriately Indian tone to match the generally meditative mood. As "Eternal Caravan of Reincarnation" takes shape, with the sounds of double bass, phased piano and jazz guitar, the listener is forcibly reminded of Pharoah Sanders' "Astral Travelling" and their own "Singing Winds, Crying Beasts". The Mahavishnu influenced "Waves Within" is where the emotional action cuts in, with a simple two-chord concept, startling time signature shifts and intense percussion. Most noticeable was the sound and performance of Santana's guitar which hits the listener with a more refined brand of passion, a clear advance in technical control and a less blues-based, more horn-like tone. Whereas he would have gone for the jugular straight away in the past, here Santana develops an expressive, story telling improvisation which builds tension to a strong climax. The album then moves into a brief Latin-funk-rock segment, starting with "Look Up (To See What's Coming Down)" which calls to mind influences like Sly Stone, War and Tower of Power, but is altogether more dirty, fuelled as it was by wild wah-wah guitars, Hammond and Chepito's fervent timbales break. The first vocal on the disc is the simple but atmospheric "Just In Time To See The Sun", a tune driven along by the percussionists and more fine guitar playing, which again builds to a virtuoso climax. It moves into a lush segue which introduces the sublime "Song Of The Wind", one of the finest Santana recordings. This guitar duet between Santana and Schon created a style of guitar playing and music that was unknown before, except perhaps in the work of Gabor Szabo, whose approach it recalls in spirit. Over a sumptuous cushion of Hammond, Shrieve's beautifully sensitive drumming and Mingo Lewis' lithe conga, the two guitarists weave long, free, airy melodies, each of which might have been the starting point for a new composition. In some senses, it is a more refined version of the samba section of "Samba Pa Ti" and is definitely a close cousin of the last part of "Incident At Neshabur". There are no fretboard histrionics here, just a panache and expression that brings to mind a Miles Davis or Freddie Hubbard solo; Schon would subsquently ditch this feel until he recorded "Szabo" for the Abraxas Pool years later, but "Song Of The Wind" was the template for Santana's style for many years to come. Drummer Shrieve took the master tape home to record his drum part again, a risk worth taking, as the final drum track reveals. After six or more gorgeous minutes it gives way to the less moving "All The Love Of The Universe", a clever mix of flamenco moods and the nearest to straight ahead Latin-rock on the album, which gives Rolie and Schon room to deliver burning solos.

The advent of compact disc in the 1980s didn't serve albums like *Caravanserai* especially well, as it tended to blur the clear distinction between the two sides of the record, which were obviously programmed for effect. It was clearly the producers' intention that there should be a natural break between "All The Love Of The Universe" and "Future Primitive", which had entirely different moods. The latter was the introduction to the intensely percussive and experimental second side of the album and it is an alarming juxtaposition of New Age electric piano sounds and one of the hottest percussion breaks ever committed to tape. This volcanic interlude blows away any doubts of Mingo Lewis' skills and reaffirms Chepito Areas' invention and virtuosity. "Future Primitive" is clearly the vision of Michael Shrieve and offers a pointer to his later solo career. Above all it creates a tension between the meditative and the physical as did the entire album. Shrieve and Santana were sharing music like brothers in this period and the drummer was instrumental in introducing the guitar man to new sounds. Amongst these was music from Brazil where African, indigenous Indian, Romantic European sensibility and jazz had fused to create a unique musical form. Soon, the pair were enthusiasts and "Stone Flower", a subtly unique rhythmic work by legendary Brazilian composer Antonio Carlos Jobim, was taped and incorporated into the new Santana sound with masterful ease. Indeed, rhythm is the main feature of Santana's "Stone Flower", introducing the cuica, a distinctive Brazilian percussion instrument which creates a chattering, laughing sound. Keen listeners would have detected other interesting tones, like Tom Rutley's bowed acoustic bass and the single occurrence of a Santana-Shrieve double vocal, on what was one of the few truly light hearted tunes on the album.

As soon as James Mingo Lewis had joined Santana he proved his suitability for the role and exhibited a talent which burst through on his excellent "La

Fuente Del Ritmo". It has the structure of a Cuban jam or "descarga", with its catchy piano line over which some of the finest improvisations on any Santana recording are heard. Two key players were introduced here, Armando Peraza and Tom Coster, both of whom would form critical relationships with Carlos and both of whom would permanently change the band. Mingo Lewis was key to Peraza's arrival. As soon as Mingo realised that he was heading back to San Francisco as a part of Santana, he made it known to the others that he was going to find a master Cuban conga drummer who lived there, Armando Peraza. Carlos Santana had also recently come across Peraza at a street arts fair in the Mission and took the opportunity to invite the maestro to the recording studio. Coster was invited along with Doug Rauch one evening and recorded his solo on the spot, without ever hearing the music before. He soon felt the tensions, "The overall atmosphere in the band initially was somewhat hostile because there were a lot of personnel changes being made and not all the changes were agreeable to everyone. I, for example, was made to feel as if I was not really wanted in the band initially and at first I did not know whether I had the gig or not. One of the people who really fought for me being in the band was Carlos which is why I got to stay." "La Fuente Del Ritmo" established Santana's credentials as a Latin-jazz outfit, largely down to outstanding solos from Santana, Coster and Peraza. Peraza's bongos dominate the entire track, revealing an astonishing level of virtuosity and expression, whilst Coster's break was simply magnificent.

The entire record seemed to be heading for a climax that was reached in the stunning "Every Step Of The Way", which closes the album and includes a horn orchestration by Tom Harrell that recalled Gil Evans' "Las Vegas Tango" and his *Sketches of Spain* orchestrations for Miles Davis. The music was tense, a deeper examination of the relationship between darkness and light. The darkness comes in a menacing opening section where guitars and percussion conjure a stabbing, compelling edginess, whilst the light is found in an exultant second part which features thrilling percussion and outstanding solos by Santana and flautist Hadley Caliman. This was exceptional music that contained a level of emotional exposition associated with jazz together with a fierce spiritual intensity.

Santana and Shrieve had conjured a masterful production which segued the music on side one into a continuous suite and, importantly, achieved the most focused recording of percussion of any Santana album. Above all, it is the emotional impact of *Caravanserai* which makes it stand out from everything else in Santana's canon and confirms it as one of the more important recordings of the early 1970s. The album held its own with contemporary releases from Miles Davis, The Mahavishnu Orchestra, Weather Report and all the other leading players in the jazz-fusion field. This was due to the new, higher level of musicianship of players like Caliman, Coster, Rauch and Peraza who could and did play straight jazz for a living. Beyond all of this, it was the transformation in Carlos Santana's playing that was the most astounding. He had certainly done all that any rock guitar player could do and more, but here he was crafting solos that "told stories" and conveyed complex emotions in much the way that a jazz player would. It is likely that it came from his being captivated with the power of jazz improvisers like Coltrane, coupled with his sheer determination to become an even better player. It was this struggle to reach higher levels that captivated the listener to *Caravanserai*. Even if Columbia Records were concerned that the music wasn't commercial, Santana and Shrieve would have consciously lost the audience to satisfy their emotional urge to record this music. Shrieve revealed the pair's innocent naiveté, "We thought it was appealing, to the ear and to the soul. It made me feel good inside. There's a certain purity in the music that it seemed had to be recognised that would touch people if they really listened to it."[32] Naive or not, millions were touched by an outstanding musical and emotional statement.

However, not everyone was happy. Rolie and Schon had heard enough and split. Rolie retired from the music business and went to run a restaurant with his father. Nevertheless, his contributions to the album had been strong and his Hammond sound a key part of the disc's success. Schon helped out on the first album by Azteca, a band Coke Escovedo put together with many Santana alumni. Later he joined Michael Carabello in the studio on the conga drummer's solo album, which crept out years later under the title *Giants*.

With the release of *Caravanserai* in November 1972, Santana took to the road in the USA, revealing a new line up that retained Rauch and Mingo Lewis and introduced Malo pianist Richard Kermode. He had caught the guitarist's ear during the Luis Gasca recording in the summer of 1971, "Richard was a very earthy piano player. When Michael Shrieve and I changed everything in 1972 with *Caravanserai* we worked with Tom but felt we needed another person for the "guacheos", the "tumbaos", the Chick Corea, Eddie Palmieri kinda piano company, because he knew it from within. He had a beautiful natural way of swinging and he wouldn't mind sacrificing not playing solo for just swinging." Armando Peraza and Tom Coster had been invited to join and their introduction left the band permanently changed. Peraza was already a legendary figure in Latin percussion and the most gifted improviser of any of the conga greats. Listening to Peraza was akin to hearing Allah Rakah, the great master of the classical Indian tabla drums. He was and remains the Latin percussion equivalent of a concert pianist; with Peraza in tow, Santana had to be taken seriously in Latin music circles. Tom Coster was a jazz musician with a Mediterranean heritage that found voice in an elegant melodic sense. His technique and musical imagination were up there with the likes of Chick Corea who admired his work. His recollection of the Santana scene in 1972 is telling, "The people who stood out the most as far as being in charge of the New Santana Band direction were Carlos, Michael and Doug Rauch, they definitely had a vision of how they wanted the band to sound. Carlos always looked real cool to me and there was a certain aura about him that commanded respect, when he had a vision, which he had with the new band, he worked relentlessly to make it a reality. Mike Shrieve eventually became my best friend in the band, he too was an authoritative figure but in a more pleasant and gentle manner, Mike really worked hard for the band to be successful." Coster was a key find for Santana, his playing was superb and he was just as much at ease arranging and interpreting the most complex musical ideas. He also shared an interest in meditation and understood John Coltrane and Miles Davis. He was to become Carlos' closest musical friend for the next six years.

When the new band was unveiled US audiences were literally stunned by the new music and some walked out when they realised that "Evil Ways" wasn't on the menu, but "Welcome" and "La Fuente Del Ritmo" were. However, the band were greeted by standing ovations and, by the time they reached Europe for a month of shows across November and December, they were being hailed as heros. Always liable to extremes, the British music press in particular took it upon themselves to "discover" the new Santana.

The music on this 1972 tour was culled mostly from *Caravanserai,* its heady brew was recaptured with shuddering intensity in the live arena; Carlos was playing like a new man and the double keyboard partnership of Tom Coster and Richard Kermode was stunning. Even more impressive was the magnetic three man percussion hot house of Chepito, Peraza and Mingo Lewis, as they ran through classic material expanded to the new jazz sensibilities of the band. "Samba Pa Ti" and "Incident At Neshabur" in particular were perfect for the new approach. There were no vocals on this tour, apart from the guitarist's occasional forays to the microphone on "Just In Time To See The Sun" and there were almost no concessions to audience expectation. In fact, the musicians seemed oblivious to the crowds – too caught up in the thrill of musical creation. And, it was an approach that worked.

Chapter 9

At the end of the US tour, late in October 1972, Carlos Santana found himself in New York City for a pair of meetings that were to literally change his
life. First, he met the master English guitar player John McLaughlin for their
inaugural joint live date. McLaughlin originally hailed from Yorkshire in the
North of England, but after stints in London and Germany, found himself in
New York and the sessions for Miles Davis' classic *In A Silent Way* album.
After playing on a number of Davis' ground-breaking albums, he formed his
own band, The Mahavishnu Orchestra, which played with a virtuoso intensity that stunned audiences. Carlos Santana was amongst them and he followed the group live whenever he could. As ever with a new Santana craze,
there were to be no half-measures. The second meeting was an encounter
with McLaughlin's spiritual teacher Sri Chinmoy. In 1972 the one thing that
Carlos Santana needed above all was some discipline in his life and an
awareness that being the latest hot property in the facile and ephemeral
world of rock music was no guarantee of, well anything, except for a few
million in the bank. Sri Chinmoy was exactly what Carlos had been looking
for at the time, a strong father figure to lead him away from the excesses of
the rock life towards the search for inner fulfilment and spiritual peace. In
his spiritual search Santana had passed through Jesus, Yogananda and finally
arrived at Sri Chinmoy, "Since I was a little boy I aspired to Jesus, I always
dug him. Sri Chinmoy teaches that Jesus is a window like Buddah and
Mohammed, but the light that comes in is from The Supreme."[33] Thus,
Carlos was accepted as a disciple of Sri Chinmoy and took the final step of
renunciation against the Woodstock counter-culture, he cut his long hair off !

There was certainly no lack of discipline in the lifestyle, "At that time, because of the relationship with Sri Chinmoy, we thought that's what we needed to do; learn to meditate; get up at five, six o'clock in the morning and meditate, not eat fish, chicken or anything. It was kind of like a West Point."[34] As ever, Carlos entered into his new found obsession with his customary 150% commitment and for the next ten years was a main cheerleader for the Bengali mystic. Once he had surrendered to the guru his commitment was total and by March his goal was, "to open up a spiritual centre in San Francisco. Yes it's true, I can be a bridge for many Spanish-speaking people who have never heard of the master." Clearly this enthusiasm made the guru very happy, "I called Sri Chinmoy a week ago. He said John and I were his greatest pride, he says we're taking him to the masses." However, whatever else is said about this period, it is clear that Carlos was entirely sincere in his spiritual quest and it did move him to create some exceptional music.

It seemed inevitable that McLaughlin and Santana should record together and this is exactly what they did in between tours, starting in November 1972 and finally finishing in March 1973. The album was quite literally a gift from God for Columbia and they moved quickly at the highest level in the organisation to suggest such a pairing, as John McLaughlin recalled, "I was in California with the Mahavishnu Orchestra, Carlos was following us around because he was crazy about the band. Then I went back to New York and I had a dream about making a record with him. The next day Clive Davis spoke to my manager and said 'Why doesn't John make a record with Carlos Santana?' It's amazing how these things happen. So I called him up and he came to New York and by the time we'd finished he'd become a disciple of Sri Chinmoy." The album was released in June 1973 and included contributions from Armando Peraza, Doug Rauch, Don Alias, Mahavishnu drummer Billy Cobham and organist Larry Young. Carlos Santana's brief for the record was, "that I mainly wanted to get closer to Sri Chinmoy and make the masses aware of the Mahavishnu Orchestra."[35] In the event the duo's disc was an explosion of pure emotion. At times it seems that the pair have so much passion to express and so many musical words to get out all at once, that they are about to burst. And burst is what *Love, Devotion, Surrender* does into the listener's consciousness with massive eruptions of desperate belief. The music they chose reflects the journey of discovery Carlos Santana had been taking. There was an ambitious cover of the first part of John Coltrane's masterpiece "A Love Supreme", a moving acoustic reading of his "Naima" and an Afro-Cuban working of the gospel spiritual "Let Us Go Into The House Of The Lord" (based on Pharoah Sanders' version on his *Deaf,*

Dumb, Blind LP). All featured lengthy guitar improvisations, alternating between McLaughlin's devastating volleys of ecstatic notes and Santana's more lyrical style now infused with a new euphoric mood. Armando Peraza adds his customary classic conga improvisations and Larry Young his ethereal organ interludes. Doug Rauch seems particularly at home in this setting and was a big fan of the Mahavishnu Orchestra. Indeed, Santana thought that he would have fitted in well with McLaughlin's band, "If he had joined Mahavishnu they probably would have kept it together longer, him and Billy Cobham really got along."[36]

It was a bold album to put out, but commercially a very successful one as it quickly went gold around the globe. It's not a comfortable disc to hear and "enjoyment" seems a hardly relevant expectation for what is a statement rather than an entertainment product. "Compelling" would probably sum it up, plus "beautiful" for the acoustic interludes. The cover shots of McLaughlin, Santana and a beaming Sri Chinmoy, who looks as happy as a lottery winner, were bound to generate some sniggers. The guitarists could not have cared less. This was a hot, new, overwhelming passion and no-one could stop them. The pair were like brothers, but it appeared that McLaughlin was playing big brother to his new friend, leading the new disciple into the life of discipline and musical complexity; at first Santana was ready to accept it, so overwhelmed was he by enthusiasm for his spiritual path, "John is further along than I am. But I aspire." A tour was planned but cancelled as Carlos was at the point of getting carried away with it all, "eventually we might quit our bands and do our own band together, John and I. We were working together on a tour but it fell through. All these money cats think with their minds, not with their souls. But we need people like that to attend to those things."[37] Eventually, a short replacement tour was hastily arranged to support the album, which was racing up the charts and some masterful schedule juggling conjured up a two week slot in August when the two guitarists' paths could collide. Taking with them the basic album unit of Peraza, Young, Rauch and Cobham, the two set off on an intense tour which saw extended solos and more giant steps in Santana's technique. Drummer Billy Cobham was already a legendary figure on account of his hyper-fast technique, but he met his match on this tour in the person of indefatigable Armando Peraza, who was delighted when Cobham told him that nobody but nobody could keep up with him. Naturally the Cuban master proved the hot mouthed youngblood wrong.

The basic format of the band's set included extended improvisations on "Flame-Sky", "Let Us Go Into The House Of The Lord", "The Life Divine" and "A Love Supreme"; new compositions were brought along by Larry Young ("I'm Aware Of You") and Billy Cobham ("Taurian Matador"), along with lighter moments in "Meditation" and "Naima". One of these two usually opened the show for a moment of reflection before they launched into "the three hour fuck", as one Columbia representative described it. Indeed, the fervour of the music was up a notch or two from the studio work and more was heard from Larry Young's dervish-like organ, which gave audiences the chance to hear the Hammond turned into a wild canvas onto which he painted John Coltrane's sheets of sound.

There is no doubt that Carlos Santana felt intimidated by the extravagant technical genius of McLaughlin, possibly the most accomplished guitarist of the century, but he came to learn that his voice had its own intrinsic value, "When we were on the road, I thought, 'Man, what am I going to do? I should just shine his shoes.' Then I found out that I may not play as many notes, or know as much as he does, but three notes – if you put them in the right place at the right time – are just as important."[38]

As the LP was released and the tour progressed the two guitarists became the targets for accusations of hypocrisy and ridicule for their spiritual views – with Santana bearing the brunt of the criticism. It just didn't fit with the rock life. Carlos knew that had he been a jazz musician with strong spiritual beliefs, like Pharoah Sanders or Yusef Lateef, he would never have to explain himself, but as a "rock star", an identity he did not recognise or want, he was expected to play a certain role. Spiritual disciple was not it. The music critics balked at Carlos' naive sounding devotion to the guru and pondered that rock'n'roll wasn't supposed to be like this. Gurus, white clothes and short hair were hard to take and Carlos Santana has faced this mistrust ever since. The truth was that the Mexican had simply stopped playing the part of "rock star guitarist" in the music media circus. In rejecting the established rebellious image of a rock star, Santana effectively ensured the rock establishment's scorn.

☯

Whatever anyone else thought of him, Carlos Santana was inspired to near super-human levels and, between October 1972 and the last day of December 1973, carried on a recording and concert schedule that should probably have killed him outright. He barely had a day off in the whole period and jumped straight from touring Europe, to the McLaughlin sessions, to a massive US tour and then to Japan and beyond. The Mexican was a man possessed with spiritual vision that bordered on the messianic and his urge to take his new music to the world could not be contained in a normal schedule.

By now, the Santana band was formed around a nucleus of Carlos, Mike Shrieve, Tom Coster and Armando Peraza. Chepito hung around for the money and the girls, whilst Richard Kermode and Doug Rauch were fine players but had some lifestyle problems. Mike Shrieve was critical to the whole thing, it was his closeness to Carlos in terms of musical vision that had allowed the guitar player to separate the old from the new Santana and Carlos came to rely on the drummer for support and, to an extent, direction.

Before hitting the road, Carlos pulled off one more coup by securing the presence on the tour of legendary New York soul-jazz vocalist, Leon Thomas, who had been a long-time collaborator of Pharoah Sanders and a major figure in jazz in his own right. Thomas was a master vocalist and innovator. He mixed street-style, black power politics with a heavy sense of the spiritual. Though Carlos had always been a big fan of the New York "Soul-Jazz" scene, it was a spontaneous flash of inspiration that led him to invite Thomas aboard, "I was in a restaurant in New York with my wife," he explained, "and I went over to the jukebox and there was this record by Leon Thomas and just then I decided to look him up and see if he wanted to join the band. When I called him he said he had just had a dream about me. I told him we were going on a tour of Japan and he said he'd always wanted to go to Japan, so he joined." A magical, if brief, liaison was born, though it was not all roses as Tom Coster recalled, "I didn't care for Leon Thomas, he is definitely a very talented person, but he was very difficult to have on the road. He was never happy with anything and was always asking what the band could do for him and never what he could do for the band."

At the end of January 1973, Santana embarked on their first ever world tour. The massive 312 date excursion would take them to every corner of the globe on a schedule that would have left most other bands breathless! In the middle of it, on April 20th, Carlos Santana married Deborah King, the daughter of blues guitar star Saunders King who had famously played with Billie Holiday. King was one of the first stars of blues music in the period around the second world war and he became an important musical influence in Santana's life.

The tour started with a massive trek through the USA, interrupted by the recording of their next album, *Welcome*. Then it was on to stops in Japan and the Far East, Australia, New Zealand before finally, taking another turn around the USA. Santana's new spiritual commitment led him to ask the audience for a minute of meditative silence before each show, something that was sometimes unwelcome. Once underway, the Santana set was a heady brew of a musical stream of consciousness that checked in at neo-classical gospel ("Going Home"), laid down some dirty funk ("A-1 Funk, "Free Angela"), gave a new slant to Brazilian jazz (a hot take on Airto's "Xibaba" and the newly heard "Promise Of A Fisherman"), revealed new friendships ("Castillos De Arena", a collaboration with Chick Corea), gave a musical nod to Michel Colombier ("Wings") and launched Santana rock favourites as jazz-fusion epics ("Se A Cabo", "Incident At Neshabur"). New material from *Welcome* was introduced and a number of Leon Thomas' classic features were included in the set, "The Creator Has A Master Plan", "Um,Um,Um" and a Thomas vocal arrangement of Pharoah Sanders' "Japan".

In spite of the new developments, the Afro-Cuban flavour was far from lost and the Peraza-Areas partnership set new standards for Latin percussion around the world, they were simply inspired and it was showcased in numbers like "Batucada", "Bambele" and "Savor". The other musicians like Tom Coster were entranced and invigorated by the pair, "Armando and Chepito were two of the finest percussionists I have ever performed with, they were monster players and when I would take a solo the two of them were right there with me. They both would listen carefully to what I was playing and complement each and every musical line that I played. Together we would reach musical heights that were unbelievable !" The group was interacting like a jazz band; when Santana or one of the pianists took a solo, the drummers would instantly reproduce the rhythmic pattern of the solo on their drums, creating a conversation in music. It was as if the players were communicating with each other through telepathy.

Santana, in 1973, were consistently conjuring a brew similar to that being concocted by Miles Davis. The band often played a two-hour plus set, which ran together in an almost uninterrupted flow, joined together by cunningly inventive musical segues. Santana's guitar playing had, in the space of a year, risen to a new level of control and expressiveness. He emerged with a new, fuller tone that conveyed the force of his spiritual passions, as well as sounding just a little more like a tenor saxophone, the jazz soloist's greatest tool. His technical ability seemed to have taken a massive leap forward and the fluffed notes disappeared, to be replaced with controlled be-bop style runs. In addition to this, he had begun to emulate the jazz player's device of cleverly incorporating musical quotations from other players' tunes into his solos and, so, on this tour, Santana's solos were liberally sprinkled with short extracts from the work of Coltrane ("My Favourite Things" and "Afro Blue"), Jimi Hendrix ("3rd Stone From The Sun"), Freddie Hubbard ("First Light"), Airto Moreira ("Jive Talking"), The Beatles ("Within You Without

You" and "Fool On The Hill") and Weather Report ("Boogie Woogie Waltz"). It would become a trademark of the Santana guitar style.

On the stages of the world the New Santana Band continued to present the old duality quite starkly, with Carlos Santana dressed entirely in white, occupying one side of the stage, gazing heavenward for inspiration, whilst at the other side of the stage, Chepito Areas leered at the ladies in the audience and continued his favourite party piece, phallic innuendoes. Nevertheless, Areas' *musical* thrusts were outstanding and in the Coster-Kermode keyboard partnership, the guitarist had found two contrasting, uniquely well-suited stylists. Leon Thomas and Armando Peraza were genuine jazz innovators, Doug Rauch, a street-funk master and Mike Shrieve had finally found a true home for his wonderful jazz-rock drumming. All of this band's massive energy is captured on the classic – and lavishly packaged – *Lotus*, a Japanese live album featuring material from a pair of concerts in Osaka. When it made its way around the world as an import, *Lotus* polarised Santana fans, who either loved or hated the new musical direction. Still, regardless of one's personal preferences, the record is undoubtedly a document of a group of musicians working together at a peak of creativity.

September and October took in the most significant portion of the tour, an unheard of month of dates throughout Latin America. It was a significant homecoming for a band which boasted three famous Latinos, Carlos Santana, Chepito Areas and Armando Peraza. But it would also be one of the most stressful and important tours in Santana's history.

The month-long tour took Santana through Mexico, Guatemala, El Salvador, Costa Rica, Panama and Nicaragua, then into South America with multiple dates in Venezuela, Colombia, Argentina and Brazil. This was uncharted territory for a major band and fraught with danger. Whereas the politics of Mexico and Costa Rica had been stable for over half a century, the rest of the region was in turmoil; Guatemala had been under military rule since 1954 and a low level civil war had raged ever since. El Salvador likewise enjoyed military rule, whilst Nicaragua revelled in a US-backed dynasty of government by Generals. The South American continent was fairing worse still, Chile had just experienced a barbarous military coup which left thousands dead and the country could not be visited. Brazil was booming economically, but the price was military rule and brutal repression of "leftists". Meanwhile, Argentina was fracturing under the pressure of conflicting military and Peronist factions. On reflection, it is extraordinary that this tour took place at all, especially given the 1971 experiences in Lima, one city that was definitely not on the tour itinerary. Still, for all the political upheaval in the region, the concerts themselves were greeted with hysteria in bulging soccer stadiums packed with 30,000, 40,000 or 50,000 people.

The group's arrival in Managua, Nicaragua saw the tour turboprop surrounded by press, a Mariachi band and a mass of humanity, milling around, *just being there*. Returning to his native country, Chepito Areas attracted most attention, fans surrounding the diminutive percussionist with stories and requests for tickets, signatures, anything. The musicians reached the relative safety of a bus and they were soon on the road into the capital. The fans were still there, riding pillion on motorbikes, leaning over to the bus to pass tatty pieces of paper for autographs. Inside the stadium, the crowd demanded a revival of the Woodstock moment. Chanting "sacrificio, sacrificio, sacrificio"; the throng ebbed and flowed just as a huge standing soccer crowd would. Mostly young men, in the volatile crowd, one man made some space for himself by spinning a six-foot long wooden bench above his head.

The concert opened with Carlos addressing the audience. He asked for the customary minute's silence, pointing out that music was like a mango that God had given to them, not an ordinary mango, but one filled with significance and spiritual energy. The other members of the group looked on askance as the guitar player folded his hands in prayer and appeared to bless the crowd. Meanwhile, in the boiling stadium, fans get carried out semi-conscious from the crush. The juxtaposition of the ethereal and brutish economic reality was staring the Mexican in the face. "Samba Pa Ti" elicited a wild reaction, fans pressing up to the wooden barrier between them and the stage- a sea of manic flesh which the seated guitarist appeared not to notice. The concerts climax with "Toussaint L'Overture" as Coster and Santana dredge out every last ounce of passion. Those who can, dance, the rest get pressed together like a box of bacalao. They say some died in the crush.

Whilst Michael Shrieve and Carlos Santana expressed the wish that the music would help each member of the audience realise their own "spiritual being", running battles between the police, military and the fans were underway at some concerts. The band were in the middle of political turmoil. There were rumours of demonstrations against the price of concert tickets in Nicaragua – the people from the barrio couldn't afford to get in. And, for all their spiritual intent, Santana and Shrieve couldn't live people's lives for them, or change their economic circumstances. They were just musicians. They would be back in California within a month and Latin America would return to another two decades of torment and violence. The whole sorry, but captivating, mess was captured in an extraordinary film, *Santana En Colores*.

When the band finally got back to the Bay Area, they were completely emotionally drained and later admitted that they had contemplated giving up the tour such were the pressures. Tom Coster was certainly deeply affected by the experience, "The tour in Latin America will always be in my memories, some good and some not so good. The music was great and so were a lot of the experiences, but the craziness that went on with the people of the various countries because they were so excited to see and hear the band was very dangerous. People lost their lives trying to get into the concert stadiums and were also crushed to death because the crowds became so excited trying to get close to the band. These are experiences I would like to forget." It was clear that the intensity of the 1973 tour could not be sustained and, after another visit to Europe in November and December, the year and the new Santana band came to a close at The Winterland in San Francisco on New Year's Eve.

The achievement of this incarnation of the Santana band cannot be overstated. In the space of eighteen months they had come to rival Miles Davis' group and Weather Report as one of the most innovative, exciting and accomplished fusion bands. Nobody played Latin-Jazz-Fusion as well as Santana. The band included an embarrassment of virtuoso musicians – Peraza, Chepito, Shrieve, Coster and Thomas were all leaders in their fields and Carlos Santana had emerged, after his exposure to McLaughlin, as one of the most exquisite guitar players and instrumentalists. His technique was light years from the guy who recorded "Waiting". His detractors, and there were plenty of them, may have scoffed, but *it really was* the same Chicano kid they had known bumming around the Bay Area playing the blues, who was now in company with Chick Corea, John McLaughlin and Miles Davis. If there was one skill Carlos had that enabled him to reach up to the higher level of playing jazz, it was his innate ability to deliver a melody, which he had learnt from his father. Weather Report's Joe Zawinul, one of this era's greatest musicians, suggests this is Santana's greatest gift, "I have always been a fan of Carlos Santana. The main reason is he knows how to play a melody and he makes every note meaningful and therefore I would call him my favourite guitar player for that reason. There are many, many guitar players in the world who would probably outplay him in terms of sheer technique, but that's not music anyhow." Being able to hold a melody is the first skill that a jazz musician needs, followed by a feeling for the blues and then strong technique. Carlos had the first two in abundance and was rapidly building on the third. His apotheosis was complete.

☯

Though the new Santana of 1973 may not have been as much of a collective as the original band, it was still very much a group affair. All the musicians made significant contributions to the arrangement of the music and were by no means simply a backing band for the guitar player. This is the spirit that characterised the next group LP which was recorded over a period of three weeks in May and June, between the numerous live dates of the period. There were new compositions from Tom Coster, Richard Kermode, Doug Rauch and Chepito Areas, as well as Santana and Shrieve. The record covered a dizzying spectrum of musical styles in a cohesive series of performances, which found Carlos, who had just assumed the spiritual name Devadip, taking surprisingly few guitar solos. This may have been a reflection of a sudden diffidence about his playing arising from close contact with jazz virtuosos like McLaughlin, Corea and Alice Coltrane. Another feature of *Welcome* is the remarkably light, airy production which creates a comfortingly warm atmosphere, making it a pleasure to hear. It certainly lacks the pure emotional clout of *Caravanserai,* a reflection of the more stable situation in which it was created, rather it evokes a calming peaceful mood that makes its title highly appropriate. Much of the credit for this goes to engineer Glen Kolotkin, who handled the complex instrumentation masterfully.

The music opens with the moving "Going Home", which originated from an Afro-American spiritual. The Santana version is based on a recording made by Alice Coltrane on her 1972 album *Lord Of Lords* cast in a classical setting, reflecting the song's appearance as the second movement of Dvorak's famous "New World Symphony." On the Santana album the strings are replaced by majestic organs and sinuous percussion, to create a dreamy but quite beautiful mood. "Going Home" is a warm, loving embrace set in music. The album moves on to a new kind of Latin-pop with Santana's typically uncomplicated "Love, Devotion and Surrender", which is introduced by a gorgeous guitar passage and becomes a feature for no fewer than three vocalists, Santana, Wendy Haas and Leon Thomas, who delivers a characteristically off the wall performance. A feature of this song and the whole album is the constant colouration provided by the two keyboard players, who complement each other perfectly without any hint of clashing as they do to great effect on Chepito Areas' upbeat salsa groove "Samba De Sausilito", a tune which actually emerged from a studio jam the band did with drummer Tony Smith. It's a feature for Tom Coster, who shines on a delightful electric piano solo. The first real chance to hear Leon Thomas comes on the light "When I Look Into Your Eyes", on which the Santana audience is introduced to his African throat vocals, resonant bongos from

Peraza and a curious moog-driven, funk coda. One of *Welcome's* highlights comes on the Brazilian influenced bossa-nova, "Yours In The Light" – an outstanding Richard Kermode composition with a rich melody delivered with supreme grace by the incomparable Brazilian singer Flora Purim, who had recently come to general attention through her work with Chick Corea. Carlos Santana's guitar solo on this piece is one of the best of his career, it's perfectly constructed, richly melodic and highly expressive, whilst Kermode reveals why he was considered one of the best exponents of Latin piano.

Side two of what was already a fine record is more complex, opening with "Mother Africa", a percussion showcase during which Peraza, Areas and Shrieve set out their stall as leaders in the field. The use of marimba and the flutely synthesiser conjure up the spirit of the continent, before a compelling soprano saxophone is heard over Tom Coster's piano chords, which call to mind the spirit of Pharoah Sanders' "Deaf, Dumb, Blind". The saxophone was played by Jules Broussard, an old Bay Area jazz colleague of Coster's, who began a relationship with the group at this point. Coster shows his abilities as an arranger with the resonant strings on a soul track "Light Of Life", which has a wonderfully open, echoey weightlessness, as does Leon Thomas' restrained but rich vocal. The instrumental showcase of the album arrives in the shape of "Flame-Sky", which is very much set in the style of the Mahavishnu Orchestra. The opening section finds Carlos and Shrieve in a remarkable duet, both playing with passion and invention before one of the guitarist's legendary sustained notes moves the track into a more forceful section driven by commanding keyboard breaks. Santana's guitar takes up the more urgent mood, before John McLaughlin's solo roars in like Dante's "Inferno" and the music climbs to a series of shuddering climaxes. After the passion comes the meditation and the album closes out with a peaceful reading of John Coltrane's classic "Welcome", a highly sensitive performance which sees Santana calling on his in-built ability to deliver a melody in a version far less strident than Coltrane's original.

The Santana Band were at the height of their musical powers when they recorded *Welcome*. Its seemingly effortless mood belies a creative musicianship of a very high level and an empathy between the players usually reserved for the jazz arena. Even though the best place to hear this band was in the live setting, this album gives a hint of their style in neat, bite-sized chunks. All the key elements are here, Santana's romantic, expressive guitar; Rauch's exuberant, bubbling bass; a unique multi-keyboards partnership between Coster and Kermode that provided texture and interest with nearly every chord; Thomas' unique vocals and in Peraza, Areas and Shrieve, one of the most accomplished and loose percussion sections of the period. *Welcome* remains one of Santana's finest moments, with its almost tangible air of peace.

Chapter 10

As far as the world of jazz-fusion was concerned, by the end of 1973 Santana had arrived and were to be taken very seriously indeed. As Carlos Santana became a disciple of Sri Chinmoy, he seemed to have come full circle in his fascination with John Coltrane and Pharoah Sanders as they had both been seekers of spiritual "truth" too. Now that Carlos had established himself as an exquisite instrumentalist, he was ready to work in earnest with a major figure in jazz, the wife of John Coltrane. Alice Coltrane had been the spiritual soul-mate of the legendary saxophonist and she had taken his legacy forward, recording a series of striking albums that brought the spiritual element of jazz straight into the listener's home. Her albums oscillated between heady free-jazz group sessions (*Journey In Satchidananda* and *Ptah The El-Daoud*) and dense orchestral expressions (*Lord Of Lords*), she enjoyed all the respect due to the widow of John Coltrane but was also an innovative and excellent musician herself. Again, it was the Sri Chinmoy connection that brought Santana and Alice Coltrane together to build on the collaboration on "Going Home". Joined by his two main musical brothers of the time, Tom Coster and Armando Peraza, and fired by spiritual energy, Santana and Alice Coltrane entered the studio in the spring of 1974, having played a couple of US concerts together in March along with John McLaughlin. One of these shows in New York left the *Village Voice*'s Frank Rose almost speechless in admiration, "Santana, McLaughlin and their wives came out to join Alice Coltrane for 'A Love Supreme'. The experience was unforgettable. After McLaughlin introduced it as a tribute to John Coltrane the musicians gradually picked up the air as Mahalakshami and Urmila began chanting.

Santana's electric guitar soon took its own course leaving the others far behind before it fell back into place; when it did the assemblage appeared to lose all earthly bounds."[39]

The Santana-Coltrane collaboration was titled *Illuminations*. When it was released in September 1974 it revealed just how far Santana had come, on an album that stood comparison with any of Alice Coltrane's own discs and a good many of Pharoah Sanders'. Most of the material was written by Santana and Tom Coster exposing a level of depth and empathy in the pair's composing that was well beyond what either had achieved at that point. It crystallised the relationship between the two, Coster having the background in musical theory to give realisation to Santana's ideas. Alice Coltrane added one composition, "Bliss : The Eternal Now", played mellotron and harp and added string arrangements that recalled her own classic albums. Her orchestrations tended towards the dramatic and grandiose and they had reference points in the work of modern American composer, Alan Hovhaness, who had developed a sweeping, sheets of sound symphonic palette to reflect the majesty of nature in musical form. Jules Broussard's dramatic flute is the first instrument heard on "Angel Of Air", before it is swept up into the warm embrace of Dave Holland's bass and the richly textural orchestral arrangement. Carlos' melody on his ringing guitar again recalls "Astral Traveling" and his playing here is strong and inventive. The bass line is actually rooted in Latin music, but the music's climactic twists and turns give plenty of room for the soloists to demonstrate their dynamic range. Jules Broussard is outstanding throughout, whilst Alice Coltrane's presence is signalled by the sweeping strings and occasional harp figures. It is challenging, difficult and sophisticated music. Initially, the sessions found the Mexican's jazz diffidence rising again, until the pianist encouraged him to play more than he had originally intended, "I had written most of the songs for this album with notations for other people around me to play at the designated spots. But I wasn't playing that much. She said, 'No that's not what's happening. You've got to play because your presence is needed.'"

Alice's piece, "Bliss: The Eternal Now", has a very free and open orchestral arrangement, which takes the music into the realms of modern composers like Stravinsky. This track also has quite a dark sense of foreboding, perhaps revealing the other side of the spiritual coin – the struggle for attainment.

The second half of the music opened with "Angel Of Sunlight", a startling piece of raga-imbued Latin-jazz, with Santana, Alice Coltrane and Jules Broussard all playing intense improvisations against the thunderous and compelling backdrop of Jack De Johnette's drums, Peraza's furious congas and Phil Ford's tabla, set against a forceful ostinato bass line. The depth of this piece captures something of the spirit of John Coltrane and Carlos plays a quite extraordinary modal solo set in a scale imbued with Indian quarter tones. Alice Coltrane travels on a Wurlitzer Organ which has a distinctly other-worldly tone, moving the music into a trance-like state. The outstanding rhythm section of Jack De Johnette, Dave Holland and Armando Peraza matches the intensity of the soloists by creating a musical sub-text within the main piece. All are heard taking chances and Broussard for one felt like a man jumping out from a plane, not knowing whether the parachute would open or not. "*Illuminations* was a real challenge for me because I hadn't done anything like that before but it was always fun even though it was intense. Alice Coltrane helped me, I would bug her all the time, she had a cassette recording from her keyboard and she would be playing all kinds of stuff, I don't know if anyone knows how well she can play. On that album I was playing out of limitation and I have never thought of myself as a flute player but they taught me to believe. That's what it was, believing." Broussard's playing on this track threatened to establish him as a major force in the world of jazz saxophone, and "Angel Of Sunlight" is amongst the most significant single recordings in the Santana canon. Tom Coster was equally moved by the *Illuminations* sessions, "The whole experience of working with Alice Coltrane was amazing, I loved talking to her about her late husband John Coltrane who has always been a truly inspirational musician and person to me. Alice had a very special aura about her when she spoke of John and it very much captivated me, I remember always wanting to learn even more about him and couldn't wait to talk to her more about John. I also loved the way she played organ, her concept was unique and her feel for the instrument was amazing. We recorded the string section in Los Angeles, and it was exciting to hear her string arrangements come to life!"

The album closes with a return to serenity on the rhythmically free "Illuminations", which sets a rich, but oblique, Santana-Coster melody against an equally lush string section, revealing a challenging series of counterpoints, where the first and second strings appear to clash harmonically but create an overall sense of spiritual serenity. "Evil Ways" it most definitely was not!

Illuminations is a remarkable recording for Carlos Santana to have made, mixing as it did his lyrical feel for the guitar with the melodies he and Tom Coster worked on, juxtaposed with Alice Coltrane's difficult, almost atonal orchestral structures. It stands comparison with much contemporary jazz of the period. It appeared that Carlos and Coster had finally taken off for the spiritual, but hardly commercial, realm of music. Still, it was clear that Columbia Records would soon want a pay off for it. The Santana band albums were paying for solo projects like *Illuminations* and so, when the group reconvened to record their next proper album – which would be called *Borboletta* – the pressure was on to shift some vinyl. This was emphasised by the August release of the first Santana *Greatest Hits* album which focused entirely on material from the first three Santana Band albums and quickly went gold.

Carlos Santana was becoming used to pressure and there was more on the horizon as a new band LP was due, the problem was there was virtually no band! Indeed, judging from his feelings in the spring, it looked like the Santana group was finished, "Actually, the [1973] band to me, is gone. My whole being demands something else. Last year, that's what it was for last year and it was really, really good. The energy was still there, energy is still there but I can see Chepito and Michael going in different ways from me. They are both working on albums of their own." With Shrieve and Chepito destined to go their own ways, the final links with the original Santana were virtually severed, which would leave Carlos totally in charge. However, the guitarist couldn't ditch the Santana Band just yet and in May he put together a studio band to record some new vocal cuts. The line-up included David Brown, Chepito, Shrieve, Coster and Peraza and added a Larry Graham style vocalist, Leon Patillo. The sound of the music was Stevie Wonder soul mixed with Sly Stone and gospel. Singer Patillo was a critical find, he had grown up with Sly Stone and was steeped in the black gospel tradition, "Gospel music has always been a part of my roots," Patillo explained. "I used to play organ for a church which my parents attended in San Francisco. Carlos and I discussed gospel music together, he is a very spiritual man which shows in his unselfishness towards his group." Leon Patillo also majored on electric piano, the instrument which had been the dominant sound of Stevie Wonder's recent albums *Talking Book* and *Innervisions*. In response, Santana's autumn release *Borboletta* would feature Patillo's electric piano high in the mix. Other than soul, the key ingredients on *Borboletta* would be jazz and Brazilian and a further two sets of musicians were recruited to work on these moods. They included drummer Ndugu Leon Chancler and the remarkable Brazilian husband and wife team, Airto Moreira and Flora Purim. Sax man Jules Broussard was retained and performs superbly. It seemed that Carlos was trying to match Chick Corea's Return to Forever band.

In spite of the congestion in the studio, the resulting album flows together very well and is certainly one of Santana's best. Highlights include two Brazilian improvisations, a nod to Wonder's "Superstition" on "Give And Take", plus some climactic gospel moments on "Life Is Anew" and "Practice What You Preach", the latter featuring a classic Santana blues guitar passage. In general, the guitarist's playing on this album is rarely far from stunning. Tom Coster also shines on a lush canter through the tropics ("Canto De Los Flores") and there was the startling "Aspirations", a free-jazz mode which captures some of Jules Broussard's best playing against an ethereal canvas of nature sounds, organ, conga and bongos.

However, the real highlight of the album was a segment of experimental music, which is one of the best sequences to be found on any Santana recording. It kicks off with "Here and Now", a series of echoes of Alice Coltrane, McCoy Tyner and The Mahavishnu Orchestra, with its mix of esoteric riffs, abstract piano and heavy drums. In some ways it's an introductory filler to the exceptional "Flor De Canela", a left over from the 1973 tour, which finds Armando Peraza and Airto Moreira taking Santana's music into new territory. The Santana keyboard canvas of organ and electric piano underpins a beautiful, enigmatic melody of blue note reference points, welling up in interplay between guitar and organ. The climax of *Borboletta* is found on "Promise Of A Fisherman", a devotional Brazilian adventure which came from Dorival Caymmi, catching the guitar man's ear whilst on holiday in Hawaii the year before. In an almost possessed performance Carlos, Coster, Armando, Stanley Clarke, Airto and Flora create an ecstatic, dreamy classic. The mix of Flora's ethereal vocal, the percussion of Peraza and Airto, coupled with a funky, urban Coster organ solo would have been a big enough draw, but Carlos adds to it with one of his best and most intense passages. The sheer emotional and spiritual impact of this improvisation cannot be overstated, it exceeds many of the more self-consciously spiritual encounters on *Love, Devotion, Surrender*, at times seeming wild and out of control. If this was Santana taking on Return To Forever at their own game, it was a close run thing and another major advance for the group.

Little on *Borboletta* has much to do with rock music. The musicians on the session knew that the guitarist was creating something special, as Airto Moreira recalled, "We did "Spring Manifestations" and "Borboletta" free in the studio, free music, I did it as an introduction and then Carlos worked on it and mixed it really well, added some stuff, put his own touch into it and it sounded much, much better when he finished. When I recorded they were just improvisations, he turned them into songs and he gave me the credits."

The album failed to go gold quickly in the States causing some serious hand wringing in Columbia's offices. Hence it has often been overlooked, largely because of the poor sales in the USA – around the world, however, it was a massive success with chart topping status achieved in Yugoslavia, Australia, New Zealand and Italy, where it was the number one album for fourteen weeks!

Nonetheless, the international success of the album could not wholly make up for its relatively poor American sales and further problems loomed with a US tour that was scheduled for August 1974. This would mark Santana's live return after a break of over nine months. Then two days before the first date calamity struck when Mike Shrieve quit the band. "I had been thinking of leaving the band for some time to work on solo projects," Shrieve explained, "but I was going to wait until the current tour was over before I left. But like, a week before the tour started I started getting these pains until I was rushed to hospital and they found out I had kidney stones. The tour was looming ahead while I was recuperating, then it all came to me at once in my hospital bed. All the changes and reasons for me to split from Santana suddenly came out in the open and I called the band two days before the tour to tell them that not only I couldn't make the tour but I was leaving the band as well."

Shrieve's departure was a major blow for Carlos Santana, he had, after all, been his main partner and guide to the world of jazz. Although Carlos would always appear to be "the leader" to the public, Shrieve had provided much of the direction for *Caravanserai* and *Welcome* and the success of the 1973 tour was as much his triumph as the guitarist's. However, fundamentally, Michael Shrieve (and Gregg Rolie for that matter) had no innate passion for Latin percussion or Afro-Cuban music, so he had no particular reason to remain wedded to the Santana musical concept. Carlos Santana, on the other hand, had become an aficionado of the Afro-Cuban legacy and understood the role the Santana group had in taking it to audiences around the world. Even forgetting the band's name, the guitar player was the only member of Santana who couldn't leave the group without it ceasing to be Santana. He was stuck with it and now he had to direct it on his own.

The frantic search for a new drummer began and, as Bernard Purdie wasn't available, they settled for Ndugu Leon Chancler. He was, perhaps, the obvious choice as he had played on some of the exploratory tracks that found their way onto *Borboletta*. His pedigree as Miles Davis' drummer in 1971 and having just completed *Tale Spinnin'* with Weather Report gave him the kind of credentials Carlos was looking for. Ndugu was to be a strong force in Santana for the next two years, as the new unit took to the road in August

1974 for a US tour that lasted until the end of October and a Japanese tour that ran from November into December. The touring line up included Armando, Tom Coster, Ndugu and, perhaps surprisingly, Chepito Areas, who had just released his own solo album. Maybe the Santana tour was a good way to promote his album and, indeed, the tour publicity from Japan prominently featured the album's cover. Leon Patillo joined the tour on vocals and second keyboard – he was more of a mainstream gospel/soul singer than Leon Thomas and his keyboard versatility helped to compensate for the loss of Richard Kermode. Jules Broussard was invited to tour and was given plenty of room to stretch out which he did superbly – adding a brilliant new spark to the band. Original bass man David Brown replaced Doug Rauch. Strangely, a large portion of the US tour took place before *Borboletta* was released in October, so the show was as much to promote the *Greatest Hits* album that had just been released. As such, the live set consisted of Santana standards and a surprisingly limited number of selections from *Borboletta* itself, and for the first time, it seemed that the introduction of new tones like Broussard's saxophones and flute, was a way of masking the fact that the music was essentially the same as from the year before. Still, as the touring progressed it was clear that the percussion section of Peraza and Chepito was on a new high and Santana's own playing, coupled with Tom Coster's and that of the highly under-rated Broussard, was getting better all the time. The reeds player has fond memories of the tour – and not all of them musical: "Touring with Santana was altogether different to what I had done with Ray Charles, I mean they were paying more, we went first class and everything was paid for. It was just wonderful, especially going to Japan, they treated us real well, they even rolled out a red carpet from the plane to the terminal and gave us roses." For singer Leon Patillo, working with Santana was a matter of fate, "I was in L.A. playing with Creation when I got a call from Bill Graham asking me to sing on *Borboletta*. My feelings were of completion, contentment and excitement. I felt it was destined to happen."

As the year ended, the relatively low sales of *Borboletta* in the US made Columbia apply massive pressure to Santana to revive their chart status. The run of three band albums that had seen US sales steadily fall didn't bother Carlos Santana as he was fulfilling his musical vision. He was aware that the world-wide sales of these records were consistently high. In fact, the global stock of the Santana band was close to its apex in this period, at exactly the time that their commercial potency in the USA was at its lowest ebb. Around the world Santana was rated as one of the greatest musical outfits though this meant nothing to the record company. Tom Coster summed it up, "I always felt "commercial" pressure my entire time with Santana, from the first to the last day I was in the band. When a band decides to venture in newer music to broaden its musical horizons, you usually lose some of your audience on the way. This, of course, results in lower record sales which prompts the record company to put some real pressure on the band. Columbia Records was constantly on our case to get back to our "roots". Record companies are not interested in a creative project, but rather one that sells lots of units. To quote Bill Graham, 'It's not the money, it's the money!'" It was clear that in 1975 Santana would be required to deliver something palatable in the market place. The creative honeymoon was over.

Chapter 11

Pressure was the key theme for Carlos Santana's life in 1975 – a year during which he would find his musical concepts repeatedly questioned and his leadership of the group challenged. Rightly or wrongly, he was perceived as the main architect of Santana's move away from commercially potent Latin-Rock, to a situation where sales of *Greatest Hits* had outstripped the sales of *Borboletta* many times over. Maybe Carlos had the wrong idea and, as his record contract with Columbia was up for renewal, some serious questions were about to be asked about the group's American sales. However, in the first instance the guitarist needed a break. He was exhausted, the pace of touring and recording that he had embarked upon since the release of *Caravanserai* had been staggering and so, at the end of 1974, he took three months off. He still enjoyed playing music for Sri Chinmoy's cause and participated in a concert with John McLaughlin at New York's Central Park for a Chinmoy celebration known as Jharna Kala. This involved vocal duets between the two guitarists on top of a parade float, as a troupe of Chinmoy disciples paraded through the streets of downtown New York City, Madison Avenue. When they reached Central Park, they played "A Love Supreme", "Naima" and "House Of The Lord", just the two guitars and no accompaniment to the thousand or so who'd turned up. They seemed to enjoy playing for free – as if it were giving something back – and the guitarist's commitment to Sri Chinmoy remained strong for the next five years at least. He would meet the guru whenever he could, perhaps after a show, perhaps after a special trip and continued to play free concerts for Sri Chinmoy Centres.

Above: Santana in 1968: (l-r) Carlos Santana, Marcus Malone, Gregg Rolie, David Brown and 'Doc' Livingston (foreground). *Photo: Michael Ochs Archives*
Below: Classic urban image of the "Woodstock" Santana band: Mike Shrieve, Carlos Santana, Gregg Rolie, José Chepito Areas, David Brown and Michael Carabello. *Photo: Michael Ochs Archives*

Opposite left: Carlos Santana: as the 1970s became the 1980s. *Photo: Garry Clarke*
Above left: Tom Coster. *Photo: SSL.*
Above right: Greg Walker. *Photo: Garry Clarke*
Below: Chester Thompson. *Photo: Josephine Peraza.*

Above: Seeing the sights in Jerusalem, 1987: Chester Thompson, Graham Lear, Alphonso Johnson, Carlos Santana, Orestes Vilató, Buddy Miles and Alex Ligertwood. *Photo: Josephine Peraza*
Below: The *Freedom* Tour in action. *Photo: Garry Clarke.*

Above: Learning "Angel Negro", Mexico 1988. (l-r) Jorge Santana, Alphonso Johnson, Chester Thompson, Gregg Rolie, Carlos Santana and Chepito Areas (back to camera). *Photo: Josephine Peraza*
Below: Carlos Santana at the time of *Zebop! Photo: Garry Clarke*

Above: Carlos enjoying the tour in Germany, 1991. *Photo: SSL*

Above: Searching for the soul in the 1980s. *Photo: Garry Clarke.*
Below: Two greats of Latin Music,
Armando Peraza and José Chepito Areas in Mexico, 1988. *Photo: Josephine Peraza*

Above: Carlos Santana at home in his "Electric Church" in February 1996. *Photo Simon Leng.*

Santana, the band, returned in April minus Chepito Areas, for a limited tour of California and major cities on the mid-West accompanied by Journey and they participated in Bill Graham's massive SNACK Benefit concert at Kezar Stadium in San Francisco. This was a pointer to improving relations with the impresario and a further clue to the future was the inclusion of New York timbales master, Orestes Vilató, for this one-off date. Carlos tried to get Vilató to join full time, but this was not to happen for a while yet. Later that year the band stepped onto the road as a support act for Eric Clapton. It was the first time the group had not headlined since 1969 – a development that probably came as a shock to Carlos. The commercial realities were simply that Clapton had sold more records recently than Santana in the US. The tour extended over two and a half months in the summer and the outfit were cut down to an hour long set, which covered mostly greatest hits with "Give And Take" and a couple of new songs. One was an early version of "Let The Music Set You Free" (called "Brown In London" at the time) and a never released blues, "Time Waits For No-One". Every night of the tour, Carlos, Armando and Ndugu would join Clapton on-stage for wide ranging jams which, on one notable occasion, also involved John McLaughlin. Maybe, just maybe, Carlos was beginning to enjoy playing with another rock musician.

Just after this tour, in August, Carlos and Armando Peraza took time out to play on *Eternity*, a new LP by Alice Coltrane, one of the last she was to make before retiring to a life of spiritual teaching and contemplation. There was no guitar on the record but Santana was there on timbales and percussion, appearing under the name "A Friend", an oddity amongst all his guest appearances. Rumours seemed to be rife about the Mexican's plans and reports also filtered out that he was about to record with pianist Chick Corea. The two had collaborated on compositions and got on well when the guitarist had sat in with Corea's Return To Forever group in 1974. The recording never happened as Carlos later lamented, "because time was so tight. I hadn't got a band and I was trying to get *Amigos* together."

The annual Santana band album was needed soon and it needed to be a smash. The band had few new songs and the pressure was intense. It was time for Carlos Santana to look for outside help. Since 1973 the mercurial Bill Graham had had a toe-hold into Santana's affairs as one of his associates, Barry Imhoff, managed the group. By the summer of 1975 the guitar player was again looking for a manager, having parted ways with Imhoff. He first approached road manager Ray Etzler to take on the job, but Etzler turned the job down and suggested the more heavyweight Graham. Carlos and Bill had not spoken much since 1970 when the Santana group had mistakenly dropped Graham's services, but after four years of coolness, Santana and Graham met again and buried the hatchet. Columbia needed to do something with Santana to keep them in the public eye world-wide. At the time the label had a hot new act they wanted to break in Europe, an exciting and talented funk-soul band called Earth, Wind & Fire, who had just released their first US chart-topping album *That's The Way Of The World*. Having started life as a pure funk outfit, they had passed through many incarnations before arriving at a very pleasing and commercial mix of soul and funk.

Carlos Santana liked Earth, Wind & Fire, having always loved soul. Stevie Wonder, Aretha Franklin, Bobby Womack and Dionne Warwick were major heroes and influences. Earth, Wind & Fire had the requisite ability, sincerity, drive and composing skills to turn Carlos on and they had a guitar player who was clearly a Santana pretender. With Bill Graham just about back in the driver's seat, a tour of Europe with Earth, Wind & Fire, was seen as a winner. The tour, which took place over September and October, has passed into legend. The story goes that the funk outfit could have blown Santana off the stage whenever they chose. Down to a five-piece, Santana were stuck between turning out the greatest hits and searching for new material and a new direction. The shortened set did not allow for the expansive approach of the *Lotus* period and Ndugu's trips to the front of the stage with his portable Roto-toms were no answer to Earth, Wind & Fire's theatrical stage-show.

For all this, the tour did have some highlights, not least a jam with Eric Clapton in London and a stop in what used to be Yugoslavia, but the entire venture told Carlos that a change was needed – Santana appeared to have lost its umbilical connection with "the people" and "the street". They needed to get back to the people and when Eric Clapton took him to a London night club, he was invigorated by the people's reaction to "Jingo". It sparked a chain of thought that led to him considering the power of the original Santana band, especially as a number of the current band members were starting to voice dissent. The drummer Ndugu was a strong-willed individual who was in no way awed by Carlos Santana, after all he had played for Miles Davis! He had no qualms about telling Santana what he thought and, for the first time since 1972, Carlos found himself openly challenged about the group's musical direction. Tom Coster observed the emerging tensions, "I personally liked Ndugu very much, he played great every night and worked hard and contributed a lot to the band. What he didn't do was agree with everything Carlos said or wanted to do and this was certainly not a common practice in the band and certainly caused tension between Carlos and Ndugu.

I felt that once Ndugu broke down the barrier in letting his feelings be heard, other members began doing likewise." Leon Patillo saw the turmoil as a reflection of the guitarist's determination to succeed, "Carlos is a very hard worker. If one thing does not work, he keeps regrouping until it does." A major regrouping was on the cards.

Back in San Francisco in mid-October, Santana immediately set about a major pow-wow with Graham, during which the far from shy impresario told Carlos that he should get his head out of the clouds and play some no-nonsense, street flavoured Latin music, just as the original Santana band had done. He also suggested that David Rubinson be brought in to produce and direct proceedings. The guitarist still had poor memories of working with Rubinson on those early sessions, but acquiesced after a meeting to patch things up. It's a testament to Carlos' insecurity in this period that he allowed his band's direction to be taken over by Graham, Rubinson, Tom Coster and, to an extent, Ndugu Leon Chancler. Santana didn't know which way to go and, just as in 1972 his desire for a guiding hand had led him to Sri Chinmoy, now he was letting go and taking the lead from others. Things started to change; Leon Patillo had received an offer to take up a career in gospel music and in his place came a friend of Ndugu's from Los Angeles, a young soul singer named Greg Walker. He was a rookie, known in L.A. only where he sang with a unit called A Taste Of Honey. For Walker, the audition experience was daunting, "It was the latter part of 1975, I received a call from Ndugu asking if I wanted to audition to sing with Santana, I replied "sure". He said I had to learn two songs "Give and Take" and "Black Magic Woman". I flew to San Francisco, was picked up, taken to S.I.R. on Folsom Street, walked into the studio and there they were. Of course I was nervous, very nervous. Carlos was very gracious and kind, I guess he could see that I was scared, he introduced me to everyone and proceeded to play the songs. Right after, they asked me to leave the room and ten to fifteen minutes later I was asked to come back and the manager told me they would let me know. The next day I was asked to pack enough stuff to come back to San Francisco for a few weeks, they were about to record the *Amigos* LP and I was going to be singing on it."

Santana had written new material in Europe and at the beginning of November they set about rehearsing and recording it with Rubinson. The resulting album was almost a Santana album with Carlos Santana as guest guitar player! Rubinson, Tom Coster and Ndugu took the reins and produced material to suit the rebirth of Santana, reflecting the Latin style and taking on-board the prevailing musical wind of the time, which was funk. A key event had occurred not long before in 1974 when Herbie Hancock released the massive-selling *Head Hunters*, which was an album of jazz improvisations played over extremely catchy funk themes and rhythms – the producer was David Rubinson. The jazz world had all but rolled over and died at this "aberration" from one of their brightest stars, but Hancock correctly reflected that he had never called himself a "jazz musician" and that soul/funk had always been a part of his musical life. In Carlos' eyes, if funk was good enough for Herbie Hancock, one of his heroes, it was good enough for him.

Originally to be named *Transcendance – The Dance Of Life*, the less spiritually named *Amigos* was released in March 1976 and instantly headed for the upper reaches of the album charts world-wide. So, what was the result of all the plans and calculations? Well, to an extent, *Amigos* sounds like a calculated album, there was a slab of good-time Latin anthem ("Dance Sister Dance"), a re-run of "Neshabur" ("Take Me With You"), a version of Hancock's riff from "Chameleon" on *Head Hunters* ("Let Me"), two funk-soul workouts ("Tell Me Are You Tired" and the poor "Let It Shine") and a re-write of the "Samba Pa Ti" formula ("Europa"). Along with Armando Peraza's earthy, Latin-folk "Gitano", the album should have appealed to everybody and it nearly did. Calculation and cynicism aside, *Amigos* is a very good album. "Dance Sister Dance" did have a real spirit about it and a sublime run-out section, "Take Me With You" worked well, inducing some real passion through fine playing and "Let Me" also generated some steam and showed that Santana could pull off the funk trick. "Gitano" and "Europa" in particular were great tracks and allowed the real personalities of Peraza and Santana to shine through. For those who understood Spanish, Peraza's tale of his life as a wandering musician and encounters with beautiful women was charming, fuelled as it was by his own excellent playing. "Europa" was to overtake "Samba Pa Ti" as many fans' favourite Santana guitar ballad and it took Carlos' lyrical approach to new heights, his ability to conjure gorgeous melodies that recalled his soul heroines, Aretha and Dionne, was uncanny. It is often overlooked that "Europa" was written by Santana *and* Tom Coster and it is a fascinating example of what happens when two musicians steeped in the melodic sensibilities of their parent's cultures get together. Coster's parents came from Malta and this strongly influenced his general approach to music, "I am a strong believer that melody is everything! Without melody there is not much to grab on to, I acquired my melodic playing because of my Mediterranean upbringing, the music I was brought up with had strong melodic qualities. I feel that Carlos is a very melodic player and that his strongest and greatest strength when playing the guitar is his ability to play melodically along with his lyrical soloing. The best writing experiences with Carlos also produced the best songs, "Europa" being one of them, Carlos and I wrote that tune together effortlessly and the final product radiates exactly that."

However, Carlos was not entirely convinced by the new direction and the cracks that were to appear in earnest in the late 1970s were already there. Referring to "Europa" being his favourite track on the album he said, "I only know that it had hit me more sincerely than any other song on that album. I like to play funk but it takes more of an effort for me to be sincere about the phrasing in funk than in ballads."[40] Actually, the two most prominent players on *Amigos* were Tom Coster and Armando Peraza. Coster's keyboards dominate the disc, from the lush, almost symphonic synthesiser colours in the coda of "Dance Sister Dance", to his fine jazz organ solo on "Take Me With You" and a fluid electric piano break on "Tell Me Are You Tired". Peraza, too, was prominent. The richness of his conga and bongos provide many of the LP's highlights, not least his outstanding textures on "Dance Sister Dance", the Domincan merengue rhythms of "Let Me" and a marvellous performance throughout his own "Gitano". Without doubt, as a commercial prospect, *Amigos* worked and upon presentation of the tapes to Columbia the guitarist was rewarded with the biggest contract they had ever given an artist. Crucially, the contract would allow Carlos the latitude to release three solo albums on which he could explore his private musical vision.

Clearly, the next thing to do was tour in support of the album and yet another new band was revealed at the San Francisco Winterland in November. A short tour of California followed, during which they took the unusual step of playing no new material from *Amigos*. However, they were just keeping their powder dry as February 1976 saw the band step onto a jet for the long haul to New Zealand, Australia and a 20-date trip through Japan, where Santana were becoming ever more popular. *Amigos* was voted Japan's album of the year.

As soon as the tour was over David Brown left Santana and so a new bass player was needed for the spring and summer US dates. The burgeoning influence of Ndugu came to the fore again, as the new bass player turned out to be another friend of his, Byron Miller, who had latterly been playing with Roy Ayers. As Carlos attempted to bring in a new percussionist in the shape of the master-drummer Francisco Aguabella, tensions surfaced. Since Chepito's departure, Ndugu had been handling drums and timbales but this wasn't satisfactory. Like the fans, Santana wanted to hear a real timbalero in the band. Obviously, this didn't sit too well with Ndugu and Aguabella only played a few dates with Santana. Harmony was not in the air.

The Santana band appeared to be split in two – Carlos' half and Ndugu's half. The sound of the group was changing too. It was veering strongly towards soul-funk and much as Carlos was a fan of this music, it was becoming too dominant in the Santana gumbo, which had always had its own identity and absorbed influences without being overwhelmed by them. The situation was tense and becoming childish. Ndugu, Miller and Greg Walker seemed to have formed a clique and appeared to mock Santana and Coster's spiritual outlook. Greg Walker tried to play it down telling a reporter that, "We may razz each other a little bit, but we want you to understand it's not so much in bad feelings as horsing around", but this was clearly not a tolerable situation. At the end of July, Santana fell apart again, Carlos wasn't going to be told what to do by anyone anymore or be laughed at, he knew he needed Coster and Peraza more than the others. Bill Graham did the rest. In the summer Santana looked for inspiration from his Sri Chinmoy connections. The guitarist attended conferences held by the Guru and played devotional music for them. Meanwhile he was also developing a close friendship with a young drummer who was also a Chinmoy devotee, Narada Michael Walden. As the replacement for Billy Cobham in The Mahavishnu Orchestra, Walden had taken on a difficult task, but miraculously succeeded. Now, he was working on a solo album to be called *Garden of Love Light*. Having known Walden for a while Carlos set about working on a ballad, "First Love", which showcased some of the guitarist's most sensitive playing.

Narada had secured a contract with Atlantic Records and the release of his album seemed to run smoothly. Carlos however had no such luck and the summer of 1976 saw the band in crisis again. By now the band consisted of just Carlos and Tom Coster, Peraza had been forced to quit on health grounds. Carlos and Coster decided to look to inject some young blood and the San Francisco family of bands came to the rescue. Carlos' brother Jorge had a rather good band called Malo, which had recently broken up after the release of their fourth album *Ascension*. Amongst its past members had been a fiery twenty-two year old conguero Raul Rekow and bass player Pablo Tellez. Raul Rekow recalled his introduction to Santana, "I got a call from Santana management in 1976, they said that they might want me to record on a new album on one or two songs. They asked me to come down, to check me out and see what I sounded like, I went to the rehearsal studio and it was just Carlos and Tom Coster. They asked me and Leo Rosales to come in, so

Leo and I went over there, they loved both of us and they wanted both of us to join the band. Leo was hooked up with some religious cult and was not allowed to leave town. So he passed on it, which he regretted later."

Rekow and Tellez were the first new recruits and, at the last minute, singer Leon Patillo returned, he could be relied upon to sing, bring in a few new songs and not rock the boat. The same could be said of Gaylord Birch, a drummer who was known to David Rubinson from his liaison with the Pointer Sisters. A consummate soul professional, Birch could adapt to the Latin sound and would not insist on having his own way! And, as one final twist in the tale, Chepito Areas was back, his solo career having never really taken off. He and Carlos had hooked up again after bumping into each other in the street. The sessions were held in September and October 1976 in the usual state of flux and the aim was to continue the successful Latin emphasis of *Amigos* and mix in some instrumental and soul grooves. The title of the album indicates the intention, *Festivál* was meant to be party music and the sound was immediately the most Salsa-based that Santana had ever achieved, coupled with a heavy Brazilian influence. Latin music commentator John Storm Roberts, noted the significance of *Festivál* pointing out that "Carnaval", "was a piece of almost-straight Rio carnival music played, so to speak with a Cuban accent. Another cut "Verão Vermelho" made use of a classical-style acoustic guitar and a strong Brazilian feeling in the vocals." The strong salsa feel was also to be found on "Let The Children Play" (a Santana/Patillo composition revived from 1975), and on the album's best moment, the wonderful "Maria Caracoles". This was a cover of a Cuban song based on a unique rhythm, "the mozambique", invented by the great Cuban musician Pello El Afrokan. Santana created an authentic, joyful Cuban mood through a breathless Pablo Tellez vocal, the power of Chepito Areas and Raul Rekow and intense work by Santana and Coster. Fusion got a nod in the form of the steaming "Jugando", funk was represented by "Let The Music Set You Free" (recalling Sly Stone and War), the filler track "Reach Up" and Patillo's "Try A Little Harder Now". A pleasant soul number was rendered with feeling by Patillo ("Give Me Love"), there was also an excellent gospel tune ("The River", again with a strong vocal and lyrics from Patillo) and a guitar showcase, the haunting "Revelations". All in all it was an enjoyable album, marred by less than top-quality material. Still, it established Santana's credentials again as a force in Latin music, mainly through the fearsome vigour of Raul Rekow and Chepito, particularly on "Maria Caracoles". The album was also a massive hit and Carlos professed to be very happy with it, "To me, *Festivál*, is the best of all the albums, plus a new fire and a new energy. I wouldn't say it's a new direction... it's just the best of all the directions I've taken. On other albums I like some songs better than others, but on this one I like them all."

It was another near miracle that the new and quickly assembled Santana line-up had come up with a new album at all. Patillo and Gaylord Birch weren't interested in touring, so the search for a new singer and drummer began again and it needed to be quick. The band was due to play New York's Central Park in October. The basic line-up was Carlos, Tom Coster, Raul Rekow and Pablo Tellez to which they quickly added studio vocalist Tom Croucher and drummer David Prater, who had only played in a cabaret band in the Bay Area. It felt a bit like desperation. Naturally, they didn't make Central Park and were replaced by the Average White Band. The next crisis loomed in the shape of a two-month European tour with Journey, due to start in London in early November. A new line-up was put together no more than ten days before they got on the 'plane and featured a young drummer from Gino Vanelli, Graham Lear, and a soul-funk singer called Luther Rabb, who had been getting down with an outfit which delighted in the name Ballin' Jack. One of the roadies, Joel Badie, who had sung some vocals on *Festivál* doubled up as a part time percussionist and cheerleader. The estimates of how much rehearsal they had had before they stepped onto the London stage ranged from three to seven days. As such it could have been a disaster, but in reality it was far from that and helped to push the band to a new peak of popularity. Roughly a year since he left Europe with the Earth, Wind & Fire experience ringing in his ears, Santana was back with a band that took the audience not just to the street but to Rio for a carnival. They seemed to have found a whole new energy much to the credit of young bloods like Raul Rekow and the dynamic Graham Lear. The new material blended in well with the old favourites and the band gelled superbly, apart from Luther Rabb whose vocals just didn't work and who would not last long. Santana and Tom Coster must have been mightily relieved, the pressure had really been on. Not only had they needed to find a band and record an album in two months, they had to go on the road and play a series of huge concerts that were going to be taped and filmed for a live album and maybe a movie.

The band was filmed by Columbia in Paris and most spectacularly by the BBC at London's Hammersmith Odeon on December 15th. They sounded good. Opening with "Carnaval", the new line-up signalled its intention to play fast and furious with the emphasis on rhythm and percussion. There was no time to think whether the band was cutting it or not, but they were, just about, by creating an irresistible party music. There were obvious problems with the singing, although many of the songs were Spanish group vocals. On the other hand, the percussion was fiery, Chepito Areas playing as well as ever while new man Raul Rekow generated plenty of excitement with his full-tilt approach to the congas. Graham Lear was an accomplished rock drummer who didn't appear to have too much difficulty adapting to playing beneath Latin percussion.

Throughout the shows, Santana could be seen constantly egging the percussionists on to produce more and more excitement and they delivered, particularly on "Dance Sister Dance", which closed with no fewer than four percussionists making hay; Rekow on bongo, Areas and Santana on congas, and roadie Joel Badie tickling the timbales. Likewise on "Maria Caracoles", amongst the most pure Afro-Cuban of all Santana pieces, both Santana and bass man Pablo Tellez gave every appearance of genuinely enjoying themselves – the guitarist actually dancing around the stage. It was a far cry from the intense seriousness of the *Lotus* tour. As ever the shortened set ended with "Soul Sacrifice", following which the lighter atmosphere around the band is amply revealed by the sight of the band members being variously manhandled by roadies dressed in monkey, gorilla and lion suits – no doubt the idea of Bill Graham. The first TV and radio concert simulcast closed with the scene of Chepito Areas and Graham suspended in a jungle net, twirling round and round as the diminutive Nicaraguan intones his favourite catch phrase, "Hey, gringos!" The show brought the year to an end on a happy note, but it also found Santana as ever caught between the old and the new. Exciting as the new salsa direction was, it was no indication that anything genuinely innovative was on offer. It was the same package as before with a slightly different emphasis – on these old songs Santana and Coster were relying on new arrangements rather than new ideas. Tom Coster thinks that the speed and power of this band might have been a mask for a reduction in quality, "This was a difficult time since Carlos and I knew we had to keep things together, the band was weak musically, but we had made a commitment to tour and we had to get through it. This was definitely a tough time in Santana history and I was happy to see it end."

The reality was that the band was utterly dependant on the rich, ringing guitar of its leader and Coster's keyboards to hold the whole thing together. The guitarist's playing was especially good on this tour. His new Yamaha guitar produced one of his classic tones – full, fluid, jazzy with a resonant sustain and his technique was fast, full of confidence and expression. He could still deliver a melody with passion as evidenced by the new piece,

"Revelations", which built to a tremendous climactic exchange between guitar and synthesiser.

The tour garnered good reviews, but after the customary New Year's Eve show in San Francisco, Santana split again and Rabb and Badie were left to their own devices. By then *Festivál* had been released to large sales but mixed reviews, some of which characterised it as an example of commercial sell-out. Whatever the critics thought, Santana were back on the road to another re-birth as world stars.

Chapter 12

There was no doubt that the return of Bill Graham, and the work with David Rubinson, had forced Santana to deliver the goods in the commercial arena and after the upheavals of 1976, it looked like the group was back on solid ground. They began the year supporting *Festivál* with a major series of North American shows which saw the return of singer Greg Walker. When the tour finished in April, Chepito Areas left the band yet again and after a few weeks' rest, Santana and Coster put together yet another new unit which hit the studio in June. The line-up now included ace timbalero Pete Escovedo and teenage bass player David Margen. The band already had enough live material from the previous winter's European dates to fill an album, and having summarily guillotined Luther Rabb's vocals and dubbed on the rather more successful efforts of Greg Walker, a strong set of tracks was ready for selection. Santana had always – and would always – be known primarily as a live act, but the only Santana live album at this point was *Lotus* which, outside Japan, was only available as an import at a mighty price. Perhaps because of this, the decision was taken to release a specially priced double album, which would mix the live cuts with new studio material. Santana and Coster chose the running order with Bill Graham and Ray Etzler. It proved to be a very successful mix. The result was Santana's most successful album since *Abraxas*, which they named *Moonflower*.

The live cuts on the album provide an overview of Santana hits old and new, newer numbers from *Festivál* and *Amigos* mixed in with older chart successes from *Abraxas*, plus two old war horses from the first album. All the live cuts put the emphasis on excitement and strong soul/funk elements.

Indeed "Black Magic Woman" had almost completely lost its Latin-Blues mood and taken a strong turn towards funk. There were showcase solos for Coster, Rekow and Lear which worked within the tight album context – both Lear and Rekow show how well they can cut it in their cameos with highly enjoyable, melodic workouts. Carlos Santana's guitar playing was ringing truer than ever and the whole album represents one of his finest sets of guitar performances. The highlight was a truly beautiful rendering of "Europa" that matched a typically romantic Mexican melody (shades of "Y Volveré") with a middle eight that recalled classic pop-soul before moving into a faster Latin section that was built around climactic sustained notes. "Europa" fades out to statements of a simple soul call and response melody, closing a breath-takingly emotional performance that is probably the quintessential Santana guitar track. Everything that makes Carlos Santana what he is appears on "Europa"; the real sentiment of Mexican music; ecstatic blues and gospel flourishes; his talking "soul singer" guitar; his love for Jimi Hendrix and Gabor Szabo; and finally his passion for jazz, a technique he built into his armoury over a number of years. Because of its multi-faceted origins, "Europa" has become an almost universal folk melody, as much loved in Japan as it is in Caracas.

Aside from these live tracks, *Moonflower* included Santana's strongest studio set since *Borboletta* just about reflecting all the stops on the Santana musical journey and providing something for most of their fans, old and new. There was another excellent guitar ballad, "Flor D'Luna" – one of Tom Coster's finest compositions, delivered with elegant grace by Santana, and a convincing Afro-Cuban fusion sideline on "Zulu", which showcased Pete Escovedo's heart and soul timbales. Coster also shines on "Go Within", which updates his electric piano sound of "Canto De Los Flores" to take account of the new soul mood. Another piece, "El Morocco", reminded listeners that Santana hadn't forgotten how to keep up with the lions of jazz-fusion with its extravagant solos and convincing funk backbeat while soul leanings were found on "I'll Be Waiting" and "Transcendance", the latter being Carlos Santana's musical manifesto for 1977, heavy with flamenco-style climaxes on vocal, guitar and keyboard. Singer Greg Walker stated that, "I felt as if I could fly while singing it. When I'd re-enter to sing 'it's time for us to say good-bye' I could feel the guitar in my voice come out. You know how Carlos would hold a note and that note would pierce your heart and make you tremble? That's the way I felt singing 'Transcendance'. I felt just as if I were doing what the title says... transcending..." It's what set the Santana of *Moonflower* apart from later incarnations of the band – on this album they were doing it for real.

In the middle of these spiritual musical orgasms was one curious song choice, a cover of a 1960s English pop hit, "She's Not There", which in many countries provided Santana with their biggest hit single. Whilst Italian record buyers were sending the exquisite "Flor D'Luna" to the number one spot, their British counterparts were propelling this Latin-Soul-Rock cover of a Zombies tune to number 11, an unprecedented chart position for Santana. In a repeat performance of his 1969 suggestion of doing "Evil Ways", it was Bill Graham who rang Carlos Santana up in the middle of the night to suggest the song as a recording prospect. Once the initial reluctance was overcome, the old Santana cover versions success formula came up trumps again. A smooth Walker vocal, brief but impassioned solos from the guitarist, a couple of old Cal Tjader riffs would help to propel the band to a peak of popularity around the globe that they would never better. *Moonflower* found the group millions of new listeners around the world and represented the band's third re-birth. The album hit number 10 in the USA, selling the same number of copies as *Santana*, and number 7 in Britain, equalling the position of *Abraxas*. It was also the Bay Area album of the year and sold by the juggernaut load in Japan, Australia, Latin America and Europe. It repaid Columbia Records for their faith in the commercial appeal of the band. Such was Santana's popularity around the world that they had sold 10 million records world-wide by the time of *Moonflower*.

As ever with Santana the album's enormous success was tinged with regret as it marked the end of the line for Tom Coster who, despite his pivotal role as arranger, director and songwriter probably knew that in the tail end of the guitar hero era, he would never get the kudos he deserved in a band like Santana. *Moonflower* had showcased his playing and his instrumental solos were mostly played on a new type of keyboard called a mini moog, which allowed him to bend notes and add vibrato just as a guitar player would. His sound on the album is so close to Carlos' guitar sound that they almost appeared to be two aspects of the same musical personality. However, Coster might well have arranged the album's music, but Carlos would get the plaudits, it was, after all, his name on the album cover. Add to this the success of his composition "Flor D'Luna" and thoughts of a solo career were beckoning. Nevertheless, it was all roses as Santana prepared for a series of huge world-wide concerts and, as the album was being prepared for release in September, the throng jetted over to Europe for a few dates in the company of Chicago. These dates were largely a success except for a nasty incident in

Italy where molotov cocktails were launched at the band. Carlos and his men swiftly exited the burning stage, not to set foot in Italy again until 1983. A less violent reception awaited them in Australia where they played a series of huge outdoor festivals. At these dates, and those that followed on a tour of Japan – which saw the return of Armando Peraza – Carlos and Coster started to showcase some of the new spiritual music they had written and some of it was recorded live. This aside, the success of *Moonflower* ensured a rapturous reception for "Transcendance", "She's Not There", "I'll Be Waiting" and "Flor D'Luna". Santana's stock in Japan was incredibly high and the tour included no fewer than twenty five dates, one of the longest tours ever undertaken of the country. It seemed that, internationally, Santana could do no wrong.

But internally, all was not well and the musical schism with Tom Coster was looming. Coster was ready to embark on a solo career and this left Carlos in something of an awkward spot. He had never learnt to read music in the conventional Western sense of studying form and harmony and had always relied on a fully trained keyboards man to assist in the process of taking the music in his head and putting it down on paper and arranging it for other musicians. Coster performed this role in the band as Pete Escovedo succinctly described, "Tom is probably the most important part of the band because he is most responsible for keeping the music end together." The pianist fulfilled a vital role in Santana, which grew into a remarkable musical relationship which he valued deeply, "Carlos and I were not only compatible soloists, but we complemented each other musically in a way that has never been duplicated since my departure as far as I am concerned. I feel this happened because it simply was meant to be, I will always believe that Carlos and I were meant to play together. You can hear it in the music, especially in the ballads, I do feel however that even though our backgrounds were very different, they somehow complemented one another."

All this made it hard for him to leave the band but Coster's mind was made up, "I was getting tired," he explains, "I was under a lot of pressure and a lot of people depended on me each and every day to keep things going smoothly. I also felt that I was not growing as a musician, the record company kept up the constant pressure of "being commercial" and that was really getting to me. I also was tired of being involved with Sri Chinmoy, not that I thought anything negative towards him but I felt I was already a grounded person and had always been grounded and that being in his fold was a waste of my time. The problem was that I didn't know how to relate this to Carlos and I didn't have the guts to tell him how I felt because I knew it would hurt him. So, I took the easy way out and left the band." The loss of Tom Coster was nearly fatal to the Santana band. Until the unions with Herbie Hancock and Chester Thompson in the 1980s, the absence of Coster left Santana, man and band, rudderless.

☯

With the US tour over and Coster departed, Santana were required to set about recording a new album. The success of *Moonflower* had amply demonstrated the world-wide appeal of the band and they were selling millions of records around the globe. However, decisions at Columbia Records weren't taken in Tokyo, Milan, London or even San Francisco, but New York and the perspective they had of the world was very much an American one. Big sales in Japan, Australia or the Netherlands weren't at the forefront of their mind, it was US sales they were interested in. Even though *Moonflower* had sold well in the USA, it was no guarantee of keeping up with the market in the future and the formula of that album, half greatest hits live and half new music, could not readily be repeated. As ever the marketing men were looking to fit Santana into the latest musical fashions that were filling the concert halls and cash registers, namely disco and AOR. Carlos Santana's difficulty was that he didn't think like American business, he wasn't actually interested in selling anybody anything. Sure, he had made a fortune from playing music, but it was never his main motivation, the altruism of the late 1960s was a greater part of his thinking. By the late 1970s the rock industry had become such a monster that Santana hardly recognised it and certainly didn't like what he saw. Despite sales that eventually topped two million in the USA, Columbia managed to convince themselves and Santana that *Moonflower* was not a success!

All this pressure made Carlos even keener to embark on a solo career under the name of his spiritual alter ego "Devadip" using the Santana group as the commercial wherewithal to fund this more artistic path.

"At that point Devadip was in one place and Santana in another," he explained, "in two different buildings. I have to do a Santana album where Columbia tell me what to play and what and when to play, so that I can go into the studio as Devadip. If Santana was to remain successful in Columbia's eyes and I was to maintain a certain integrity within myself, reaching all the people who come to see us in Europe and the few that come to see us in America, we had to get somebody like Lambert and Potter, someone who knows *Billboard*. Those people know about the radio and they gave us another perspective on putting Santana back into the auditoriums. So we did it consciously."[41] It was this mindset that led to the first musical mistake in Santana's career, *Inner Secrets*. The background to this poor album was a major economic recession in the USA, which fuelled the music business' conservative outlook and increased the need to back chart winners. In this context the targets of *Inner Secrets* were the disco and AOR crazes that were sweeping the States in 1978. To complete the album, the guitar man would change his entire way of working as the band's manager Ray Etzler noted, "This is the first time in Carlos' career he's really let outside producers work with him. He was open to learning from them and the band. For example, this is the first time he's just laid the basic tracks and then done overdubs; usually it's live-in-the-studio recording."[42]

Two new faces recorded on the LP, keyboards man Chris Rhyne and second guitar player Chris Solberg, who came out of another of Bill Graham's acts, Eddie Money. The double guitar approach was not to capture the spirit of *Santana III*, but to ape the multiple guitar riffing of bands like The Eagles and Styx. The positive aspect of *Inner Secrets* is Greg Walker's vocals, the rest is insubstantial, contrived pop music. There were tracks where Santana sounded like a disco group ("One Chain" and "Move On"), one which was similar to George Benson's pop hits ("Stormy") and a pair where this once great band were cast as Foreigner ("Well All Right" and "Open Invitation"). There was a half-hearted attempt to create a guitar showcase ("Life Is A Lady") and a truly dismal Lambert and Potter original, "The Facts Of Love", which wasn't even passable cabaret fare. There were three classy percussionists on the record but they were largely inaudible. Santana's guitar performances were still attractive, but that was about it. *Inner Secrets* is far too contrived an album to survive much close scrutiny and is so far away from reflecting Santana's musical vision that it sounds like he popped in, recorded his parts and went off again – which, of course, is pretty much what he did. After the artistic and commercial triumph of *Moonflower* this latest effort was a spectacular fall from grace. The music sounded better live, but it was at this point that the music press gave up on the Santana band. The inescapable fact was that though *Inner Secrets* was another gold record and a relative commercial success, it had seriously damaged Santana's reputation.

☯

By this time Carlos' real musical passion was concentrated in another direction, music that was born from and reflected his spirituality. To achieve this he was to create a new sub-set of the Santana Band known as The Devadip Orchestra (just like the Mahavishnu Orchestra) and whilst the Santana band was churning out the tepid *Inner Secrets*, Carlos was thinking about a new solo album, *Oneness*. As if to underline the almost fundamental split between The Santana Band and Carlos Santana, The Devadip Orchestra were the support act on Santana's 1978 tour of Europe. The Orchestra consisted of Carlos, Chris Rhyne, David Margen, Graham Lear and reeds player Russell Tubbs, another Chinmoy disciple. In front of massive audiences waiting to hear "Black Magic Woman" and "Dance Sister Dance", in the biggest venues across Europe, the Devadip Orchestra ran through thirty-five minute sets comprising music that would appear on *Oneness* and its sequel *The Swing of Delight*. The audiences were a bit shifty in their seats, half of them not even realising that it was Carlos Santana, but they were mostly won over by the sheer musicianship. In fact, the *Inner Secrets* European tour epitomises the difficulty that has plagued the guitarist's career since 1972. What did he do when in his heart he wanted to play *Illuminations*, *Borboletta* and *Oneness* and the majority of his audience wanted to hear "Black Magic Woman"? In 1978 he split himself in two and led two bands comprised of the same musicians.

Oneness was originally conceived as a double album which would contain material that was to eventually appear on *The Swing Of Delight* and the subsequent *Havana Moon,* but it was eventually reduced to a single disc. A live segment was recorded in Osaka, Japan in November 1977 under one name, "Prelude". The studio elements of *Oneness* were recorded in February of 1979 and really saw Carlos striding out on his own. This was his first solo album proper; there was no Buddy Miles, no John McLaughlin and no Alice Coltrane. Accordingly, the music is an intensely personal inner view of Carlos Santana's private vision, not one conceived in any respect for commercial purposes. Most of it can be characterised as jazz fusion and much of it is adventurous and entirely distinct from anything he had recorded before. The recording starts with a mini-suite of themes which mix dramatic, orchestral overtones with syncopated jazz rhythms, providing the structure for accomplished improvisations from Santana and Coster (for whom this was the last substantial recording with Santana). The styles of these two musicians now appeared to be locked telepathically together. "Arise Awake" comprises a brooding, rising melody which gives way to a slightly dissonant bass figure ("The Chosen Hour"), before an uplifting cover of Chico Hamilton's modal hard-bop chart "Jim Jeanie" (from Hamilton's 1966 album *The Dealer*) that draws rapturous solos from guitar and keyboards. It is one of the very few times Santana has recorded a straight jazz piece and, in a fine solo, he proves he can play bop. There are strong classical elements to this opening music, most notably in a successful adaptation of passages from Alan Hovhaness' modern American symphony "The Mysterious Mountain" (which Devadip called "Transformation Day"), on which Santana's natural preference for melody over complex harmony compelled him to work with Tom Coster to select certain themes from the Hovhaness work and emphasise their melodic content. Coster builds a luxuriant synthesised string section that cushions the natural harmony of the music, rather than suggesting discord and other abstract tonal clashes.

Other clear classical influences are found on a segment led by David Margen's bass that clearly recalls a motif from "The Firebird", an intensely modern, almost abstract Igor Stravinsky opus. There were plenty of reviewers who were queuing up to dismiss such fancies as pretentious, but the rationale for these ventures clearly comes from the orchestral adventures of Alice Coltrane, most notably her *Lord Of Lords* recording which itself included an adaptation of "The Firebird". Her own orchestral arrangements, which can be heard on that album or *Illuminations*, and are clearly influenced by the work of Stravinsky and, perhaps, Hovhaness who works in a similarly difficult, if more accessible, vein. The classical moods were also partly the result of influence from Santana's wife Deborah (who at the time was known as Urmila), who shared his spiritual leanings and was a trained classical musician. She would often accompany the guitarist in the devotional music settings that he favoured in this period. It is also likely that she introduced him to the work of Hovhaness, which even now is far from mainstream classical music – and the lush orchestral setting for her narration of a Chinmoy poem later on the album leaves no doubt about her affect on aspects of the record.

The opening devotional music is followed by a feature for Santana's father-in-law, Saunders King, for whom the guitarist and Tom Coster create a convincing pastiche of a 1940s jazz-blues ballad ("Silver Dreams, Golden Smiles"), which King delivers with aplomb.

Narada Michael Walden's presence is keenly felt on *Oneness*. He and Santana were particularly close during this period and often appeared together at concerts of meditative music. "Guru's Song" was one of the pieces they played at these private occasions and they reflect a general simplicity of approach, emphasising the melody through Santana's beautifully controlled and expressive guitar and Walden's dramatic, sweeping piano. The major key setting of "Cry Of The Wilderness" is unusual for Santana who nearly always favours more romantic minor keys. The result is an urgent, forceful segment that conveys a sense of striving for achievement. The second half of *Oneness* is more straightforward, containing elements of funk, Latin and folk. The title track is a tour-de-force, opening in a meditative mood showcasing an emotional guitar passage then builds through Graham Lear's fine drumming to an ecstatic climax created by an outstanding Tom Coster solo. It is a dramatic piece and a good reminder of Coster's qualities. "Life Is Just A Passing Parade" is a lighter affair – essentially the story of Santana's childhood told in gauche lyrics set to a disco funk backbeat, it features an excellent vocal performance from Greg Walker and more roaring guitar.

The guitarist's disaffection with Mexican music had caused him to virtually bypass acoustic music but "Golden Dawn" – a one voice and sole acoustic guitar piece – possesses a simple lyricism that mixes the Mexican melodic style with blues flourishes and because of its simplicity conveys a greater sense of contentment than any number of Santana's Chinmoy inspired lyrics. More than this, "Golden Dawn" reveals some very precise jazz influences, Gil Evans' masterwork "Las Vegas Tango" and Chico Hamilton's "Thoughts", a tune that had captivated Carlos in the mid-1960s. The only piece of Latin music on the album is the joyous "Free As The Morning Sun", which also manages to convey a sense of spiritual freedom by using mostly acoustic instruments. Greg Walker again forges an excellent vocal, whilst Tom Coster's piano provides motion and colour under the light orchestral blanket and Peraza and Rekow's virtuoso percussion adds to the pleasure of a highly enjoyable piece.

"I Am Free" seems somewhat self-indulgent in retrospect but it does not minimise the impact of the album's closing track, Narada Michael Walden's "Song For Devadip". This rapturous selection is probably amongst Santana's finest recorded guitar performances, helped by Michael Walden's keen empathy with the guitarist's melodic needs. The opening melody recalls classic soul passion, before a middle eight of aching beauty that Santana emphasises by repeating the bittersweet guitar harmonies he used in "Samba Pa Ti". His closing improvisation in a voice-like tone is a stunning display that recalls the impact of Coltrane's soprano or Pharoah Sanders' blistering tenor. There is a strong sense of the musician laying bare his soul to the listener through his instrument; there is a yearning, pleading tone to some of the passages. This was something that the guitarist recognised too, "A lot of my best solos remind me of when my mom used to scold me, 'Dit-doo-dup-dat-doo-doo-*bah!*"[43] Largely because of its emotional nakedness "Song for Devadip" is a majestic performance that almost erases the horrors of *Inner Secrets*.

In retrospect *Oneness* is amongst Carlos Santana's most personally revealing recordings and it must be viewed as his attempt to be taken seriously as a thoughtful musical architect. Whilst his association with the Sri Chinmoy empire resulted in drum-beating gaffs such as "I Am Free", the overall impact of the album is positive. In the ten years that had passed since the creation of the Santana band, his own guitar style and technique had developed to the point of almost being something entirely new. His skills were probably at their peak, he was close to reaching the jazz player's technical level and could handle be-bop complexities. Nevertheless, the same basic foundations of his style underpinned his new virtuosity. He still relied fundamentally on melody, he still had the ability to uplift the listener with the power of just one note and he still crafted passages that had the lyrical soul music qualities of his favourite singers. Above all, *Oneness* demonstrated that he had acquired a deeper musical maturity and was at ease working in diverse musical idioms. Stripped down, the grooves of the record contain most of Santana's musical roots, the blues are still heard in his guitar licks, but there's also devotional Indian music, Western classical music, jazz in romantic and hard bop guises, soul-funk, plus a simple, acoustic melody that reflected his Mexican roots and a lively dose of Afro-Cuban. In this way, *Oneness* was much more than a guitar album, it was the story of a musical journey.

The gulf between *Oneness* and the limp *Inner Secrets* was massive and it seemed that the two simply could not be reconciled. The Santana band had almost become a monster that Carlos could not control and which hardly reflected his musical interests. In 1979 the band was almost an entity outside of Carlos Santana, he felt detached from it and was almost the guest guitar player in his own band! Throughout this period the real Santana could be found occasionally appearing at Sri Chinmoy meditation concerts as "Devadip", events largely for Chinmoy devotees that might be held in schools or colleges around the USA. These might be solo performances, or performances with other devotees like Narada Michael Walden or John McLaughlin. On other occasions he might be accompanied by a group of disciple musicians called Sri Chinmoy Rainbow or solely by saxophone playing disciple Russell Tubbs. A typical performance found Devadip alone with a guitar, a drum machine and his own voice running through "Love, Devotion and Surrender", "Spartacus" or "Swapan Tari". The freedom of the scene gave the listener the feeling of being present at a private practice session where he might include a simple rendition of Luiz Bonfa's "Manha De Carnaval", "Song For My Brother", "Hannibal", "Gardenia" or even "Samba Pa Ti" and "Europa" or a new vocal entitled "Angel Negro", performed as early as 1980, with just guitar, voice and drum machine. His commitment was not in doubt and the lack of a group seemed to give him more freedom to explore the instrument without the need to go into amplified overdrive. The solo performances would last only one hour and Santana's intent was set out in a flyer that was handed to those present, "Tonight Devadip will be performing some of his favourite songs on solo guitar. This is a new venture for him and it is his wish to perform free for his brothers and sisters as his soul's offering." It was at these Devadip recitals that interpretations of Sri Chinmoy's compositions were worked through, having been "translated" from Indian form by Carlos and his wife. These included many themes that would appear on *The Swing Of Delight* and it might involve Devadip playing alongside the Guru, who accompanied himself on harmonium or esraj, a violin-like instrument of mild tone. One example was a long, linear, traditional melody played on esraj with Devadip accompanying on well crafted guitar chords; eventually, the recognisable sound of "Guru's Song" emerges, but in a far less rhythmically bound way than that demanded by Western music. In this setting, "Guru's Song" reveals its genesis as a religious melody firmly anchored in the traditions of Indian devotional music. There was an innocence to these free Devadip performances which was a refreshing change from the indulgence and hype of the rock world. Fellow Chinmoy devotee Narada Michael Walden reveals the naiveté of the period, "Well Devadip was always in love with Guru. He would say "I'm coming to see Guru with my shovel, to put spiritual light on myself with my shovel, so that I could go back into the world and be full of light ." He was always happy to come to Queens, he'd come up to my room and jump on my bed, wake me up and we'd hang out and either write songs or drive around and talk. There's a song called "Guru's Song" where I play piano, he played guitar, beautiful. That was on one of his solo albums. There were quite a few pieces of music like that we would play together, for either meditation, or the parades or concerts or if Guru was having a meditation somewhere we would play together."

☯

There is little doubt that by 1979, Carlos Santana was seriously considering ending the Santana band and escaping from "Black Magic Woman" once and for all. As early as 1977 he said he hoped that the release of *Moonflower,* with its live hits mix, would allow him to "seal the package and get away from playing a few of the older tunes. I'm not sure people are going to let me get away with it."[44] It was in this hardly enthusiastic frame of mind that Santana entered the studio to write and record the annual album, "I told the band that if the Santana band was going to continue, that they'd have to keep me interested and I told that to the management and to everybody else too."[45] A new singer and keyboard player were required as Greg Walker had left (was he just too popular for comfort?) and Chris Ryhne had returned to session duty. Carlos had heard the work of a Scottish singer, Alex Ligertwood, on an album by David Sancious. The Scot, who was also known as a song-writer from his Brian Auger days, was asked to join – as was Alan Pasqua, a talented jazz pianist who had most recently worked with Bob Dylan. There was nothing in the can, so the band set about writing a whole album and the result was one of only two Santana albums entirely consisting of newly writ-ten material. Carlos was passive again as Columbia appointed Keith Olsen to produce the record; Olsen was another of those Los Angeles professionals who had worked successfully with Fleetwood Mac and The Eagles, but his preferred method was some distance removed from Santana's approach of trying to get a live feeling to the music, as Carlos later reflected, "with Keith we did it extremely the opposite way. It was mainly like tracks. You do gain a lot in the sound but you lose a lot of emotion. I prefer to go for the feeling with minimal dubbing." The omens were not good and some of the new material was of marginal quality, tending towards the heavy guitar rock pop-ular during the period.

The album was finally named *Marathon*, after Carlos' wife's recent achievement in completing the New York marathon and, indeed, the short title track has an invigorating feel of motion, as did an accomplished show-case for bass player David Margen, "Runnin". However, the album was let down by weak songs like "Love" and "Hard Times" and a banal attempt at cracking the AOR market with "You Know That I Love You". "All I Ever Wanted" had some clever riffing and powerful bongos but was an oddity for Santana and there were a couple of OK ballads in "Summer Lady" and another of Carlos' Stevie Wonder infused efforts, "Stay (Beside Me)". This lilting tune had one of the most convincing melodies on the album and a fine solo from Alan Pasqua. Still for all its shortcomings, *Marathon* was some way better than *Inner Secrets* and included the sublime "Aqua Marine" and a strong piece of Latin-rock in "Lightning In The Sky" – a showcase for Alex Ligertwood's extraordinary four octave vocal range.

The release of the LP in September found the band in the middle of a major US tour which included Madison Square Gardens in New York City, where Sri Chinmoy attempted to lead the 20,000 crowd in a meditation before the concert. As ever the set was a mix of old favourites and selections from the new gold LP, except that this time they didn't play too many of them! As the band went on to Japan and Australia, in the company of Eddie Money, their set even included a version of The Beatles' "I Want You (She's So Heavy)" and the musicians appeared full of energy. Some like Chris Solberg had reached the peak of their life's musical achievement and knew it. Alan Pasqua was an accomplished musician and when he got the space he shone, as did a reduced percussion section of Raul Rekow and Armando Peraza (the latter now handling timbales since Pete Escovedo's departure and doing it with aplomb).

Marathon may not have reflected Carlos Santana's real musical vision but the equation was clear. It was albums like *Inner Secrets* and *Marathon* that literally paid for *Oneness*. It was a pact the guitar man was prepared to make. The truth was that Santana had been rudderless since Tom Coster's departure and the guitar player had to look beyond the confines of the group to find musical satisfaction. Santana and Devadip were still worlds apart as the group celebrated its tenth anniversary in what seemed to be the normal state of flux.

Chapter 13

A bright spot came in the autumn of 1979. After the release of another ho-hum album, Carlos was in Los Angeles with the band that bears his name, when he got a call from jazz star Herbie Hancock. Hancock was about to record a new album and once again it was David Rubinson who would be providing direction and pushing the buttons. The record was to be a R&B, dance album and Hancock had written a song with Carlos Santana in mind. Rubinson suggested that one-time Santana singer Greg Walker would be just the man to sing it. The result appeared on the *Monster* album in the form of an enjoyable Latin workout, "Saturday Nite", which was considerably lifted by Walker's smooth vocals and great guitar from Santana. This included an exchange of notes with Herbie Hancock who was playing the latest guitar-imitating synthesiser. This venture, and the new friendship between Santana and Hancock paved the way for a new project, the follow-up to *Oneness* which would be called *The Swing Of Delight*.

Once again, David Rubinson was to be at the helm at his Automatt studio and Herbie Hancock brought along three of his old cohorts from his Miles Davis days, Tony Williams, Ron Carter and Wayne Shorter. Carlos was ecstatic, the very thought of making his record with all but one of the members of Miles Davis' legendary 1960s quintet was enough to send him into paroxysms of joy. In addition to the Miles Davis musicians, Carlos enlisted the peerless Santana percussion section plus David Margen, Graham Lear and Russell Tubbs. The result was a musical treat comprising a mixture of Santana originals, a superb Wayne Shorter composition ("Shere Khan The Tiger") and a number of examples of Sri Chinmoy's writing: "Jharna Kala",

"Swapan Tari" and the sublime "Phuler Matan". These emerged from devotional themes performed by Sri Chinmoy at meditation concerts. The guitarist would take the basic linear themes of Chinmoy's ragas and develop them into full-blown compositions, but it was no easy process as he recalled, "Three times a year a lot of people from the San Francisco centre of Chinmoy disciples go to New York to study with Guru and all the girls learn fifty songs and all the boys learn fifty songs. The songs are usually little melodies and singing them is a sort of meditative action. Some songs are very foreign to me, my mind is very Western and they go over my head. But others are catchy, I'm hooked on melody and they jump out at me. I'll hear my wife singing these songs and I get the melodies from her."

Once the melody was planted in his head, Carlos Santana's great ability to take a musical idea and turn it into something new, took over. Herbie Hancock and David Rubinson were also crucial to the arrangements, Rubinson in particular providing a bridge between Santana and the jazz players, as he explained, "Devadip is not a studio musician, Ron Carter on the other hand does a lot of record dates. Devadip is a musician who is very instinctive, the flow from his feelings to his fingers is very direct; his feelings are beautifully expressed musically and very fast. He's very creative but he's not someone who can go, 'I see, bar 55, the Bb7, we should play that Eb7 with a D in the bass.' So, on "Shere, Khan The Tiger" it was all written out and it went 5/4 for eight to ten measures and changed to 6/4, but the 6/4 was weird because a lot of the accents came on the fifth beat. As good as these guys are (Hancock, Carter etc), they were all counting the whole time. Now Devadip had to play this song and he played it beautifully. But in order to do it, I had to sit with the music and every once in a while just nod at him." Carlos elaborated on his approach, "I make my own sort of charts and it's like chicken scratch. I did learn how to read music when I was a child but I dropped out of it, but I remember the fa-so-la-ti-do kinda thing and I write my own charts around that. What I'm lacking is the bar structure, I just write the notes and memorise the first note of each phrase, so to speak." For all this, the learning wasn't all one way traffic and Herbie Hancock noted that, "even in a short space of time I learned so much from him (Carlos)."

The music on *The Swing Of Delight* reflects the Santana approach to jazz expression; simple, effective melodies couched in jazz-funk, Latin or Brazilian settings. There were three pieces of more or less straight jazz ("Jharna Kala", "Gardenia" and "Shere Khan The Tiger") – the rest was close to the standard Santana concept. All the Miles Davis musicians on the disc were experienced players of fusion and blues which provided the common ground on which they could meet the guitarist who, by his own admission, was not about to turn into John McLaughlin and surprise us all with a flurry of technically advanced be-bop runs.

Carlos Santana had been friendly with Herbie Hancock for less than a year and had never worked with Tony Williams or Wayne Shorter before. Given this, the obvious musical empathy is a clear testament to how highly regarded Carlos was by these true jazz masters. There were beautiful solo passages from Santana and Shorter that flowed effortlessly into each other on "Gardenia" and "Spartacus", a persuasive, powerful ensemble approach on "Phuler Matan" and some hedonistic telepathy between guitarist and drummer on the exciting "Swapan Tari" which opened the album. However, most of the work was the result of a close musical partnership between the guitarist and Herbie Hancock, who worked closely together on the arrangements. They revived their "Saturday Nite" high stepping solos on the lightweight "Golden Hours", whilst Hancock provides some horn-like synthesiser on "Song For My Brother". The best moments came on "Gardenia" and "Spartacus" which found the chief head-hunter's Fender Rhodes prompting and cushioning some of Santana's exquisitely expressive guitar, before setting off on dancing, probing musical explorations of their own.

Of course, Santana had some prime musicians of his own to introduce to his new friends. Armando Peraza updates his jazz contacts list in style with more virtuoso bongo performances, while reeds man Russell Tubbs suggests that he might have been a serious contender had he not chosen the disciple's life. His solo on "Jharna Kala" is outstanding. The Santana bass/drums team of Graham Lear and David Margen isn't quite able to match Tony Williams and Ron Carter, but who could, especially given Williams' outstanding playing on "Gardenia"?

As his playing clearly demonstrates, Carlos Santana's confidence in his own musical abilities was high during these sessions. "When I recorded *Caravanserai* I felt insecure," Santana explains, "I was moving into the unknown, I didn't read music. I was working with advanced musicians like Hadley Caliman and I was trying to stretch myself beyond rock'n'roll. When I recorded *Swing Of Delight* I did not feel so insecure because I have learned a great deal through the years."[46] One feature of his musical growth was his improving writing skill as evidenced by "Song for My Brother" and, particularly, "Gardenia" which were both mature compositions. The final Santana composition was the Mexican folk song "La Llave", which included a fine conga break from Francisco Aguabella and Carlos' own guileless vocal.

The highlights of the album were "Shere Khan, The Tiger" and the best track, "Phuler Matan". Wayne Shorter' s "Shere Khan" is a complex, tricky composition that is a fitting close to a fine album, showing as it does how Santana's approach to even the most heady music can be a humanising one. "Phuler Matan" opens with a serene rendering of the basic theme on Spanish guitar before it is turned inside out into a fiery piece that recalls the power of "Mother Africa"; there are no solos, but all the musicians play with exceptional fire, particularly Tony Williams who is inspired. The music unfolds in wave after wave of collective passion and energy that moves towards an ecstatic embrace. The lyrical undercurrent of the session is best demonstrated by the delightful "Spartacus" which had become a jazz standard through interpretations by Bill Evans and Carlos' enduring hero, Gabor Szabo. Santana's musical approach influences Hancock and Shorter who both add beautiful passages of their own to the track.

The Swing Of Delight is an important record, it emphasises Carlos Santana's unique ability to deliver a melody and draw great expression from his instrument. It would have been impossible to "fake it" in the company of jazz masters of this stature. If Carlos Santana was not able to cut it on this session, the presence of musicians of the calibre of Hancock, Shorter, Williams and Carter would have starkly revealed any deficiencies. The album also highlighted his improvement as a composer and, given that it received a five star review in *Downbeat* magazine, it just showed what he could do when left to his own devices.

In May, the guitarist joined a Hancock live gig in Berkeley for a lively session with the pianist and a band which included Stanley Clarke and John McLaughlin. Carlos was clearly so much a part of the jazz scene in this period that the question remained: would he kill off the Santana band and go it alone, or would he continue his schizophrenic musical life?

❧

By 1980 the music business was a very different beast to its 1970s counterpart. The late 1960s and 1970s were Santana's era and, as the new decade broke, the guitarist would have to ponder how a band like Santana could remain relevant. As far as the Santana band was concerned, 1980 was a make or break year and it was probably Jimmy Page who saved it from an early demise. The group was in Frankfurt, Germany, midway through a middling tour of Europe, when they invited the Led Zeppelin guitar man to jam on "Shake Your Moneymaker" at the end of one show. This passed off peacefully enough, but after the show Page enthused about the band to Carlos and this had a remarkable effect on the ever-impulsive guitarist. Only a couple of years after threatening to pack it all in, Jimmy Page convinced him that it was "significant to play rock'n'roll" and suddenly Carlos was full of enthusiasm to revive the Santana band as he told the BBC, "I got together with Jimmy Page and he charged me up by certain things he said to me about Santana, he liked the band, he came and saw us and liked us a lot. Now when we play live, there's Santana and Devadip happening together with this band because they're so versatile."

The true highlight of 1980's tour was the introduction of New York timbalero Orestes Vilató to the band, which completed one of the greatest percussion sections in the history of the band. Vilató was already a major figure in Latin music when Carlos Santana asked him to join his band in 1975, but having just left Ray Barretto and started his own band, Los Kimbos, Orestes had too much to lose. By 1980 hassles with record labels had told Vilató that it was time for a change, so he moved to the Bay Area and joined the band. Raul Rekow remembered how it happened, "Pete Escovedo left after a short period and Carlos asked 'which timbalero would guys like to play with?', we said 'Orestes Vilató, he is the guy.' Carlos called Orestes and talked him into moving out to San Francisco to play with us, I was in complete heaven then. You know they were very nice to me, I know that I am not at the level of musicianship as either Armando or Orestes, both of them are innovators, they changed the instrument, both of them."

Orestes is one of the great leaders of Latin music and highly regarded by his peers and his dynamic stage personality enhanced Santana's reputation as one the most exciting live acts. His style is more "classic" than, say, Chepito Areas' and he took seriously the fact that within the Santana band he could take the culture of Cuban music around the world. He was to prove a very influential figure and was responsible for introducing a number of chants from Yoruba culture that began to permeate the band's music from 1981 onwards. These chants derived from West African religious rituals which reached Cuba through the slave trade. They were mostly spiritual invocations. Also joining the band was Richard Baker, a Canadian keyboards man who knew Graham Lear from the Gino Vanelli days. Baker was a fine musician, comfortable with rock, Latin and jazz.

With the new men on board, the tour trundled on through Europe and played to large houses with a set that took in a wide view of Santana's music, including seldom heard material like "Just In Time To See The Sun" and "You Just Don't Care". This was quickly followed by a fairly brief tour of the USA in the company of another "guitar hero", Al Di Meola. The year closed with a newly energised Santana setting about the quest for new songs to populate what they hoped would be a big album. The San Franciscan was under massive pressure to come up with a hit record and that meant forgetting Devadip and writing some commercial material, but this time he was reconciled to the market place, "We're right in the middle of the next Santana album. We've got close to fifteen songs and out of them I only like six. But see, I like commercialism, only when it's insincere does it offend me."[47]

The album-to-be would have a chequered course. It started life under working titles *Conquerors* and *X-Man* in sessions held with Alan Pasqua and Chris Solberg. These sessions resulted in songs like "Searchin'", "Tales of Kilamanjaro", "Primera Invasion" and "Hannibal" (another album title at one time), as well as tracks that never appeared such as "Diamond Heart" and "Drums Of Victory". The band even tried a version of an old Marvin Gaye hit from 1967, "You". Completing the album in the new year, it was on the verge of being released under the title *Papa Ré*. Test discs were pressed, as were covers, but the album was pulled at the last minute as the record company's search for hits became paramount. "I haven't been under this kind of pressure before," Carlos explained at the time, "I feel the pressure from Columbia and from around the world to get people listening to the band again. It's not so much finding an audience but we want a new audience. I want to reach more people and to play with bands like The Police and not sound like an antique."[48]

He chose not to face the pressure alone and considered working again with Coke Escovedo, choosing the old Tito Puente song "Azukiki". Sadly, this didn't bear fruit. Equally unsuccessful were his concerted efforts to coax his brother Jorge to join Santana full time as second guitarist. Jorge had just finished promoting his second solo record, but again, this plan didn't work out. In the end Bill Graham was given the chance to do what he had always wanted to do which was to produce a Santana album, even though he would take some convincing that this was a co-production. His presence brought dividends in the stronger Latin feel and a powerful performance of the old 1940s Tin Pan Alley tune, "I Love You Much Too Much", which he literally drummed into the guitarist's head so that he got it right. Graham had always loved Latin music and the blues and both are heard on the resulting album, which also makes much better use of the percussion section, which can actually be heard after its conspicuous absence from half of *Marathon*.

Finally given the curious title *Zebop!*, the disc appeared in April and the result of all the efforts is half a fine album and half a poor one. The poor half was a depressing blanket of AOR pop songs, which included true rubbish like "Winning", "Over and Over" and "Changes". The good half was represented by exciting percussion and strong, but rough, guitar performances on the Afro-Cuban flavoured charts, "É Papa Re", "American Gypsy" (a great, Cuban style descarga), "Primera Invasion" and the excellent "Hannibal". "I Love You Much Too Much" was a moving ballad and equally satisfying was a recollection of the mid-seventies Latin-Jazz on "Tales Of Kilamanjaro" ("Astral Traveling" revisited... *again*). The remainder was average. Without doubt, "Hannibal" was the album's best moment, almost being a summation of 1980s Afro-Cuban rock. It was uplifting, exciting and passionate music which quietly spread a little of Afro-Cuban culture as the lyrics were a chant which originated in the Afro-Cuban cult religion, the santería.

The new percussion section was outstanding and Armando Peraza's conga break on "Hannibal" was worth the purchase price alone. Despite the general animation and the roaring guitar, there was nothing really new on offer. The album was fundamentally a more enthusiastic rehash of the old formula, but *Zebop!* gave Columbia, Bill Graham and Carlos Santana the hit they were seeking, hitting the *Billboard* top 10 and staying on the chart for 21 weeks on the back of the awful "Winning" single which somehow made the top 10 singles chart. Santana as Cliff Richard was a true low point. It made observers wonder if Carlos was really prepared to sacrifice his reputation as a musician for chart success. In the harsh reality of financial survival it was probably expedient and might guarantee a fan base for another ten years. The glorious musical invention of *Abraxas*, *Caravanserai*, *Lotus* or *Borboletta* seemed very distant and, when he heard "Winning", Tom Coster must have been relieved that he'd jumped when he did.

Meanwhile, fortunately, as a live band, Santana were still delivering the goods and the live setting considerably improved most of the *Zebop!* material. The album's US success was helped by a massive 60-date tour that lasted from February well into July. This trek not only saw Santana back in the auditoriums, but in the stadia too. 46,000 fans turned out in Detroit, there was a nationally broadcast "4th of July" special from Cape Cod Coliseum, two mega-dates at Puerto Rico's Roberto Clemente Coliseum and a hot jam with the stars of Latin music, Tito Puente and Eddie Palmieri, in New York. This date gave the Santana percussion section the chance to take-on New York's finest on their own ground and they were well equipped to do it. The combination of Peraza, Vilató and Rekow set a consistently staggering standard – their live performances were a magnet for the eyes and often threatened to upstage Carlos. Raul Rekow for one will never forget that summer night when they came face to face with "El Rey": "Tito Puente, when he heard that rhythm section, said it was "the greatest percussion section in the world" at the time. That's a hell of a compliment coming from Tito Puente, because Tito doesn't like to really give up too many compliments. That was after a gig in New York at the Pier, and Tito, Nicky Marrero, Eddie Palmieri, all the cats came out to jam with us. You know Orestes and Armando are very territorial, and myself as well, I've kind of learned that from them. People come up to sit in at your gig and there is a bit of competition that goes on, so you have to play your ass off, you got to give them everything you've got, you can't let someone come up and play better than you. So that day at the Pier we kicked some ass."

The Santana set at this time was the standard mix of old favourites and the better material from *Zebop!*, but it worked really well and the new enthusiasm of the band's leader made for some exciting shows. Carlos' guitar sound was sharper and harder than in previous years. He had a new guitar handbuilt for him by master craftsman Paul Reed Smith, and this new instrument had a more direct sound than the warmth of his old Yamaha. He had rediscovered the blues and the set often included tunes he used to play in Tijuana like "Shake Your Money Maker" and "Help Me", as well as the band's own classics like "Incident At Neshabur" which gave Richard Baker room to show that he could cut it with Santana. The pace of the touring was hectic and after a break of only a few weeks the band was off to Japan for a series of interesting encounters. Firstly, Carlos had a special series of three dates with Herbie Hancock, Ron Carter, Tony Williams and Wynton Marsalis where they ran through some material from *The Swing Of Delight*. Next, he joined Journey on-stage in Tokyo for a reunion with Neal Schon and then it was the start of a special five city tour of Japan for the band in the company of Japanese guitar player Masayoshi Takanaka – Santana were still very much able to pull a crowd in Japan and the opening date at the Yokohama Stadium was the biggest concert in the country's history. Next, the band enjoyed a three week break before embarking on a 33-date tour of Europe which lasted nine weeks and played the largest halls. To cap it all, Bill Graham's links with The Rolling Stones saw the year's touring close with two dates in support of the Stones at massive US arenas. After all the pressure, 1981 had brought what Santana and Columbia had hoped for, a big selling album and successful tours that put the Santana band back in the mind of the public. Carlos settled into a four month break with well-earned satisfaction, and if he had the inclination he might have counted the seventy five gold discs the group had earned in Europe alone up to this point.

Chapter 14

Zebop! had seen Santana gain a new army of young fans around the world. However, his appetite for chart success and media celebrity was sporadic and he quickly grew bored of the demand to record pop music. Increasingly he turned his attention to the equally over-hyped world of tennis, which provided him with new friends like John McEnroe and Vitus Gerulitas who were fans of the Mexican's music. Genuine as these liaisons were they could never replace the thrill of playing music and 1982 provided Carlos with a chance to record with one of the true giants of jazz, the pianist McCoy Tyner, on his album *Looking Out*. Tyner had even written a song dedicated to the guitarist and included an extravagant version of Santana's song "Hannibal", which coupled an inspired performance by Carlos with Tyner's billowing piano. Although he could never aspire to the heights of a jazz master like Tyner, his innate melodic sense and highly expressive style stopped him from sounding out of his depth. In fact, he sounded quite at ease.

The reluctant guitar hero also participated in other sessions with Leon Patillo, Stanley Clarke and José Feliciano (a dramatic vocal version of "Samba Pa Ti"). The reunion with Patillo revealed how much Carlos meant to the singer, "I was so honoured and privileged to have him on my album, when he walked into the studio you could see the smile on my face a block away." Another reunion was in the air as the late spring found Carlos working again with his original musical partner, Gregg Rolie. The keyboards man had enjoyed a second dose of massive chart success with Journey, but by early 1981 he had grown tired of the constant touring and left the band. Santana and Rolie had barely spoken for years and tension remained right into the early 1980s. Now, however, Rolie decided to build bridges with the guitar player by suggesting that they work together on a new concept to be called, appropriately, Friends Again. Appropriate or not, it never really left the ground. Rolie's idea was for a new band which would bypass all Latin percussion and operate in a straight rock vein. To achieve this he recruited Journey's talented drummer, Steve Smith, whilst Santana brought along David Margen to handle the bass. Democracy aside, Gregg was adamant that there would be no Latin percussion. The venture started with rehearsals at the singer's Novato home, but they soon encountered difficulty in coming up with good new material and the relationship between the two main protagonists remained delicate to say the least. Carlos had been the undisputed leader of Santana since 1974 and Rolie had been the main force in Journey with Neal Schon, so, once again, the meeting of two strong personalities led to a minor revival of the old power struggles. For all this, Friends Again made some progress and the unit even cut some demos at Fantasy Studios in Berkeley, but as Steve Smith recalls, success was never really likely, "I was still in Journey, so I wasn't really free to spend a lot of time on the project and I don't think I was really all that excited about it musically. It was a good idea, but needed a lot of work."

Little is known of the musical output of Friends Again, but it was the trigger for Santana and Rolie to start writing material together as the Santana Band's leader sought Rolie's assistance in giving some impetus to the follow-up to *Zebop!*. As ever the pressure was on to create another hit record. In 1982, the two most fashionable groups in popular music in the minds of Columbia's executives were the British groups – The Police and Dire Straits. The former played a catchy form of pop-rock that made clever use of reggae rhythms, whilst the latter originally played a kind of light country-blues-rock based around the twanging Stratocaster sound of guitarist Mark Knopfler. The clear business logic was that if the Santana band were to maintain contemporary appeal, they would have to incorporate some of these sounds into their music. They also needed to continue to take into account the continuing success of FM bands like Journey, REO Speedwagon and Foreigner. To achieve this Columbia recruited a new clutch of producers to work on Santana's next album and the result sounds like an attempt to ape new styles whilst still retaining a little of the Santana essence. The names included John Ryan, who had tasted success with Styx, and Bill Szymczyk who had been responsible for The Eagles and the J. Geils Band. Gregg Rolie would co-produce some tracks with Santana and was involved on all the arrangements, which accounts for a harder rock sound. The procession of producers brought in to manufacture a new sound left the guitar man in a state of supreme indifference. He later reflected, "We got such massive amounts of money from Columbia; we got a fat, juicy contract to make up for how cheap they got us at first. For a while they wanted us to play the game. I would just play tennis, show up at the studio, play the music and split."[49] It was a sorry state of affairs.

Nevertheless, there was a style of contemporary music that was interesting Carlos Santana, namely reggae. It was an infectious and spiritually inclined music from Jamaica whose figurehead, Bob Marley, had recently passed away. In the years before his death Marley had become a world superstar and many rock musicians championed his music, not least Eric Clapton who had a hit with Marley's "I Shot The Sheriff". Santana was soon enthralled with Marley's highly melodic *and* rhythmic music. No doubt he identified with the Jamaican's status as a "Third World Star" and his strong spiritual beliefs. As the years went on he became more and more fervent in his admiration for the Jamaican, playing his songs live ("Exodus" and "So Much Trouble" were the favourites) and becoming friendly with Marley's widow.

Armed with help from Rolie, the band entered the studio in April to record the new LP which they called *Shangó*. That title and the charming Mexican cover art might have suggested to the prospective purchaser that a cornucopia of ethnic musical delights awaited them on the enclosed vinyl. It didn't. There are two good tracks on *Shangó*, a Latin jam "Nueva York" that saw the return of Gregg Rolie's Hammond to a Santana disc and the title track which was a brief but uplifting Afro chant. The rest was modest pop music which sought to be contemporary by mirroring the sounds of reggae, The Police, Dire Straits and AOR. Particularly awful was a mind-numbing, would-be rock anthem, "Nowhere To Run" which left the listener feeling exactly that. Santana's guitar was still worth hearing and the percussion section battled gamely with the formula music, creating some imaginative charts, but most owners of *Shangó* listened to it for a few weeks and returned it to the shelf to gather dust. The band were in the middle of another massive US tour when the LP was released in August, but the basic lack of quality halted its chart climb at number twenty-two on *Billboard*. It was obvious that after the surge of enthusiasm he felt at the time of *Zebop!*, Carlos Santana had little enthusiasm for *Shangó,* a point further evidenced by the fact that within a month of the tour only three songs from the record were being played live. *Shangó* represented a natural turning-point in Santana's career, and a change was overdue. In his heart Santana knew he was a musician and not a tennis player. There might have been a temporary attraction in turning up to dub on his solos and collect the money, but this was not the do or die attitude to music that had driven the guitarist throughout his life.

Carlos was also dissatisfied with his spiritual life and the end of 1982 saw him move away from Sri Chinmoy, and instead he seemed to have become more interested in the "born-again" Christianity movement that was sweeping the world at the time. It was his first step towards freedom and reflected a new found confidence; it had been ten years since he was first introduced to Sri Chinmoy in New York and in that period he had developed into a highly regarded musician feted by many of the major names in jazz, the musical form that he most aspired to master. His musical-spiritual journey had been charted through work with John McLaughlin, Alice Coltrane and eventually his own important albums *Oneness* and *The Swing Of Delight*, which had revealed how he had matured tremendously as a player and composer. His recent session with McCoy Tyner must have been a major boost to his confidence. In addition to his personal confidence, he had also begun to have doubts about the Guru's motives, "I found God in different ways than a Guru, swami or yogi. It's good to learn from them, but they get in the way, especially when they start lusting for immortality. You should always be suspicious of anybody who is lusting for immortality by burying their writings under the ground and shit like that."[50] So, having left Sri Chinmoy, Carlos Santana was free of that discipline, but whilst he might have had doubts about the extent of the Guru's egoless state, the period had had a profound impact on him and continued to influence his life and spiritual outlook.

Meanwhile, Santana had the US tour to complete which included a one-off TV date in the Dominican Republic where the band were greeted by a crowd nearly hysterical with excitement. This was Santana's first date in Latin America since the 1973 tour and it almost ended in disaster. A tropical storm hit virtually as soon as the band took the stage and the entire ensemble were almost electrocuted and washed lock, stock and barrel into the Caribbean as they attempted to play on. In spite of the difficulties, this return to Hispanic America after an absence of nine years would signal the theme of Carlos' music making in the next year. Santana was going back to his roots.

☯

1983 was Carlos Santana's year of freedom and a year to reflect on his musical roots. He had some breathing space, he was free of Sri Chinmoy's discipline and had the room to make a solo recording of his own conception to complete his current record contract. He was also about to become a father. At the turn of the year he was in the studio recording an album which looked back at the musical influences of his days in Tijuana, artists like Bo Diddley, Bobby Parker, John Lee Hooker, Booker T. Jones, Chuck Berry and Lightnin' Hopkins. To do this he enlisted the producers *he* wanted and what better choices than Jerry Wexler and Barry Beckett? Wexler was the mastermind behind the careers of Santana heroes like Wilson Pickett, Aretha Franklin, Ray Charles and Otis Redding. Barry Beckett was the piano player and de facto leader of the legendary Muscle Shoals Rhythm Section. No longer Devadip, Carlos recruited Booker T. Jones himself to play organ on the album and, at the insistence of John McEnroe, recalled Greg Walker to the microphone who delivered the goods in no small measure. The resulting album, *Havana Moon*, is amongst his most "different" albums and is really a glimpse into the Santana musical photo album of the 1950s and 1960s. It was twenty years since he had left Tijuana and now at the age of thirty four he was ready to look back and pay his dues to the R&B champions from that era, who he still admired.

The result was an enjoyable "roots" album which moves from the strong R&B flavours of "Watch Your Step", "Who Do You Love", "Lightnin'" and "Mudbone" to the soul feel of "Daughter Of The Night" and even a taste of country and western on "They All Went To Mexico" (which included a Willie Nelson vocal). Booker T. Jones is prominent on a seductive jam, "One With You", and a remarkable reworking of an old Chuck Berry hit "Havana Moon". Carlos' animated guitar was blended throughout with Jones' Hammond organ, fine Greg Walker vocals and the instrumental talents of the key players from Texan band The Fabulous Thunderbirds – in general the music conjured the mood of a sleazy bar in 1960s Tijuana.

Another track of note was a jazzy version of "Tales Of Kilimanjaro", an alternate take from the early *Zebop!* sessions. It has a cooler, more spiritual feel and provides the best opportunity to hear Alan Pasqua's excellent piano stylings. However, the most significant cut came with the finale "Vereda Tropical". This track is the only time Carlos has recorded a classic romantic Mexican melody, thus taking the listener back to his pre-Tijuana days. What this sweet tune reveals are the building blocks of a melodic sensibility that would one day lead to "Samba Pa Ti" and "Europa". Carlos' father José Santana is heard on violin and vocals, leading a classic Mariachi band over which Clare Fischer prepared a romantic string arrangement. Listening to this music, it's hard not to consider how the young guitarist rejected it to go off and play *pachuco* music. Now older and wiser, Carlos Santana no longer chose to ignore the part this had played in the musical development of his country and in his development as a musician and was ready to celebrate it. On an album of musical reconciliations, this is the most significant.

The album, which effectively documented Carlos' musical roots, came out quickly and was on the shelves by April. It didn't exactly fly out of the stores, but sold well nevertheless. It seemed to be the signal that the guitar player was moving away from the self-conscious sombreness of the Devadip image and no longer saw a separation between "spiritual" music and "street" music, but above all, it showed that when left to his own devices Carlos Santana could make very good records.

He had always been able to produce *great* live shows and the band was committed to a heavy tour of Europe throughout March, April and May, which was to be swiftly followed by a trip to Japan and Australia. To reflect his new found musical freedom he brought in some new faces, having ditched Ligertwood, Baker and Margen. Tom Coster was back having just completed his second solo album, which heavily featured his trademark moog solos. This was the sound that he would bring to the 1983 tour. Greg Walker had impressed with his newly gospel-infused vocals and made the tour, as did an excellent Jamaican bass player, Keith Jones. Clearly Carlos wanted to get closer to the reggae sound and as luck would have it, Jones could also handle jazz, Latin and blues with consummate ease. As the band started the European dates, Carlos remembered Chester Thompson, the hot organ player he had known from his many links with Bay Area funk outfit Tower Of Power and invited him to join the tour. Thompson jumped at the chance, "It was an idea Carlos had of having two keyboard players or going to a two keyboard set-up in 1983. It was a lame period during the Tower Of Power days and I wanted to just move a little bit further, an opportunity came and I took it." Thompson flew out to Europe to start a musical partnership with Carlos that would last for more than a decade. This two-keyboard line-up was the strongest Santana had assembled since the heady days of the *Lotus* tour and was possibly one of the strongest line-ups ever to bear the group name. The new Santana band comprised a legendary percussion section, one of the world's great guitar players, two outstanding organists, an accomplished bass player and the charismatic Greg Walker.

The sound of the new band was far less "rock" orientated than its previous incarnation, but the range and capability of the musicians was such that they could cover almost anything from the Santana repertoire. They reflected the loose R&B feel of *Havana Moon* and Carlos even handled the lead vocals on spirited renditions of the Mexican folk classic "La Bamba", it was hard to imagine Devadip doing that. In addition, there were surprise choices like

Billy Preston's gospel hit "That's The Way God Planned It" which sat easily alongside Santana's new John Lee Hooker style "Super Boogie" and a new rap-fusion tune, "Brotherhood". *Shangó* was all but forgotten save for perfunctory performances of "Hold On" and "Nowhere To Run". In fact, this Santana band was so relaxed with the band's entire musical past that they even played "In A Silent Way" for the first time in years. Santana was clearly delighted to have Greg Walker back and the charismatic singer was given plenty of room to shine on a new blues "John Henry" and R&B classics like Sonny Boy Williamson's "Help Me". The range of this band's styles was extraordinary. Carlos himself was, by now, working the music like a magician, old favourites would be effortlessly invigorated by adding in different textures and styles. For instance, on this tour, in the middle of "Soul Sacrifice", the guitarist would bring the band down and start playing the famous melody from "Concierto de Aranjuez" with all the sensitivity of a true master. This would develop into a loose jam that called in at George Benson's "El Mar" and War's "The World Is A Ghetto", the band moving from one dynamic, one mood to another with a masterful ease that recalled the great days of *Lotus*.

Santana's 1983 set amounted to a history of black music covering jazz, Afro-Cuban, R&B, blues, gospel, soul, funk, rap and rock in a stunning three-hour show. As if to emphasise this the shows closed with the Afro chants of "Shangó", which moved into an extraordinary segment which took the audience to a black Southern Pentecostal church with Chester Thompson weaving a magical church-style organ outburst. The mood was taken up by singer Walker, who improvised what sounded like plantation moaning, while the band's leader beat a tambourine and introduced the band as if he were a preacher collecting new souls.

As the tour wound on through the year there were plenty of pleasing musical encounters, like a session with the great Japanese sax-man Sadao Watanabe in Tokyo where Carlos also invited Saunders King out for a run through of the old standard "Stardust". In October, having finished a short US tour, he joined piano legend McCoy Tyner on stage at the Kool Jazz Festival in San Francisco where they recalled the highlights of the *Looking Out* album in a scintillating live session. Carlos' confidence was high, he had already cut a great album with Herbie Hancock and handled plenty of live dates with that piano legend and now, here he was, working with one of the true legends of jazz who predated even Hancock. Contentment was breaking out in the guitarist's life, domestically and professionally.

Chapter 15

After the year of freedom came the return to reality – Santana as a product. A new contract was signed with Columbia and at the turn of 1984 the band entered the studio to start recording new material that was not to see the light of day for over a year. New faces appeared in an attempt to find new musical flavours, well known players and writers like David Sancious and Alphonso Johnson, plus Chester Thompson who was drumming with the eminently commercial Genesis. Work in the studio lasted from March to May and reports filtered through that a new album, *Appearances*, was slated for a summer release, but it never appeared. The release was originally planned to coincide with a stadium tour of Europe with Bob Dylan. This brief tour suited Santana's new domestic situation – his first child, Salvador, had been born a year earlier, an event that signalled a slowing down of activity that would last three years.

The Dylan-Santana tour of 1984 had the hallmark of a big Bill Graham enterprise, massive, lucrative gigs mostly held in the major soccer stadiums of Europe in front of crowds rarely fewer than 40,000 in number. They visited new countries on the Santana road map like Ireland where they made a big impact but curiously never returned. Such was the financial scale of the tour that the Santana band could afford to expand to a massive ten man outfit which included two singers, Greg Walker and Alex Ligertwood. Leaving out "Black Magic Woman" and "Oye Como Va" for just one tour the group played a set of almost all new material which seemed to have a leaning towards funk and soul, but there was still a blend of Afro-Cuban in there and a good clash of egos when Sancious took to the front of the stage with his flashy heavy metal guitar licks on "Open Invitation". However, the prospect of cashing in on the sales that could be generated by a huge European tour was not significant enough for the record company and *Appearances* was withdrawn. A short American tour followed and the musicians entered the studio to finish the recording which ran up to November. When *Beyond Appearances* finally appeared in February some new tracks had been added by a new producer. These were obviously aimed at the charts and the difference between the material written by Santana and the new tracks is stark. The result was another discouraging album.

The new producer was Val Garay, who had a good track record with chart successes Kim Carnes and The Motels. However, these were acts with a very different sensibility from Santana. Garay contributed further doses of banal pop trash, "Say It Again", "I'm The One Who Loves You" and the spectacularly bad "How Long". In the midst of this there was good music like "Spirit", "Touchdown Raiders" and "Who Loves You" which sounded something like Santana and two outstanding tracks, "Brotherhood" and "Right Now". The former was a startling mix of Afro-funk, fusion solos and rapping, whilst "Right Now" was a pleasing, uplifting melange of reggae, soul and an Afro-Cuban coda. It was clearly inspired by Third World's 1982 hit "Try Jah Love" which had been written for them by Santana's perennial hero Stevie Wonder. *Beyond Appearances* followed the usual formula of every Santana album since *Inner Secrets* in its attempt to find a way of making Santana contemporary and the end product was another poor release that saw the band's reputation sink even further. Santana was simply not fashionable and it appeared unlikely that they would ever have a major hit again. Columbia had to recoup their investment and no doubt Garay didn't come cheap, but it was really a waste of time to try. As ever the guitarist attempted to rationalise the experience and saw the benefit of the album as being a way to influence people through the songs' words, "The lyrics on *Beyond Appearances* are geared towards bringing people to a place where they can see that we do have options and alternatives." He also spoke with guarded enthusiasm about the producer, "Val Garay has a lot of conviction and I like that in a producer because I also have a lot. I got away with a lot considering it was supposed to be a Hollywood commercial concept. Well, we fought a lot, but it was constructive fighting. Like I said, he can't take me totally to his territory, it's not me. We have to find the middle place where we can find material and moods and lyrics where we can reach the younger audience."[51]

Observers knew in their hearts that Carlos Santana didn't buy this and even as the album was launched he was changing his tune, "Once in a while we go to L.A. to see if we can learn something and every time I learn that they don't have the vision, technology or facilities. Producers who don't understand the band, we keep trying, it's like dating. I learned a lot about how to use the board to get a bigger sound from working with Val Garay. Sometimes when you play live the sound goes out of the window and what you concentrate on is the performance. What they concentrate on, is the sound. So to me to try and get both is the goal. We've gotten it on some songs, "Brotherhood", "Spirit", "Right Now", "Touchdown Raiders", "Body Surfing" and "Aqua Marine"."[52] As soon as the album was released and the interviews started, Carlos was more keen to talk about a new session he had just completed with drummer Tony Williams at The Plant in Sausalito. The guitar hero was invigorated by the session, but the only fruit to materialise from it was one track "'Trane" which came out two years later. In the course of the year Carlos also found time to record with Gregg Rolie, who had launched a solo career with a self-titled album on Columbia which included contributions from a number of old friends including Neal Schon, Mike Carabello and David Margen. Between them they conjured up a collection of highly FM-targeted songs destined to find favour only in the US market.

Beyond Appearances was launched with a high profile appearance on *Saturday Night Live*, presaging a 40 date US tour. Santana's marginalised station in the world of media rock was underlined half-way through the tour, when a tragic famine in East Africa led to a multi-media, multi-national concert, Live Aid. The concerts had been conceived and run from the UK where the band was far from fashionable, so it was obvious that Santana was not exactly the first name on Live Aid organiser Bob Geldof's list. But, for the US show, Geldof had naturally enlisted the assistance of Bill Graham, the king of American promoters, and, at Graham's insistence, added Santana to the schedule. Santana repaid the effort with an "in your face" performance that gave no quarter to the kind of self-congratulation that other artists fell foul of, at an event which seemed to feature more than a hint of ego massage. As ever, Carlos was happy to share the spotlight and invited jazz guitarist Pat Metheny to join the band for a moving take of a new instrumental "By The Pool", coupled with an exciting "Right Now". Sadly, the band's multi-ethnic line-up and music attracted little attention from the assembled media, who were predictably more interested in Phil Collins.

1985 had been another year of ups and downs for Santana and with a young son to look after and another baby just born, it was time for Carlos Santana to have a quiet year. It seemed he was running out of steam, "Someday maybe I can get away with doing a sabbatical," the guitarist mused at the time, " Sometimes I feel like I need to just stop and listen for a couple of years and learn more before I can keep doing all this music. Something motivates you and I think when the joy would stop, that's when I would have to stop. Sometimes it is tempting to stop, especially now with the children." By 1985 the demands of the music business had almost turned Santana off music completely. This was a staggering situation given the man's struggle to better himself through music and his total identification with his work.

☯

As the year turned, Carlos Santana reflected on the fact that 1986 was the twentieth anniversary of the Santana Blues Band's formation and the start of his life as a rock star. At heart Carlos Santana was a live musician and the group's concerts continued to be a massive attraction around the world, but there was no getting away from the fact that the sales were dropping off; *Beyond Appearances* had just about crept into the *Billboard* Top 50 and that despite the exposure of Live Aid. The reality was that for the first time in his life music was not Carlos Santana's overriding priority, so 1986 was his lightest touring year seen since the days of the Blues Band. By the end of the year he would have played fewer than thirty concerts – clearly his new domestic situation meant he didn't want to stray too far from home for too long.

Away from the Band the new year started brightly with a significant project led by Grateful Dead percussionist Mickey Hart. Hart was recording an album of material by the legendary Nigerian drummer Babatunde Olatunji, the man who had brought the world "Jingo". Hart drafted in Carlos and Airto Moriera to help out and the result was a terrific disc, *Dance To The Beat Of My Drum*. The mix of serious African drums, choral vocals and Santana's guitar was mesmerising and includes many highlights. The Olatunji project even inspired Carlos to book some more studio time, after all it had been two or three years since he had written most of the songs that had appeared on *Beyond Appearances*. He entered the studio in February with no singer and some new songs, still smarting from the most recent recording trauma. Sadly, the trouble he had getting his new music released was to be even worse. However, another of those chance encounters gave the guitarist a lift. It turned out that Santana and his men were in an adjacent studio to Buddy Miles, the ex-Hendrix counterpart who Santana hadn't worked with in fifteen years. Both Greg Walker and Alex Ligertwood had been sent out to grass at the end of the 1985 tour, so Santana was without a singer. As Miles didn't really have a gig, it seemed logical to ask him to join the sessions and, once again, Santana was to be invigorated by a new member rather than an innovative new direction. Miles stayed for just over a year and pianist Tom Coster also returned during a mid point in his solo career.

The music they recorded was hardly a new direction but did include a strong ballad called "Personal Contact" which was the first title given to the "new album". The song was never released but was used in a TV advert for a telephone company, a piece of promotional kitsch which found Santana and Bill Graham hamming it up for the cameras. Other new songs included "Just Let The Music Speak", a complete vocal version of "Now That You Know" and a jazzy, percussion workout, "Serpentine Fire". As the sessions wound on the name of the album moved to *Songs Of Freedom* and by the spring it was completed, but once again the demo was rejected by Columbia and as the band set off for a very short tour of Japan and Australia, Carlos had no idea what would happen to the album. The tour included a single date in Japan with Jeff Beck which saw the two guitarists join forces for some good ("Super Boogie") and not so good ("Johnny B Goode") workouts. Miles' stage presence gave Santana a lift on this tour, his exuberance and post-Hendrix guitar antics pushed the Santana show towards the showier end of rock and audiences loved it, but he was not in good health. The singing could be hit or miss and he actually had to be provided with oxygen during one performance! The highlight of the tour was undoubtedly a special twenty-year celebration show held in August at Bill Graham's newly opened super-venue midway between San Francisco and San José called the Shoreline Amphitheatre. Carlos invited all the members of the early 1970s band to play and it was Graham himself who introduced the show. The first half of the evening was the 1986 Santana introducing new music from the *Songs Of Freedom* sessions while the second half saw all the members of the 1969 Santana Band playing the old favourites and some new jams. They opened with "In A Silent Way". After fifteen years it was all smiles again, the old telepathy was there. It sounded remarkably good and Chepito Areas in particular was outstanding. By the end of the show, which included some nerve-shattering percussion showdowns, the stage was thronged with Santana players old and new, plus friends like Gregg Errico from Sly Stone's band. The concert closed after three hours with a passionate and fervent rendition of "Toussaint L'Overture", which was always one of the exemplar moments of Santana Latin-rock. The band appeared to be genuinely getting off playing this music and as the show ended old friends embraced and old enmities were put aside for a moment. Santana shook hands with Rolie and stood arm in arm with Michael Carabello. Shrieve, Peraza and Areas – the powerhouse percussion section of the *Lotus* days – embraced. Things had changed, they were now a group of musicians approaching middle age, most had children, summing up the gulf between then and now. These were people with responsibilities. Music was still a passion but it was also how they made their living and supported their families. All the same, at this one-off show there was real power in each player's performance, the music still worked. For once this was a reunion concert that generated heat *and* light.

☯

If the Shoreline date was the highlight, the downer came with a disappointing show at Madison Square Garden in support of Bill Graham's latest venture which he called Crackdown, an attempt to highlight the growing problem of drug addiction. Santana was on a bill that included Run DMC and the Allman Brothers, but Graham and Santana were soon to realise that the band was no longer the draw it once was as ticket sales stalled. It was probably the first time that this reality had hit home. Nevertheless, another musical highlight was on the horizon in August as the guitarist finally fulfilled his ambition to share a stage with one of his greatest jazz heroes, Miles Davis. The opportunity arose during the closing Amnesty International concert at Giants Stadium in New York where Carlos added a few guitar runs to an aptly named fusion called, "Burn". It was something like his 1960s brief encounters with Michael Bloomfield, a few notes thrown into a musical melee of no great consequence. All that was important was to have been there and done it. After the concerts Santana immediately returned to the studio to record new material to try and get his album accepted. His bitterness with the music industry had already been vented in song ("Victim Of Circumstance" and "Songs Of Freedom"), but with Alphonso Johnson, Tom Coster and the help of Gregg Rolie, three new songs were written and recorded.

Presented to Columbia in November, the new recording, now titled *Freedom*, was finally accepted and released in February 1987. The album is more cohesive than *Beyond Appearances* and *Shangó* and gives an overview of Santana's world of music, but, sadly it is not a brilliant work. It starts by recalling Carlos' Tijuana R&B days with the modest "Veracruz" and the Fillmore jamming period on "Victim Of Circumstance". Then there was a typically romantic Latin-Mexican guitar ballad, "Love Is You", and a couple of doses of James Brown funk, "Songs Of Freedom" (shades of "Living In America") and "Deeper, Dig Deeper". These tracks were a snapshot of Carlos Santana, 1955 to 1968! Soul with gospel overtones has always been a large part of the Santana package and is represented on "Praise" and the product of a 1984 liaison with Jim Capaldi, "Before You Go". Two of the newer pieces, "She Can't Let Go" and "Once It's Gottcha", were hybrid soul-rock with reggae overtones, entirely reliant on Carlos' steaming guitar for interest. Generally, Buddy Miles' vocals sound powerful and, fortunately, he reduced the tendency for hollering that had marred the 1972 album. The percussion section, now dubbed "The Gorillas" by their leader, turn in another fine performance. The final piece of the *Freedom* musical jigsaw was Afro-Cuban jazz, which was found on its best track, Armando Peraza's "Mandela". Based on "Saoco", a tune Peraza recorded with Mongo Santamaria before he joined Santana, it finds Carlos using a guitar synthesiser to replicate the sound of Afro flutes, tones that were always a feature of Cuban jazz. Set in the classic African 6/8 rhythm, the tune harked back to Santana's glory days as the pianists recalled some of the McCoy Tyner style piano chords that were last heard on *Welcome*. It was an adventurous work and stood head and shoulders above the rest of the disc which wasn't bad, but certainly no classic.

Clearly Columbia didn't know what to make of this far from contemporary mish-mash of R&B, funk, soul and Latin grooves and the promotion was minimal. They made a half-hearted effort to turn "Vera Cruz" into a hit with some remixed versions (produced by yet another hot shot, Don Miley), but it was never going to work. The only effective promotion for the record was on the *Freedom* tour which brought the music to life. By 1987 Carlos Santana had concluded that the only true way to reach his public was on the live stage where no A&R or marketing men could get to him and tell him what to play and where he could communicate directly with his audience. It was this realisation that characterised the next ten years of Santana's career as recording became of minimal interest to him.

The long *Freedom* tour gave Santana some of the biggest highs in their career, but it was a test of physical endurance as the European leg alone included forty dates and each show lasted a minimum of three hours. Nearly every song from *Freedom* was played nightly and dominated the set, along with a selection of "old favourites" which were now compressed into medleys, but the highlights were magical versions of Leon Thomas' tunes "One" and "Malcolm's Gone". Featuring powerful, virtuoso solos and a superb duet between bass and bongos, over a driving Latin-jazz rhythm, "One" became a Santana live classic. Orestes Vilató had now branched out and played a dizzying array of timbales, bells, chimes, cowbells and electronic drums. The energy of Raul Rekow was incendiary and Armando Peraza continued to enthral audiences with his undoubted panache. It was as if Santana were turning on the percussive power deliberately, to blow away the competition.

The tour had two main climaxes, a pair of emotional dates in the old East Berlin which had seen more than 200,000 applications for tickets and two shows in Israel: one in Tel Aviv and one in Jerusalem. These shows were to have a massive impact on both Carlos and Bill Graham, as Santana took their songs of freedom to the war torn Middle East. Graham later recalled that, "Santana played the most inspirational show of his life at the foot of the great wall. 10,000 went kosher bananas." What Carlos Santana saw was Jews and Arabs enjoying the music and getting along together, even if it was only for three hours. But to him that was the point, only the universal sound of music could heal these wounds. It was fitting that on this tour they had started to play a moody selection that had a Spanish name, "Curandero", and an English name, "The Healer".

Meanwhile, it seemed that some healing of old scars had brought Carlos and Gregg Rolie back into the fold, Rolie played a part on *Freedom* and had his own album to promote which the guitarist turned out for. It was *Gringo*, his second solo release which, like its predecessor, worked in a pop-AOR vein. The record was characteristic of the genre, but did include a piece in the "Black Magic Woman" style, "Fire At Night", which showcased a Santana-Neal Schon guitar duet for the first time since 1972. In a long coda the two guitarists don't quite revive the magic of "Song Of The Wind", but it was still a reasonable encounter.

The summer also saw the release of a new film version of the life of Richie Valens, the first Chicano rock star, famous for his recording of the Mexican folk song "La Bamba". The film was given the same name and Los Angeles band Los Lobos provided the soundtrack, while Santana wrote a series of incidental musical passages, creating some empathetic guitar melodies which worked closely with the emotions of the film. For instance, the scene where Valens' mother and brother hear of Richie's demise in Buddy Holly's aeroplane is matched musically by the strains of Santana's crying guitar (the tune was a little reflection of classical composer Johannes Brahms and it would crop up again later in Carlos' music). The most interesting aspect of Santana's score was found when the young Valens crosses the border to Mexico to meet a healer, behind this visual encounter a few moody guitar chords are heard which were a taste of "The Healer". *La Bamba* was important for Santana because in his eyes it was the first time that a positive image of Mexicans had been portrayed by Hollywood. Understandably, he was none too enamoured of the clichéd "sleeping Mexican under cactus tree with sombrero" image and was therefore happy to contribute to this film which united in spirit three Chicano musical success stories – Richie Valens, Santana and Los Lobos.

It was the overture to a summer during which Carlos' Latin heritage was to the fore. His status amongst Spanish-speaking people in America and beyond was crystallised in the production of a huge wall mural of him, Armando Peraza and Eddie Palmieri, in San Francisco's Mission District. Located between 22nd Street and Van Ness in the heart of the Latin American area of the city, an area which even today tourists are invited to avoid, its prominence gives it the level of dominance usually associated with political, sporting or religious figures. The painting of the mural by local artist Michael Rios coincided with the declaration of "Santana Day" in San Francisco, which climaxed with a free Santana band concert on the streets of the Mission. Carlos Santana had returned to the streets he kicked around in as a Chicano teenager and this concert in front of 200,000 listeners perched on roofs and lamp-posts indicated the man's unique link with the streets. It was part of him and his status as a positive role model for Chicanos has been repeatedly acknowledged through awards from Hispanic community organisations throughout the USA, but particularly Los Angeles and San Francisco. Carlos Santana's importance as a Hispanic superstar has never been of any interest to the white music press, but a visit to the Mission will make it plain to any visitor. Indeed, the crowd that assembled in the Mission that day in 1987 represented about 25% of the entire population of San Francisco.

After this excitement, Santana continued a long US tour in the company of another of Bill Graham's acts The Neville Brothers. Carlos had added a solo to a track on their latest album *Uptown*, which came out in May, and signalled a new interest in the Nevilles that peaked with their *Yellow Moon* album in 1989. There was also time on the tour for a reunion with Tijuana guitarist Javier Batiz who had been Carlos' local hero many years before. As the tour rumbled on 1987 had one more climax left for Santana as they took their music to Moscow, almost as if it were part of a peace mission. They had to break into the tour at short notice to take part in the concert which Bill Graham had moved heaven and earth to organise to mark the end of a peace walk of Americans through Russia. The planning of the show, however, was a logistical nightmare that was anything but peaceful. Equipment and even food had to be brought in by road from Hungary and right up to the last minute it was touch and go whether the show would go ahead. Still, Graham and Santana were triumphant in the end as Boris Grebenshikoz, lead singer of an underground Russian rock group, pointed out, "Basically, Santana

commanded most of the admiration of the crowd. Santana is a name everyone knows in Russia from long years of listening to them. Santana, well, he's
closer to the Russian consciousness because he presents the spiritual aspects.
Carlos is something spiritual, he is so melodic and that is a sign of the
spirit."[53] A better summation of the guitarist's universal appeal is hard to
imagine. Santana certainly appealed to the Moscow audience and the impact
of the 25,000 strong crowd's call for an encore left the Mexican crying like a
baby, "When we finished they just responded. After the last note was played
and everybody was walking backstage, we started hearing all of a sudden,
"Santana ! Santana !" I turned around and looked at Bill and I just started to
cry. When I heard people who didn't want to go home start chanting
"Santana" I broke down. I broke down like a little kid and hid my head and
face in my wife's chest."[54]

The American tour concluded in September and once again Carlos was
exhausted and looking for a change. The *Freedom* tour had been a great success, both musically and financially, but after Israel, East Berlin, Mission
Street and Moscow the Santana Band had nothing more to achieve for the
time being, so Carlos put it to bed. Some of the musicians went their own
ways and some, like Orestes Vilató, expressed the frustration that working in
a band like Santana can bring, "Carlos was cool, he was into Indian meditation and musical experimentation. He had created some intricate albums with
Alice Coltrane and John McLaughlin and had advanced a lot in his music.
The first five or six years were great; we were part of the project. Then
things began to change. We didn't feel like part of a band anymore, but more
like a back-up group."[55]

After taking a rest, Carlos took time in December to join most of the members of the original Santana group in Oakland for a spontaneous musical get
together, which saw them trying to recreate the old magic by jamming on the
odd riff or half-realised chord change. The results were clearly not intended
as polished performances, but they sounded quite good with Santana and
Schon exchanging volleys of notes much as they had done on Rolie's *Gringo*
album. Carlos always had a hankering in his heart for the original band,
especially Rolie, and their paths were beginning to cross more and more frequently after Rolie helped out on *Shangó*.

Maybe Santana was coming to value his old friends and he had good reason to be reflective, as another of his musician friends, bass genius Jaco
Pastorius, had just died in violent circumstances. Pastorius was a legend for
his electrifying performances with Weather Report and on his solo records.
He died on the night of a Santana concert – an evening Carlos will never for-

get, "He came to see us in 1987 at the Sunrise Theatre in Fort Lauderdale, we heard that he was a little drunk and out. I didn't see him before we started and when the Alphonso solo came I was in the back. After the solo, Jaco jumped up on stage to hold his hand up like HE was the champion and the guards threw him outside. There was a big scuffle and he waited, then they let him in again, because probably guys from the band saw what had happened. After the concert he came over and grabbed my acoustic guitar in my dressing room and he started playing like Paco de Lucia! So we were leaving and outside people always wait for autographs and stuff, you know, and he sat down kinda close to me on a fence and then he said something weird about Sheila E and Sri Chinmoy that didn't make any sense. Then he said something about Jesus Christ while I was signing autographs. I said to him, 'I don't want to hear from you about Jesus Christ.' So he totally changed, he started calling me "sir". They went to this club, he said 'do you want to come?' I said, 'No, I don't think so, I'm not much of a club guy, I play, brush my teeth, call my wife, read a book, got a gig tomorrow.' So, I didn't make it there. And that's were it happened." Carlos was convinced by this more than ever of the perils of the rock 'n' roll lifestyle and became even more determined to balance his need for a steady home life with the demands of being a musician.

Chapter 16

Freedom seemed to bring the Santana band concept to its logical conclusion. There really seemed to be nothing left to say musically after a tour which had highlighted all the power and energy associated with Latin-Rock. It appeared that Carlos Santana agreed with this assessment and was looking for new musical avenues, away from the restriction of playing pop-rock songs and the old hits. He had tired of the "Santana as product" concept and possibly realised that the albums coming out under the Santana band name were chipping away at his identity as a musician. Only on the live stage could he get across his passion for music, so in 1988 he put Santana to bed and went solo. In the course of it he rediscovered his musical being and forgot the music business for nine sweet months.

The prelude to this year of musical freedom was the late 1987 release of his solo album, the excellent *Blues For Salvador*, which captured more of the Santana spirit than any release since *Havana Moon*. The album was mostly derived from an idea the guitarist had in 1985 to put out a solo record, which he called *Love Never Fails*. The rough demo for *Love Never Fails* included new studio tracks created in 1984, live outtakes from the 1983 European tour (including a delicious Latin number "Ya Yo Me Curé") and newer 1985 material. The main feature of all these pieces was that they were not commercial and featured strong guitar performances and plenty of percussion. Most of the tracks from the demo would eventually appear on the *Viva Santana!* and *Freedom* albums (e.g. "Love Never Fails" was the original title of "Love Is You") and the opener on *Blues For Salvador* was another one. This was the exciting "Bailando/Aquatic Park", which mixed Afro-

Cuban and blues just as the original Santana had, in a compelling collection of blazing guitar, virtuoso percussion and Buddy Miles' best Santana vocal. It was a great return to form. Another *Love Never Fails* left-over was "'Trane", which recalled the spirit of Tony Williams' Lifetime and included a choice performance from the master drummer, while "Now That You Know" was a live cut from 1985 which effectively conveyed the passion of a Santana live jam. It was a clear throwback to the days of Butterfield's "East-West" and was miles ahead of most of Santana's 1980s output. Other tunes of interest were a short but interesting guitar synth mood, "Mingus", and an early version of "Hannibal" set in a stimulating jazz context, which reveals what *Zebop!* might have been had the demands of the music business not intervened.

Good as these tracks were, they were comprehensively surpassed by two genuinely inspired works which represented the real Carlos Santana, "Bella" and "Blues For Salvador". "Bella" was a beautiful ballad that showcased Santana's best recorded jazz playing, sympathetic keyboard textures and beautifully understated percussion. The music was created as a love song to Carlos' daughter and the power of pure emotion that emerges from the man's guitar is remarkable.

"Blues For Salvador" remains one of the few occasions when the studio captured Carlos' real spirit. Chester Thompson used a range of keyboards to create horn and string-like textures over which Santana could just blow and blow in an impromptu jam that took the roof off anything the band had done for years. There seemed to be telepathy at work as Thompson's keyboards tracked and underpinned the sheer overwhelming passionate emotion of the guitar playing. It reflected urgency, spiritual longing and great love simultaneously, all within a basic blues idiom. It was astonishing, recorded live and utterly free of studio contrivance.

Blues For Salvador sold modestly, but with it, the San Franciscan regained some of the reputation that had been lost on the dreadful 1980s Santana band albums, a reputation that was reinforced when he took the music on the road in the spring of 1988. For this tour the guitarist retained only Chester Thompson, Armando Peraza and Alphonso Johnson from the Santana band and added Ndugu Chancler on drums; he dubbed the new unit The Promise Band and it found him in a musically free setting where there was no singer, no hits to play and the main voices were his guitar and Chester Thompson's Hammond organ. The music was exclusively instrumental and what most would call Latin-jazz-fusion and it was Santana's most satisfying live music since the great 1983 band and one where his true identity as a musician was found again. Most of the music was from the new solo album, plus selections from Ndugu's release *Old Friends, New Friends* and a tune Santana had just recorded with a rising jazz star, Clyde Criner ("Kinesis"). There were blues showcases, funk and Afro-Cuban jams, all served up in a loose musical setting that was magically bolstered by the surprise reappearance of José Chepito Areas half-way through the dates. Touring with Carlos for the first time since 1977, the diminutive Nicaraguan added his unique timbales sound to this combo and helped to ensure that it wasn't just "good" but "great".

Carlos Santana was enjoying his musical freedom and the time seemed right to take his liberation one step further by touring the European summer jazz festivals with the great jazz saxophonist, Wayne Shorter. The pair went back some years to the days when Weather Report had backed Santana at the height of their rock success and more recently, in 1986, the guitarist played on the fusion band's last album *This Is This*, almost seeming to replace Shorter's nearly absent saxophone on the disc. However, not everyone was enthusiastic about the Santana-Shorter Band and Bill Graham warned the guitarist that the venture would be a career mistake. But Santana didn't care, he was about to embark on what he would later call "the greatest musical experience of my life." The Santana-Shorter Band grew organically from the Promise Band as Santana told *Musician*, "We got Armando, Ndugu and Alphonso and looked for what chemistry was there. Out of a ten we were getting seven and a half, eight consistency. So, I said 'Maybe this band could accommodate Wayne's stuff.'" Shorter was equally keen on this new unit and he admired Carlos' direct way of playing, "You might say he has a kind of drive and his guitar sound was like singing. He has a way of getting to the point without revving up, without using a lot of notes." The saxophonist brought along pianist Patrice Rushen, which helped propel the band into the musical stratosphere. They opened with a try-out gig at the Fillmore in San Francisco and even though there was some obvious tightening up needed, favourable reviews flowed in the local press. One reporter opined, "This band is a mutha. They improvised from a foundation of simple melodic ideas, riding atop an explosive field of Latin, funk, Afro-Cuban and rock rhythms. Shorter and Santana improvised on top of this rumbling carpet of rhythm with consistent fire and invention."[56] Another went further still, declaring Armando Peraza "the greatest conga drummer in the world" and asserted that the unit "may be the most significant band sound of the late 1980s. By fall it will have been proclaimed the most exciting band of the year."[57] It was the culmination of Santana's jazz journey that had started with

Caravanserai and called at *Illuminations, Oneness* and *The Swing Of Delight*.

The guitarist was in heaven, freed at last from "Black Magic Woman" and holding musical court with one of the true lions of jazz in a band that allowed the full mastery of players like Peraza, Areas and Thompson to shine through. They worked new life into the old Miles Davis piece "Sanctuary" or new material from Patrice Rushen ("Fireball 2000" and "Shh", soon to be recorded for Terri Lynne Carrington) and Shorter (the imaginatively named "Wayne 1" and "Wayne 2", the latter eventually turned up as "Virgo Rising" on his *High Life* album). The shows generally opened with a jazz setting of a percussion jam which dated from the 1984 period. They called it "Peraza" and it showcased Shorter's animated, crafty tenor against Santana's impassioned style, over a magical blanket of percussion. The Mexican wasn't really meeting Shorter on his own ground, rather the sax player was coming to his. Other contrasts were provided by Patrice Rushen's modal piano against Chester Thompson's powerful gospel organ, which added to the sense that a massive canvas of Afro-American music was being painted by this band; jazz, blues, Afro-Cuban, funk, rock and gospel. Aside from those who had come to hear "She's Not There", audiences were generally enthused by a roller-coaster ride of musical passion which avoided all the pitfalls of excess usually associated with "super-groups". This was amply revealed in the true highlight of the shows, beautiful renditions of "Incident At Neshabur", which seemed purpose built for this band. The prospect of the Mexican's guitar flowing into Shorter's tenor on this classic Santana original was mouth-watering indeed and the reality did not disappoint; the lyrical aspect of the unit was also found on "For Those Who Chant", a romantic interpretation of a track from the old Luis Gasca album which was Santana's first true jazz session. This great band was recorded at the Montreux Jazz Festival and an album planned, but yet again Columbia didn't sense a hit and the Santana-Shorter live album was never released. Carlos was beginning to get the distinct impression that the record company was no longer interested in his music and Columbia were so cool about this session that, when the Californian left the label in 1991, they gave him the rights to it. He later recalled the situation, "Yeah, the Montreux show was recorded. I own it now, Columbia gave it to me, because they weren't interested in it. I'm not in a position to release it for the same reason. If I release it and it gets stocked in a New York warehouse and is not out to the public, then it is not important to me."

The musical success of the Santana-Shorter Band seemed to be a signal to pull the curtain down on the Santana band forever. The guitar man had proved that he could recapture the wonder of the *Lotus* days and it seemed inconceivable that he could go back to the musical confines of Latin-Rock. But, it wasn't to be. In the first instance music was Santana's living, it was his income and he simply could not ignore that fact. For all its outstanding musical qualities, the Santana-Shorter Band had no commercial potential as evidenced by the failure to release the live CD and fate seemed destined to revive the Santana band to support a retrospective triple album that was being prepared throughout 1987 and 1988. It would be called *Viva Santana!* and contained a blend of pointlessly remixed greatest hits with a few outtakes, including some fine live work including "Super Boogie" and "Bambele". The studio outtakes were of variable quality but did include one of Santana's best ever Latin originals, "Angel Negro", and fine percussion jams with Armando Peraza ("Bambara" and "Peraza"). The package studiously ignored all of Santana's jazz output, as did a moderately interesting greatest hits video that was released at the same time. Given that Carlos had selected the music for *Viva Santana!* himself, he clearly understood that for the majority of his public he was "Black Magic Woman", "Oye Como Va", "Soul Sacrifice", "Evil Ways", "She's Not There", "Samba Pa Ti" and "Europa". Both album and video went gold underlining the commercial realities.

Part of the reason for the success of the album was the autumn US tour that supported it, which was very much an attempt to revive the spirit of the original Santana band. For this outing the guitarist recruited old partners Gregg Rolie and Mike Shrieve. As Chepito Areas was already a fixture, this meant that four-sixths of the musicians who recorded *Santana* in 1969 were back on the road together. Naturally, Michael Carabello was just a little miffed to have been overlooked, but as Rolie and Shrieve soon found out, Carlos Santana was not about to revive the full collective nature of Santana 1969. The pair found themselves as just two more parts of the guitarist's latest backing band. Maybe the one-off success of the 1986 Shoreline reunion had lulled them into thinking it could work. This 1988 tour comprehensively proved that it couldn't. Both Rolie and Shrieve had carved out successful, if very musically different, careers for themselves after Santana and both were used to being masters of their own destinies. The pair were far from pleased with events, as the ever-tactful drummer later recalled, "It wasn't what I hoped it would be, it wasn't a band. It was like Carlos bringing in some guys from the original band and then proceeding as a band leader. I was frustrated,

I had high hopes, but it was not a band anymore. Carlos wanted to call all the shots which is understandable in a lot of ways. He's been doing that for twenty years. The original band was a real group effort but this felt like being a hired hand."[58]

The tour was reasonable from a musical perspective and it saw the revival of long redundant old favourites like "Everybody's Everything" and "Se A Cabo", but it offered nothing new and was a significant step backwards from the heights of the Santana-Shorter tour. Other than its obvious commercial value, the tour would have been better postponed as it raised expectations that couldn't be met. Nevertheless, it did include the band's return to Mexico with ecstatically received concerts in Mexico City and Leon, a major city close to Santana's Autlán birthplace. A far less hysterical reception awaited the band as they gave two free shows at San Francisco's hardest jail, San Quentin. The guitarist was impressed by the mix of black, brown and white faces that came together to see the shows, in normal circumstances the jail was divided on racial lines. After all, Carlos Santana came from the street and at the end of each show, he jumped down from the stage to sign autographs and chat to some of the area's most notorious murderers. As the show closed the year fans wondered what 1989 would bring. Many found it hard to conceive that the Santana band would go on turning out "Black Magic Woman" forevermore. They were to be surprised.

Chapter 17

Since *Shangó* Carlos' considerable passion for reggae had continued to blossom. Towards the end of the 1980s he was delighted to discover a local Bay Area reggae band called the Caribbean All Stars. The guitarist soon made contact with the outfit and used his status in the Bay Area to promote them. He even took them on the road as a support act and appeared as executive producer and guest musician on their second CD *Paths To Greatness*. Working with the reggae band was of greater interest to Carlos than the musical jail of the Santana Band and in the spring he only retained Chester Thompson and Armando Peraza as a basic working unit.

Carlos first brought the All Stars into the limelight at the 1989 Bammie Awards, the Bay Area's own annual back slapping musical equivalent of the Oscars. Santana usually participated in the Bammies and used it to showcase new music, or new ideas when he had some. This time he had arranged a jam to celebrate one of those "Lifetime Achievement" awards that he himself was to present to Armando Peraza, in recognition of the fact that the Cuban was indeed amongst the century's musical greats. The curtain went back to reveal no lesser figures than Tony Williams and the legendary jazz saxophonist Pharoah Sanders, a man who had provided plenty of inspiration and blueprints for Santana's musical explorations on *Caravanserai*, *Lotus*, *Welcome* and *Illuminations*. In particular, Sanders' LP *Deaf, Dumb, Blind* had been comprehensively plundered as the musical boilerplate for *Love, Devotion, Surrender* and "Mother Africa". As ever, the jazz champion would have to enter Santana's territory and not the other way around, especially as the jam was to be on The Temptations' old soul-rock hit "Cloud Nine"; the ensemble turned this pop tune into a wailing, free-drum orgy. This first meeting with the renowned Sanders saw Carlos moving again in the highest company and there was a notable confluence of styles.

The session went extremely well and seemed to suggest that the guitarist was moving in a new direction. This had also been hinted at in the booklet that went with the *Viva Santana!* package, which quoted him as saying, "It's a celebration and a conclusion until further notice. I don't want to just crank out "Black Magic Woman" and "Jingo" in the future. And I feel that a lot of other people are with me as far as wanting to change." But, when the new band emerged at the New Orleans Jazz and Blues festival in April, a change of heart appeared to have occurred. Alex Ligertwood was back and there was a new face on the drummer's stool, the dynamic Walfredo Reyes Jr, son of the revolutionary Cuban drummer of the same name. The group was also still playing "Black Magic Woman" and "Jingo". As ever, contradictions reigned supreme as Santana set out on a long 40-date tour of Europe, which mixed the old hits with some new jazz instrumentals and the occasional revival of an old blues classic like "Stormy Monday Blues" that called to mind Santana's passionate Tijuana days. The chance to see Chepito and Peraza operating in tandem was still thrilling, but the former had a taste for excess which reached a climax after a date in Finland. The diminutive timbalero was subsequently put on a plane bound for San Francisco, ending a 20-year relationship with Santana. It was a sad conclusion, Chepito had always been the perfect Santana timbalero and his performances were consistently good, but Carlos Santana didn't have time to be a band leader and baby-sitter. Roadies were despatched to find a set of timbales for Walfredo Reyes who spent the next eighteen months doubling on drums and timbales – though not very successfully.

Frustrated by the continuing yoke of the band, the guitarist was developing his interests outside its confines and this period saw him involved in a large number of sessions, with a varied range of artists. Foremost amongst these was the July release of blues master John Lee Hooker's first album in over ten years. It was christened *The Healer* and included the song of that name that Carlos Santana had given him in 1988. It would shoot Hooker to a new career as a major celebrity. The album made the charts all over the world and sold particularly well in Europe, as did the release of "The Healer" as a single which even hit the higher reaches of the charts in some countries. Accompanied by an atmospheric video, the strange thing was that it was basically a Santana song to which Hooker had added a vocal in a live session, the whole thing being recorded in one take. Columbia would never have taken the chance on promoting "The Healer" as a single as the Santana name wasn't sufficiently fashionable to secure the requisite radio play. By contrast, Hooker was suddenly extremely fashionable and legions of radio stations and listeners discovered him for the first time, but in no small measure it was a Santana song that relaunched Hooker's career.

"The Healer" was one of Santana's most impressive works of the 1980s which revealed Carlos' guitar drenched in blues passion, whilst the Armando Peraza-Chepito Areas reunion was mesmerising. On top of all this, Hooker added a mumbled vocal that simply stated the truth about blues being a world-wide healer. It sounded like he knew what he was talking about in a version reminiscent of a plantation work song. Carlos Santana was delighted, to discover that he was admired by one of his earliest idols from his Tijuana days. Whatever Columbia thought of him, no matter how little airplay he received, he knew that he could cut it with John Lee Hooker, just as he could with Buddy Guy or Otis Rush or, from another sphere, McCoy Tyner or Wayne Shorter. He also had their respect as a musician. It seemed to him that not just the blues, but all of music was "the healer" and there was no need to make distinctions between any music – it was all either good or bad, soulful or not soulful. This conviction in music's healing powers fired Carlos with a new enthusiasm as the next decade loomed and new experiences continued with a series of record dates with a broad range of artists, including young lady jazz drummer Terri Lynn Carrington, soul legend Bobby Womack and another African star, Mory Kante.

As the Hooker album was heading up the world's charts, the Santana band committed some of their new material to tape, after which Alphonso Johnson headed off into the light and the versatile Keith Jones walked back in. A few good Californian dates followed and gave Carlos the opportunity to invite old friends like Airto Moreira to sit in with the band. It seemed like a good new album was on the cards. As the tour proceeded a massive earthquake hit the San Francisco area in October and widespread devastation ensued; as ever, Bill Graham was on hand to muster his massive resources and network of contacts to stage a benefit for earthquake victims at one of the areas worst affected, Watsonville. As usual, Santana were free to help out. The tour completed, they went back to the studio for more recording on what was to be their last album for Columbia. Unbeknown to Carlos, a less than happy year was around the corner.

☯

The magical Brazilian percussionist Airto Moriera has a very clear view of the relationship between music and spirituality and sums it up as an entirely natural connection, "We are a spirit, but we have a body right now that we use to go through this life, that's how it works. This is what I learnt from my father who was a spiritual healer. Me and Flora and every musician, we have our spiritual guides that are with us when we play and that's what gives the audience the healing force they need. It's not coming from us, it's coming from the spiritual world which co-exists with the material world." Whilst the European and American view of spirituality has been reduced to cynicism by the likes of Jimmy Swaggart, the child-abuse scandals and rent-a-guru lifestyle, the spiritual side of life is deeply ingrained in the Latin American psyche. The late 1980s appeared to find the guitarist settling on a clear vision of a universal spirituality, which embraced all previous devotions into one pantheistic whole. He was fired again with an urgent need to express his vision to his audience, though this was an approach that left some discomforted.

Starting with concerts in 1989, the Mexican would open the shows with a kind of brief spiritual overture which came from a tape of a Pharoah Sanders live date known as "Angels All Around Us". It was the precursor to a new song entitled "Spirits Dancing In The Flesh", which the guitarist would introduce over a backdrop of lush major 7 synthesiser chords – the musical equivalent of a stick of incense. He would tell the audience the good news that, "we are completely and utterly surrounded by angels. We see them and feel them dancing in the flesh", which was the cue for the thunderous funk of the new song to start. The audience reaction to these remarks varied from place to place. In Northern Europe there was a mixture of embarrassed shuffling of feet, some applause and some hostility of the "shut up and play" variety. American audiences reacted with less hostility but some puzzlement, whilst in Southern Europe and Latin America, the vision was welcomed. The equation seems suspiciously simple, in Catholic countries he was understood, in non-conformist Northern Europe and the USA he left himself open to ridicule.

As the 1990s progressed, Santana's spiritual expositions became a staple feature of his concerts and the music press had a field day ridiculing him. Articles appeared in Britain with titles like "Beam Me Up", and European TV features ran tabloid headlines like "Yes! Carlos Santana believes in angels and UFOs." It was childish, revealing no attempt to understand the man's cultural background, but he had left himself open to it through his stubbornly honest approach. This included an intention to document his feelings on a new album which he dubbed *Spirits Dancing In The Flesh*. The main obstacle was getting it released, and the 1990s opened with Carlos

Santana on familiar ground, about to go on tour having just had a new album rejected by Columbia. Completed demos had been delivered as early as the winter of 1989 but had been turned down as too uncommercial. The demo contained too many instrumentals without hit potential. The last thing Columbia wanted were instrumentals. They wanted hits just as they had before with earlier albums like *Zebop!*, *Shangó*, *Beyond Appearances* and *Freedom*. The striking imbalances of those albums were also found on the new album which was another mixed bag swinging between spiritual exposi-tions and banal pop tracks.

Carlos' spiritual vision was unleashed on the opening music of *Spirits Dancing In The Flesh* through what sounded like an Afro-American spiritu-al, "Let There Be Light". For this track the guitarist enlisted the services of the superstar of gospel, Tramaine Hawkins. Her soaring, powerful voice, the rapturous choir and the musical arrangement create an ethereal mood which is shattered by the upbeat title track which is an expression of spiritual joy. "Spirits Dancing In The Flesh" conveys the spirit very well with its mix of a simple funk riff, Sly Stone chants, burning solos and lithe percussion. The programming of a lame cover version of Curtis Mayfield's "Gypsy Woman" as the following cut was astonishing. Astonishingly imaginative or astonish-ingly stupid. Casting Santana in the role of a Las Vegas "soulful hits" act was never going to be credible and despite some passable guitar, vocal and conga, it is best forgotten. Carlos' fascination with creating rock-funk moods comes to fruition with two pieces that include vocals from soul legend Bobby Womack, "It's A Jungle Out There" and "Choose". The former is the more successful of the two driven by Santana's fine rhythm guitar, which might have earned him a place in James Brown's backing band, and a com-pelling backbeat. "Choose" is neither here nor there. These two efforts are separated by the album's finest moment which is also amongst Santana's best recordings, "Soweto". For many this track was a glimpse of the real Santana – inventive, evocative, imaginative music that had the power to make people smile. It works in a Latin-jazz-fusion character benefiting from one of the most accomplished Santana melodies in years and outstanding performances from Carlos, Thompson (who plays one of his finest breaks), Peraza (who is breathtaking) and guest Wayne Shorter who captures the ecstatic mood perfectly. Anyone who doubts Santana's ability to create excellent music should hear this. It was just a pity there wasn't more like it.

The rest of *Spirits Dancing In The Flesh* was similarly uneven. In "Mother Earth" there was a compelling eco-rock track which mixed John Coltrane and Hendrix and featured an incendiary guitar exchange with Living Color's

Vernon Reid who, along with Prince, was now openly citing Santana as a key influence. Another guitar showcase, the romantic melody "Full Moon" was followed by another disastrous R&B cover version. The Isley Brother's "Who's That Lady" might have seemed like a good way of gaining some crossover radio play, but it was hugely out of step with the rest of the music. The rationale behind recording "Jingo" again was also not really clear. Since reviving it in 1986, Santana and Thompson had given it an Afro-funk arrangement that worked well live, but as a studio track it is less successful. For all that, it is noteworthy for being another exposition of Yoruba culture and does feature a battery of percussionists, including the great Francisco Aguabella who produces a fine performance that is just about audible in the cluttered mix. The album closes with the more fruitful "Goodness and Mercy", an intensely emotional kind of blues-gospel duet between guitar and keyboards. However, despite Santana's excellent guitar work and the mesmerising telepathy between him and Thompson, a worrying heavy-handed approach is evident in Walfredo Reyes' unnecessarily loud drum entrance which is out of kilter with the rest of the music.

So, like every one of its predecessors since *Moonflower*, this new Santana release was a very mixed bag. There's no reason why Columbia shouldn't have tried to get a hit album from Santana, but the truth was that they were unlikely to score a hit single again and the efforts to find a formula to accommodate elements of the Santana sound in a radio-friendly package were hopeless. Sadly for the Santana admirer there was much good music recorded for this album which was left behind. Some of it would be released on the *Dance Of The Rainbow Serpent* package in 1995 and, either the light rock-funk of "Sweet Black Cherry Pie", or the Vernon Reid instrumental "Every Now And Then", would have been far preferable to quite a few of the tracks that did make the album. But these were not even the best of the unreleased material, which included three instrumentals in particular that should have graced the disc. These were "Jungle Music", "Get Uppa" (a James Brown pastiche that did see the light of day on a live video *Sesion Latina*) and "For Those Who Chant".

As it was, *Spirits Dancing In The Flesh* was another half-realised Santana band album and, with more than three years elapsed since the release of *Freedom*, the new album peaked at number 85 on *Billboard* (68 in Britain). However, it did remain on the chart for more than two months and sold reasonably well over time.

By the time *Spirits Dancing In The Flesh* was finally released, a troubled Santana were in the midst of a European tour which was clouded by the poor sales of the new album. The tour saw the group playing some dates in second rate halls in second rate towns. However, it was during the long US tour, which followed in the company of reggae outfit Steel Pulse, that Carlos' problems really began. The band were powering through the new material but Armando Peraza was beginning to feel the pace. He was now approaching his seventieth birthday and had long suffered from diabetes. The tour became too much for him, but his instinct was to soldier-on and like all father-son relationships, the Peraza-Santana bond was so close that it could explosively combust at any moment. It looked as if that moment was approaching and that Peraza was going to "be retired" at the end of the first leg of the US tour in September. This was a major blow for Carlos Santana; not only was the Cuban a true master musician but Peraza had also been his role model and inspiration for years. He was a one-man symbol of perseverance and determination to overcome all the worst features of racism and prejudice. Even with the burden of diabetes the conga drummer always gave 100% to the band and if Peraza didn't show the effects of fatigue on a long tour, then how could the younger men in the line-up? He conducted himself with a mixture of pride and dignity that the guitarist greatly admired. Santana lionised the conguero in public and dedicated the *Viva Santana!* album to him, however, Peraza's beaming smile was rarely seen on-stage these days. On the other hand, Raul Rekow could have smiled for America in the Olympic Games and the ever-willing drummer was brought back in to complete the tour. Still, Rekow's return could not detract from the fact that 1990 had ended on a sour note for Santana. The saga of the album, rifts with promoters and Peraza's departure left Santana needing a big shot of inspiration.

Chapter 18

Carlos Santana has always been motivated by playing live and, miraculously, the antidote to 1990's trials came in the shape of a trip to Brazil in January 1991. Santana had been invited to play at the monolithic rock extravaganza, "Rock In Rio II". Rio was itching to see Santana who hadn't been there since 1973 and the band were hailed as the highlight of the whole event. This was partly because Santana was the only visiting musician who invited local players to sit in on his set and the Brazilian audience responded enthusiastically to duets with their favourites Djavan and Gilberto Gil. Carlos was rejuvenated by these live sessions and he found it far more appealing to jam with Djavan than to sit around listening to record company executives telling him that a cover version of "Gypsy Woman" was the thing for him to do. Accordingly, the 1990s saw Santana virtually retire from recording and concentrate on bringing the universal musical message to live audiences. As far as recording was concerned he would sit tight, bide his time and wait for a good offer.

Santana regrouped in April with some new faces, local singer Tony Lindsay, drummer Gaylord Birch (after an attempt to bring back Graham Lear failed) and the extravagantly talented timbalero Karl Perazzo. The new band played a fresh, invigorating mix of Afro-Cuban, fusion, soul and Brazilian grooves that took in Bobby Womack ("Save The Children"), Djavan ("Stephen's Kingdom" and the hot "Minha Irma") and John Lee Hooker. It sounded fresh. This new band took off for Japan and Europe, by which time Billy Johnson had taken the drummer's chair. In between these trips they played a huge show in Mexico City that somewhat whetted the appetite for playing in Latin America again. Just before Birch left Santana went into the studio again with John Lee Hooker to record new music for his *Mr Lucky* LP. By now Hooker was hot property and had signed for a major label (Charisma) and the LP shot into the charts when it was released in September. Santana had two new songs for Hooker, a similar groove to "The Healer" titled "Chill Out" and "Stripped Me Naked", which mixed blues with Stevie Wonder. "Chill Out" was the better song but was held back as the centrepiece for a 1995 album.

As well as John Lee and the Brazilians, Santana had recently been working with the African superstar Salif Keita, who had just recorded an album, *Amen*, with the help of Joe Zawinul and Wayne Shorter. Though not as great an album as his classic work *Soro*, *Amen* builds keyboard and guitar textures on top of Keita's basic songs and works well. Santana sounds at home on the disc and some real fireworks can be heard on one track in particular, a gem called "Nyanafin" which includes Santana on acoustic and electric guitars. Keita had no doubts about working with the guitarist, "I've loved the way Carlos plays for a long time. He's got such a lot of feeling in his guitar and what he plays is so simple but beautiful. He sings with it. I wrote the guitar parts for him as if he were an extra voice. I knew his music since "Samba Pa Ti". Africans loved that tune, because it was so beautiful, so melodious." *Amen* was released to coincide with Santana's European dates which Keita would open. It was all set for something great, but when Santana arrived in London for their first date neither Salif Keita nor his band were to be seen, a great chance lost.

In general, the 1991 tour of Europe was not dissimilar to previous year's, with some very big gigs (Athens and Lisbon), mixed in with some dates at smaller venues. It seemed that the group would play just about anywhere and there was a suggestion that the entire venture was lacking a little focus.

Bill Graham had often provided Santana with a much needed sense of focus and he was delighted when in the late summer of 1991 Carlos asked him to produce a couple of tunes on the new LP he was planning. One evening in September the guitarist received a phone call from Graham, at the end of the conversation the impresario parted by saying "Stay well, my friend." It was the last time the two old battlers ever spoke. The next day, Friday October 25th, Bill Graham was at a Huey Lewis concert at his Concord Pavilion venue, to the north of Berkeley. He travelled there by helicopter piloted by Steve "Killer" Khan, another old friend and aid to Santana. The weather was not good and the trip there from Graham's estate had been nerve wracking. They considered driving back, but the speed of the helicopter was attractive to the ever-active Graham. As the flight home progressed, Khan descended to get out from a blanket of clouds, but as he did this, the helicopter collided with an electricity pylon and all on board were killed instantly. Carlos and Graham were not as professionally close as they had been and the guitarist had not been represented by Graham's organisation for a number of years. Nevertheless, he knew how much he owed Graham and was personally distraught.

Looking back at Santana's career, Graham's key part is clear. It was Graham who first broke the band through his tireless promotion and in particular his insistence that they were included on the Woodstock bill. Later, he would work hard to force the band onto Live Aid, despite stern opposition and he often used his links with the Rolling Stones to include Santana on large dates with the masters of white R&B. Above all, it was Graham's sense that the segregation of music was ridiculous that struck a chord with Santana, after all, it was this spirit of Graham's that had led to him including diverse acts on his bills at the Fillmore in the late 1960s. It was these shows, featuring the rock stars of the day with the true stars of blues, jazz or Brazilian music, that exposed the young guitarist to a range of music that moulded his own approach. Aside from both being immigrants, Bill Graham and Carlos Santana were musical twins. Sadly for Carlos, the last show of 1991 was at the enormous Bill Graham tribute show. This was held in early November in Golden Gate Park and it became a celebration of San Francisco's musical heritage. Santana were joined by Armando Peraza, Bobby McFerrin (who added his own unique interpretation to "Oye Como Va") and Los Lobos. A touching performance by the band is highlighted by hearing Carlos play "I Love You Much Too Much" as a moving tribute to his friend. Later, he would play the same tune at a memorial service for Graham.

☯

On top of the personal reflection that inevitably accompanied the death of a close friend, Carlos also had his recording career to consider. His Columbia contract had expired with *Spirits Dancing In The Flesh* and he was debating which record company to sign up with. The bitterness he felt towards Columbia was remarkable, "I just couldn't stay any longer, now it's not Columbia records anymore it's SONY and it's all quantity and no quality. Every time I went into the studio to make a new album they wanted to hire some plastic producer and wanted me to sound something stupid." He had been in talks with another label, Polygram, who appeared to be offering artistic freedom, so he signed with them and entered the studio in November to record a new album which he christened *Milagro*, in English, "miracle".

Santana was very enthusiastic about the new label, "It's a total breath of fresh air to be working with people who have a big heart and big ears."[59]

The recording of *Milagro* was quick, but clouded by the death of Graham, which gave the sessions an emotional edge that was transmitted to the disc. The promised artistic freedom was delivered and Santana recorded seventy minutes of the music they had been playing live for the last year. This meant that for the first time in years, a Santana album accurately reflected the music the band was playing at the time. It turned out to be Santana's best album since *The Swing Of Delight* and *Moonflower* and there was a bonus for Polygram, as Carlos recounted, "This new album is probably the least expensive I have ever recorded, the company gave me the freedom to do it as I wanted to do it. We spent three weeks in the studio whereas in the past it usually took at least two months to record a new album. The only things overdubbed were keyboards and vocals." The guitar and organ stylings are returned to their natural prominence in the arrangements without interference and the result is a powerful, emotional session recorded almost entirely live in the studio. The sound was a melting pot, a heady gumbo of reggae, rock, blues, soul, gospel, Afro-Pop, jazz and Afro-Cuban delivered by the standard Santana arrangement of guitar, organ and percussion. Pleasingly the percussion instruments are returned to their rightful place in the sound mix, at the forefront.

Santana's affection for Bob Marley finds expression on the title track which builds in a chant from Marley's *Uprising* album ("Work") around a loose jam structure, propelled by a catchy bass line and thrilling percussion, augmented by the first horn section on a Santana band album since *Festivál*. Over this framework, guitar and Hammond breaks are heard without hindrance or studio compression so that the listener experiences the full capacity of these musicians. There is no gratuitous technique on display and both make ample use of silence as a significant element in their playing. Emotion is also evident throughout "Somewhere In Heaven" which finds Santana considering friends he has lost, whilst finding comfort in simple faith in the Christian message.

The next piece was a tribute to singer Marvin Gaye, a musician who, like Santana, mixed the sensual and the spiritual and had an immensely passionate and lyrical style. Above all Gaye was a believer. Recruiting old friend Larry Graham to handle the vocals, the group create a successful cover version of Marvin's "Right On". Introduced by a romantic Afro-Cuban melody, the track is driven by a potent rhythm which takes centre stage in the first half of the piece through the colours of guiro, conga, cowbell and timbales.

The musicians play as if their next meal depended on it – Santana's guitar roars and swoops as it recalls Gaye's scatting improvisations on the original in an exciting coda. For once Marvin Gaye is covered with aplomb in a version that actually adds something to the original.

There are lighter moments on *Milagro* that might have been excised in the days of the forty minute LP. These include "Free All The People", a worthy but unremarkable reggae fragment which understandably rails against apartheid and "Make Somebody Happy", a sweet but unrealised melody which needed more work. Nevertheless, the song includes a passionate guitar solo and fine vocals from new singer Tony Lindsay and Alex Ligertwood. Another less significant piece is found on "Your Touch", an enjoyable seven minutes showcasing fine percussion, particularly from Karl Perazzo, more sweeping guitar and a bass cameo for Benny Rietveld. Its sense of disco-funk made it a popular piece, but it is of no great consequence. There's a stab at Afro-Pop with the uplifting "Life Is For Living", a far more satisfying commercial pop-rock song than any of the efforts from the 1980s and an impressionistic fusion chart "Red Prophet", which highlights the writing talents of Benny Rietveld and some imaginative improvisations from Santana and Thompson.

"Agua Que Va Caer" is more significant, being an Afro-Cuban classic created by the conga legend Carlos "Patato" Valdes, a contemporary of Armando Peraza, Mongo Santamaria and Francisco Aguabella. Here Santana prove they still have the capacity to record convincing Latin music, something they hadn't done since "Angel Negro". It's fitting that Raul Rekow, who has been a long servant to the Santana cause, finally gets a cameo. He responds with an admirable vocal and an excellent conga solo. He is justifiably proud of what is his greatest Santana moment, finally getting the chance to express his almost scholarly affection for the roots of Afro-Cuban music. An interesting segment of Native American Indian drumming is tacked on to the end of Rekow's solo in an effort to highlight the universal nature of the drum.

Emotions run high as the guitarist says a musical farewell to Bill Graham with a touching melody, "Gypsy", again blended with an upbeat celebration in the form of a jam which he gives the impresario's original surname, "Grajonca". Another showcase for the Santana guitar-organ-percussion soup it recalls the loose, jamming days of the Fillmore and is formed around a neat guitar riff that sounds uncannily similar to one on the old disco hit "Going Back To My Roots". This jamming segment is carried over into "We Don't Have to Wait", which is more of the same, building to a frenetic, climactic guitar-drum apocalypse featuring some of Santana's most rocking guitar for some years.

The album's closer is the remarkable "A Dios" which finds Santana calling out to the spirits of Davis and Coltrane in a ritual, ceremonial, wall of sound over which a keening, fervent guitar melody emerges. This is coupled with a choral farewell which finally gives way to a sample of John Coltrane's awe inspiring tenor saxophone, sweeping over the listener with its other-worldly, powerful tone. This comes to an abrupt end after which Miles Davis' gentle trumpet is heard as if it were the last sound on earth on the day of judgement. It is remarkably powerful music.

There is a strong sense of unity and purpose about *Milagro* which makes it stand out from Santana's 1980s and 1990s releases. It is largely a powerful emotional statement which has not been tampered with in any way to meet commercial demands. As such, it provides a clear view of Carlos Santana's musical vision and is therefore a valuable musical document. The music conveys his sense of the spiritual and a universal purpose to life and music. Indeed, the whole of *Milagro* aims to show that all of this music, Santana, the blues, jazz, African, rock, Afro-Cuban, soul and gospel, along with Miles, Coltrane, Marley and Gaye, were all a part of the same universal root of music and it achieves this aim very effectively.

☯

Shortly before the album was released Santana played what are probably the most emotional concerts of his entire career, a pair of "Regresa a casa" or "homecoming" concerts in Tijuana – the first time he'd played a note in the city since 1963. The shows were held in a seaside bullring and the guitarist was received like a returning hero by a 17,000 crowd who bordered on the hysterical. The concerts opened with performances by a local Mariachi band Tequila who on this occasion included José Santana, the 44-year old's father. Tequila performed the old favourites that Carlos used to play on the streets of the city... "Son De La Negra" and others. Fans packed into the tight bullring, a small arena surrounded by sheer walls that created an intimate, close atmosphere. Santana emerged into the mayhem at half past five, through the tunnel which is usually the preserve of the bullfighters.

The Afro sounds of Salif Keita's "Sina" rang around the bullring as the local hero emerged from the tunnel surrounded by cameras, police, roadies and minders who looked around them as if they were guarding the President of the United States on a trip to an unstable third world state. The atmosphere soon reached fever pitch and a shattering roar went up as the guitarist reached the stage. He lit a cigarette, danced to Keita's funk, pointed at faces in the crowd and for once looked nervous. Even battle hardened warriors of the road like Chester Thompson looked awed by the spectacle while Raul Rekow appeared fit to explode with pent up energy. Another breathtaking clamour rose up from the cauldron as Santana strolled onto the stage and paid homage to Pharoah Sanders by opening the performance with a typically Mexican fanfare of Sanders' "Angels All Around Us". Then the opening notes of "Samba Pa Ti" resounded like a national folk anthem and by now the police at the front of the audience were turned to watch their own street hero, while two Mexicans at the front played every note with their entire bodies.

The crowd boiled and bubbled as Santana ran through the old licks of "Black Magic Woman" one more time. This was their triumph too, a matter of national pride. The noise was nuclear for "Oye Como Va" and the party was on, people danced uncontrollably as if bit players in a Bacchanalian ritual. The end of the song was greeted as if it were the winning Mexican goal in some imaginary World Cup final. New songs from *Milagro* merged with old favourites like "Savor", a dirty, percussive threat of a song, where Chester Thompson brought the spirit of rhythm and blues to Tijuana just as other Afro-Americans had thirty years earlier. Karl Perazzo, another Mexican-American, played the most intense timbales break of his life, covering every trick in the showman's arsenal. In a virtuoso display Perazzo played to the crowd with a cry of "¡Viva Mexico!" which introduced Raul Rekow's Afro-Cuban feature "Agua Que Va Caer". The friendly rumba broke into a conga duet which found Rekow possessed by the drum and playing with a mixture of craft and passion that has his percussion partner hopping up and down in admiration. The highlight of the show approached as Santana introduced Javier Batiz, the R&B pioneer of Tijuana and his original guitar hero with whom he spent those years playing the strip joints of the city. They performed "Blues For Salvador" and while Santana evoked an other-worldly passion, Batiz stuck to the blues. Almost every passage drew great cheers, but there was more to come as the two played in tandem, notes intertwined in parallel orbits. As Batiz improvised, Santana reached over and turned the volume control right up on his old friend's guitar to take the passion up a notch. Other old friends were on hand to offer support, like Larry Graham, a survivor from Sly and The Family Stone, who appeared in an all-white sailor's suit to assist on "Right On." Graham worked the throng well, but it was the classic "Toussaint L'Overture" that brought the energy to a peak.

Fireworks were let off as the main set closed after two hours of pumping street-spiritual power, but soon the illusory image of Woodstock was reborn

with the rain chant and "Soul Sacrifice". It wasn't quite 1969 but the guitarist was animated whilst the Americans frugged and the Mexicans danced.
For once everyone sang along with "A Love Supreme", led by a trio of
Santana, Ligertwood and Larry Graham who followed it with a thigh-slap-
ping "I Want To Take You Higher". Then the crunching crescendos of "Soul
Sacrifice" gave way to a climactic, moving new song, "A Dios", which had
an intense, spiritual tension relieved by "Europa", Santana's other folk
anthem. The guitarist jumped off the stage and slapped a few hands at the
front which interrupted the flow of the romantic melody, but allowed him to
see the upturned smiling face of the policeman whose hand was outstretched.
The end of the fiesta came with the original Santana homage to Africa and
the stage was packed with guests and assorted children as the celebration
reached its apogee with "Jingo-Lo-Ba". Representing the Los Angeles
Chicanos, Cesar Rojas of Los Lobos strolled on almost unnoticed just in time
to be name-checked. The introductions ended with a warm, emotional
embrace between Santana and Javier Batiz; Tijuana's first rhythm and blues
star and its most famous had come home together.

☯

Milagro was released in June 1992 and the band toured in support of it
throughout the year in Europe and the USA. On the US tour they were supported by reggae band Third World and the two groups would jam every
night, working out some of Bob Marley's classics like "Exodus". Working
with Third World ensured that Santana's passion for reggae and Marley continued at a fanatical level. Meanwhile band members came and went, particularly bass players. After Benny Rietveld left, first Alphonso Johnson and,
finally, new man Myron Dove, filled the spot. Alphonso Johnson had come
in for just three weeks to help out after Rietveld's departure, but regretted it
immediately, "To be honest, after having played with the band for five years
going back felt like a step back because the band was still playing the same
music and a lot of the things I hated about being in that band were still going
on. Just little things, you know. Once you're on stage playing things are fine,
but the long soundchecks to play stuff that everybody knows, changing parts,
all the stuff that really bugged me came back."[60] However, the lasting experience of other ex-Santana players, like Leon Patillo, is far less negative,
"Playing with Carlos was the turning point in my career as a singer and
musician. I will always live in the shadow of that great legacy."

Meanwhile, 1992 still had one more crescendo to add to the Santana legacy and, as if the Tijuana dates weren't a sufficient high, the year ended with
a quite extraordinary show in Santiago, Chile which was seen by 100,000

people. The vast audience received the band like local heroes. Current rock hot shots Guns 'n' Roses had played in the same city the month before to 30,000. Santana wasn't counting but here was confirmation of his band's fundamental importance to the people of Latin America. This enormous crowd responded to Santana's "Greatest Hits" show with a fervour that surpassed even that of the Tijuana audience as the guitarist dedicated "Somewhere In Heaven" to all the parents of the country who had lost children, an oblique but overtly political remark in Santiago. The throng behaved exactly like a huge soccer crowd, ebbing and flowing like one unit. The Mexican observed the mad crush with concern, it must have reminded him of the South American tour in 1973; he left Chile with a true sense of how deeply he is regarded in Latin America, but a stronger sense of relief that nobody had lost their life.

Chapter 19

After *Milagro*, Carlos Santana took to the road on a never-ending tour that accounted for at least four months of most years between 1993 and 1999. Even though he had changed his record label, Carlos seemed to almost hate the people he had to deal with in the music industry and virtually gave up recording so they couldn't touch him, "I told the people at Columbia one time, because they were getting in my face about doing something I didn't want to do, 'Look man, I hear the music before I play it. I literally hear the music before I play. People hear the music after I play it and you hear it after the people hear it. Don't tell me how to fucking play my music.' If Wayne Shorter was the company executive I would listen to him because it's a musician talking to me. Cats who can't play a lick, I don't give a shit what they say. I never considered myself a product. I am sound and I am colour. I am feelings, I am emotion, I am soul. I'm not a package."[61]

The reality was that the tours kept the band in the public eye – to the mass of MTV viewers Santana was out of sight. Santana's live shows were a consistent draw for large audiences world-wide (a sell-out run at Los Angeles' Greek Theatre in 1990 saw the band play to 18,500 fans and shows there in summer 1992 grossed more than $500,000[62])[63], but the audience for their new material was ebbing away. "Say It Again" was the most recent "hit" and as the group's recorded output slowed to barely a trickle in the 1990s, they were effectively only visible to those who attended the concerts and through the band's old hits. As a reflection of this trend, the release of a greatest hits package always generated considerable sales and Columbia cashed-in on this by releasing one a year, every year, somewhere in the world. It paid off.

Greatest hits packages released in consecutive years in the late 1990s in Italy and Spain were Top 10 sellers.

Santana took to the road and kept going south to Latin America where he was still big news. It was no surprise that his next project was a live album and video taped in Latin America. The intensity of the recent concerts and the audience reaction made Carlos think that he had really found his much sought after "spiritual orgasm". A South American tour was hastily arranged and the band, augmented by young rapper Vorriece Cooper, flew out in May 1993 for dates in Argentina, Venezuela and Mexico. All were filmed and recorded and the result was a live video and CD *Sacred Fire* which was released in the autumn. The video was an enjoyable overview of the considerable passion of a Santana concert as experienced by musicians and audience and although it was really a "Greatest Hits Live" package, it did include an extraordinary new instrumental, "Wings Of Grace". This mesmerising performance built on the "Blues For Salvador" concept of just guitar and keyboards. Its foundation is a two chord structure and a touching soul guitar melody which Santana delivers as if it were a human voice before it builds into an intense section, coloured with a heavy wah-wah effect and overlaid with delay that creates an almost overwhelming transcendent mood. This was the guitarist calling out musically to the spirit of John Coltrane. Santana shows his genius by moving effortlessly from this rapt mood to a straight blues passage, before taking the piece back to its soul basis. It is one of the best expositions of his uniqueness as a guitar player, there is literally no other player who this could be. There is no room for flashy technique here, just the ability to deliver a melody with incomparable feeling and the art of conveying his own consciousness through the instrument. "Wings Of Grace" is one of Santana's finest ever recordings.

South America was not the band's only stamping ground, the annual tours were world-wide and there were always highlights and always lots of new band members. Highlights included a successful musical reunion with John McLaughlin at the 1993 Montreux Jazz Festival and a great US tour with the blues champions in 1994. Working on alternate nights with Buddy Guy, Bobby Parker, Luther Allison and Robert Cray was far more important for the Mexican than hits on *Billboard*, "To play with Buddy, Luther and Bobby Parker, I'm just really grateful that I'm in a position to be able to ... share is the best way to describe it. Share with them and learn with them." Another notable event was a jam with Prince at a 1995 Miami date which set the seal on some strong vocal support the younger man had been giving Carlos in the press. In most of his interviews Prince mentioned Santana as a key influence and he even played a medley of Santana riffs in his current set; needless to say the Bay Area legend was delighted by this open flattery and soon started including the Prince version of his own licks in his set. It was Santana-plays-Prince-playing-Santana.

New faces flowed through Santana like water, and blues harmonica man Curtis Salgado soon found out that playing in the band was a matter of sink or swim, "He is an amazing cat. He just kinda puts you in a situation where you hang on and you better fucking hang on and figure it out ahead of time because he's too busy with his own shit." During a performance in San Francisco, the guitarist sprang the idea of a harp solo on Salgado as the song was playing, "First night we ever played live and I've never been with this band before. He starts playing "Chill Out" and all of a sudden he looks at me and puts his hands to his mouth imitating a harmonica and I'm like 'uh.. what?!' You know I never played on the song, I don't even know what the changes are!"

In between the tours Santana cut an album with his brother Jorge and nephew Carlos Hernandez and released it in autumn 1994. *Brothers* has three faces, one third "standard" Santana material, one third Jorge Santana originals and one third material with Carlos Hernandez. In truth it is a CD of variable quality. The Santana material was very good, Carlos' composition "Luz, Amor Y Vida" is powerful and "Blues Latino" is an archetypal example of Carlos' guitar craft. His imaginative rendering of "Aranjuez" was a refreshing change and there were two successful tracks with his brother, "Contigo"(a tune left over from Malo days) and "La Danza". Jorge contributed an interesting opener in "Transmutation /Industrial" and a strongly sensitive performance of Bola Sete's "Morning In Marin" to close the album, but the difficulty was a section of less than top quality material between "La Danza" and "Marin". The album's release passed off virtually unnoticed and Carlos noted the distinct lack of promotion it was given.

As the tours and years went by the guitarist spoke optimistically about releasing some of his new tunes on albums he imagined might be called *Harmonious Convergence* or *Serpents And Doves*, but by the mid-1990s he was unsure of his business relationships, "We're set to record around October, November, but in reality I'm recording every day. I record every rehearsal, every concert. I'm hoping that everything is mixed correctly, that the music is played correctly. This way maybe we go to the studio and record a minimum four songs. You know, there are so many new songs that we're playing, if I find the right tempos, the right balance and the right heart and soul then we're gonna be recording the whole year ! As for the release thing, right now I'm not in a position to say when – I don't need anybody to go out of their way and hype Santana. If most of our concerts that we do are sold out and we're not on the radio then any person with common sense would say, all the people left happy, so let's put the album out so that they can buy it. So you can transfer ticket sales into album sales." A neater expression of the guitarist's rather simplistic view of the music industry would be hard to imagine.

Santana's old record label continued to release greatest hits sets, like the almost entirely superfluous *Dance Of The Rainbow Serpent* and the retrospective mood of that package was mirrored by some of Carlos' old compatriots who were cooking up something new by looking back. The 1971 Santana was reforming without Carlos or David Brown under the name Abraxas. The band played a number of well received gigs around California before an album *The Abraxas Pool* appeared in 1997 with the Santana blend of Latin Percussion, guitar, Hammond organ and Rolie's strong vocals to the fore. The best moments on the disc were Chepito Areas' timbales, rehashes of "Guajira" and a fine guitar track, "Szabo". Meanwhile, the Abraxas Pool spent their time appearing to lash Carlos Santana in the San Francisco media. The *San Francisco Chronicle* was at the heart of the storm printing an article titled "All The Gang's Here Except One". This calculation seemed to forget David Brown entirely and there were some curious remarks attributed to Michael Shrieve – "Actually the sound of Santana was Chepito and Gregg" – and Gregg Rolie, "he's congenial, but we obviously disagree. He is polite to me but you can see there's no love lost here." Michael Carabello went further still, "This band wasn't created around Carlos Santana, it was created around the sound. It wasn't about Carlos, it was about the music and the people."[64] Sadly for fans of the original sound and San Francisco sub-editors alike, The Abraxas Pool never really took off again as, by the time the CD was released, Chepito Areas had received a gunshot wound and was no longer available to perform. In any event, after everyone had calmed down, Neal Schon headed off for a Journey reunion, whilst Gregg Rolie and Carlos started exchanging riffs and tapes again. Rolie showed up at Santana's 1996 Shoreline show. It seemed that no matter how little love the two would admit to in public, there was always a mutual attraction. The ire of the Abraxas Pool members was decent publicity for their Bay Area audience, but their complaints against Carlos found few interested readers outside California.

☯

Meanwhile Carlos Santana continued his endless touring, a commitment to the road that gained the guitar player the admiration of his peers like Airto

Moreira, "He's a genuine musician because he doesn't stay at home in his studio making millions of dollars, he goes out and plays for the people. That's very important for a real musician." Good it may have been from Airto's point of view, but the Santana state of mind put him on a collision course with the music business. Its attitude was alien to him and he simply could not understand why his music wasn't attracting more airplay. Sidestepping the issue of not being fashionable he put it down to racism, as he revealed in no uncertain terms to the *San Francisco Examiner* in a rare display of anger, "I can go to West Africa and play with King Sunny Ade or to Rio and play with Milton Nascimento. We are not Xerox machines, we should break down stereotypes. Why should I be limited to just playing Mexican music? To satisfy your expectations of me just because I'm from Tijuana? If you are alive and have a heart, you play what is in your soul." Perhaps the real target for his ire was his record label. He wasn't happy with Island, who had taken over the Santana contract from Polygram, even though they had launched his own label, Guts and Grace, which he used to release a CD of some of his live recordings of his favourite musicians, John Coltrane, Bob Marley, Stevie Ray Vaughan, Marvin Gaye and Jimi Hendrix. Guts and Grace also signed Italian musician Paolo Rustichelli who had coaxed Miles Davis into recording a tune of his just before his death. Rustichelli had recently created another montage of melodic snatches and Euro dance beats, overlaid with Santana's guitar and samples of Davis' trumpet. Carlos put his full weight behind the resulting CD, *Mystic Man*, which eventually achieved sales Rustichelli could surely only have dreamt of. But, in his heart, Santana didn't want to remain with Island and was eventually released from the contract leaving him free to get back on the road.

Santana's shows during this never-ending touring were, as ever, a mix of old and new. 50% of the 1990s Santana set was taken up with the equally never-ending old favourites; "Black Magic Woman", "Soul Sacrifice", "Europa" or "Samba Pa Ti". On a good night these could sound fresh and full of life, on a bad night they were perfunctory. It was simply impossible to believe that Santana and the rest of the musicians could have enjoyed playing these tunes one hundred times a year, but in the game of musical survival Carlos Santana knew that this was what a large proportion of his audience wanted to hear and it would have been box office suicide never to play them. Sandwiched in between the oldies would be new cover versions from a range of influences, including music by free jazz guitarist Sonny Sharrock ("Dick Dogs"), Funkadelic ("Maggot Brain"), Bob Marley ("Exodus" and "So Much Trouble"), Timmy Thomas ("Why Can't We Live Together"), Joe

Zawinul ("Dr. Honarius Causa"), Mama Sez (an Afro-French band led by singer Shakara who wrote the anthem-like "Yaleo"), Voices of East Harlem ("Right On, Be Free"), George Benson ("El Mar"), Gabor Szabo ("Concorde (Niteflight)") and Ray Lema ("HAL 99"). Santana had always been masterful at adapting other artists' material to his sound, now he was doing it with a vengeance.

Another portion of the set was usually given over to the jams that recalled the Butterfield "East-West" style. These might be on a John Lee Hooker boogie guitar riff, mixed with a Lightnin' Hopkins vocal, or Sly Stone's "Sex Machine", or a riff-cum-tune from the Davis, Coltrane or Hancock music book, or the classic Afro-Cuban hook "Mazacote". For the Santana listener of a jazz bent these were the moments that offered the most interest as Santana and Thompson found room to stretch out, take a few musical chances and relax into their playing. In the midst of all this there was also new material that wouldn't have been beneath release standards; some of it was created out of sound check jams, like the soul tune "When You're In Love" (which came to Santana in the shower, but had quite a bit to do with Neneh Cherry and Youssou N'Dour), some was more studiously crafted ("Angelica", "The Call-Kenya", "Serpents and Doves" and "Day Of Celebration") and some of it was only played a few times ("Children Of The Light"), before disappearing faster than a politician's promise. The end of 1996 saw a new collection of songs with titles like "I Believe It's Time" and the Devadip-like "Metatron" and at this time Santana, in tandem with Chester Thompson, was writing plenty of material, but he felt he could only express it in the live setting, hassles with record companies held no interest for him. Occasionally, very occasionally, one of the band would get one of their compositions aired. Singer Tony Lindsay had a reggae-ballad called "Spread Your Wings" which was played a few times, but generally the group was a backing band for Carlos' and Chester Thompson's ideas. There were plenty of cameos for each of the band members but in reality the showcase solos for bass and percussion might have been dispensed with. Ultimately though, on a good night (and there have always been a staggeringly high proportion of good nights with Santana), the music could provide the listener with a real sense of joy and many left the concerts genuinely uplifted. After all the years on the road Santana knew how to reach people directly and the leader's oft stated desire to "touch your hearts" was often a reality.

Santana's own guitar playing remained captivating and still at its best when he stuck close to the melodic approach and blues setting. As the 1990s progressed, he started injecting avant-garde elements into his playing, stem-

ming in no small way from his interest in the free-jazz guitarist Sonny
Sharrock, a one-time musical compatriot of Pharoah Sanders who would
lambast audiences with heavily amplified, inter-galactic chromatic runs and
musical shrieks. It wasn't really Santana's style, but he was soon to be found
running a bottleneck up and down the fretboard in a creation of pure angry
noise. However, at heart, Santana would always be a melody freak and he
could pick out a melody from anywhere, any circumstance. Fans would
occasionally give him tapes of their own melodic fragments and find them
being played by the Third World hero. Similarly, his fascination with
Hollywood epics saw him take a snatch of melody from the love scene of the
old western *Apache* and make a song from it. Watching him play this short
piece was telling, it showed that he still used the same techniques for con-
necting with an audience that he had learnt in Tijuana, decades earlier.
Sometimes he would appear to play directly for a single person in the crowd,
he might point at them or stand directly over them and eyeball them as he
played. Other times he would bend down as he executed one of the extravagant string bends he used on "Apache" and with his free right hand reach out
and take the hand of the recipient in the audience. It was as if he were trying
to transmit his feeling for the music to the listener, making a physical as well
as musical connection. Years before in Tijuana, he learnt that he could attract
people's attention by the way he played, it was a way of standing out from
the crowd. Now, he still had the need to keep people coming back to his concerts, in effect he still needed to be noticed and so these moments of musical
physicality appeared to be a way of getting the crowd to directly feel what he
feels and go away with a sense that he had been playing "just for them", one-
to-one.

At the same time, Carlos was drawing contentment from his ever growing
list of contacts with other musicians around the world. The mid-1990s
brought a crop of fine recordings with Junior Wells (a cover of War's "Get
Down"), the delightful "Chill Out" with John Lee Hooker and an incendiary
version of "Spanish Castle Magic" with Stanley Clarke and Tony Williams.
As Williams sadly died in 1997 this was the final session these two great
originals played on together and as if they knew, they light a fire which is
almost out of control.

It particularly gratified Carlos to be invited to play on African artists'
albums and he soon discovered that he and his band were extremely influential in Africa and their visit to Ghana in 1971 had become the stuff of legend.
From the moment Carlos had stepped into a recording studio with Babatunde
Olatunji in 1986 he began to see that his music and the music that he loved

like blues, jazz, flamenco, reggae, funk, gospel and Afro-Cuban, were all part of the same musical root and that root was Africa. He worked live in France with Touré Kunda, an exciting band from the Ivory Coast who mixed African percussion and pop with reggae to create a highly seductive blend of music. Carlos especially liked their tune, "Guerrilla", which he played with them in Paris in 1991 and kept in the back of his mind as a possibility for recording. It all started to fit together as he recorded on albums by Mory Kante, Salif Keita and Angelique Kidjo, the biggest international stars from Africa, it became even more clear to him that they were all playing music from the same root. An illustration of the mutual empathy between Santana and an African act like Baaba Maal, who opened the London date for them in 1996, was to be found during the Santana soundcheck for this Wembley Arena show. Maal and his band were occupying a few seats in the otherwise empty hall as Carlos drove his band through yet another try on "Yaleo". When he was finished, Santana approached the microphone and directly addressed the African musicians, whom he had never met, and told them how much he loved their music and that he hoped they would jam with him later. When he finished speaking all the African musicians stood and gave the Mexican a warm and spontaneous round of applause. The jamming that resulted that night reflected this happy and wholly natural connection.

At the end of 1996 Santana finally started recording the material they had accumulated over the past three years, but by the end of the year Carlos had changed the band again and brought in a new Cuban drum hero, Horacio "El Negro" Hernandez. They returned to the studio and set about retaping the material they had just recorded, but this time with a view to making a demo for a new release. The impetus was the negotiations for a new Santana record deal that were going on throughout this period. The talks extended through another massive bout of US touring in the spring and summer in the company of new age jam band Rusted Root, whose audience brought plenty of new faces to the Santana party and boosted attendances to the point where this was the most successful Santana tour of the US since the early 1980s. Finally, in the autumn Santana signed a new record deal with Arista Records which saw him reunited with Clive Davis – the president of Columbia way back at the start of Santana's career. Davis was now the head honcho at Arista and it was probably his presence that swung the deal and so the guitar man, shortly after his 50th birthday, set about writing new songs throughout the winter of 1997 in the expectation of finally putting out a new release in 1998.

Chapter 20

Of course, no new Santana music did appear in 1998 – a year which saw the band embark on no fewer than three separate European tours and the customary late summer pull through the US, showcasing another clutch of new songs that sounded like they were aimed at the three minute market. The band was invigorated by two new faces, who took the virtuoso levels in the group to new heights. They were bass man Benny Rietveld and drummer, Rodney Holmes. Both had been in Santana before and both were regarded by Carlos as just about the best in their fields. The two were jazz players by training and had a technical facility that was well beyond the norm. They were Carlos' dream-team.

With the new men on board, the year saw the band's activities split between recordings and live dates. All the material that had been recorded the year before at Fantasy Studios was recorded again with the new rhythm section and, as the year progressed, a clutch of rumours emerged about who was involved in these sessions. Initial reports suggested that Gregg Rolie was collaborating on one track and the Santana engineer from the '70s, Glen Kolotkin, was also working with Carlos again. Another suggestion was that Mick Jagger and Dave Stewart of the Eurythmics had written a song for him called "Blind Leading The Blind". It was one of the pieces recorded at the Fantasy sessions. On a more contemporary note, it was said that Santana was collaborating with Lauryn Hill of Fugees fame and they'd cut a version of The Beatles' "And I Love Her". The working title for the album was said to be *Mumbo Jumbo*.

However, thoughts of the new album would have to wait, as nostalgia was back on the agenda. January 1998 saw the 1969 Santana Band inducted into the "Rock'n'Roll Hall of Fame" and for this massive New York ego-orgy all the musicians except Chepito Areas were reunited. David Brown, looking frail, didn't play but the others did, performing the old favourite of old favourites "Black Magic Woman". Carlos also invited the song's author, Peter Green, to play it with them. Green had only recently revived his career, after surviving the living hell of schizophrenia for over a decade and it was indicative of Santana's admiration for the Londoner that he was invited to join them that night. As the taste for nostalgia was gaining hold, Columbia didn't miss a trick by releasing yet another "Best Of Santana" package and yet more remastered versions of the first three Santana albums. These were releases with a difference as each came with bonus live tracks (including unreleased goodies like "Gumbo") and a tie-in promotional CD even contained "Folsom Street", an outtake from *Abraxas*. It seemed that Columbia would never give-up on the Santana back-catalogue.

In the midst of all the nostalgia, two key releases kept Carlos Santana in the public eye; first, he played on an album by Mexico's most popular rock band El Tri. This band, led by singer Alex Lora, are well-known throughout Latin America and despite their many years' service, still fashionable with youngsters. Unthinkable in a "Western" rock context, their latest CD *Cuando Tú No Estás* opened with a passionate tribute to Mexico's patron saint, the Virgin of Guadelupe, and Santana's guitar added a notch or two to the passion Geiger counter. Such is El Tri's standing in Latin America and the success of the song, "Virgen Morena", as a single and video, that Carlos was thrust into the consciousness of Latin American youth in no small measure. Meanwhile, the guitarist was about to make the right decision by agreeing to add sympathetic guitar to a tune on a solo album by the new queen of soul, Lauryn Hill, who, having ditched the Fugees, struck out on her own account with the astonishingly successful *The Miseducation Of Lauryn Hill*. Clive Davis had spoken to Hill about Carlos Santana and she revealed her love for his music, recounting that as a teenager she used to write lyrics against Carlos' guitar lines on *Abraxas*. There was an amazing logic to this; Carlos Santana's guitar style has always been heavily influenced by soul vocalists' lines and here was a soul singer putting lyrics to his soul guitar licks! When the singer finally phoned the guitarist, a new musical union was born. Lauryn Hill's album made her the most visible and successful female soul artist in the world. When she appeared at the Grammys in February 1999 to pick up a hatful of awards (including Best Album), she performed a charming ballad "To Zion" and the man on guitar that night was Carlos Santana, putting him back in the Hollywood public eye. Times had changed. When he won a Grammy for *Blues For Salvador*, Santana received his award in the post. Despite playing second fiddle to Hill (Santana was not even name-checked by the singer), his musical empathy with her found the guitarist going back to his roots, as the singer delivered an ecstatic, near-gospel rendering of her song. Ever since he discovered the blues as a teenager in Tijuana, Santana had been immersed in a forty year love affair with black music. His own music was essentially a cross between black forms (which naturally includes Afro-Cuban) and Mexican romanticism, now the wheel had come full circle as he found himself feted and supported by the black music icon of the late 1990s. Hill's album had almost appeared to document black music forms from doo-wop to soul and beyond to hip-hop; these were as much Santana's roots as hers. It was also interesting to hear the new mega-star being so open about her obviously strongly-held spiritual beliefs at such a blatantly media-hype event and, it was hard to suppress a glance back to the Devadip days as Hill and her backing band took the stage dressed all in pure Sri Chinmoy white!

The guitarist's increasing US media profile was the ideal foundation for the relaunch of his recording career and throughout this period he was busy in the studio cutting and re-cutting tracks for a new CD that he hoped would surprise everyone. But, the genesis of the album was not a real surprise. At most of the key junctures of Carlos' career there has been a strong, guiding hand directing him behind the scenes. In the past this role had been played by the likes of Stan Marcum, Bill Graham, David Rubinson and Sri Chinmoy. Now, with his career at a real cross-roads, it seemed that the guitarist was ready to be directed again and, this time, the guiding hand was to come from Clive Davis. But, the ball was in the guitarist's court as it seemed that Davis would act on instruction, "Mr. Clive Davis came really close to my face, eyeball to eyeball, and said, 'what does Carlos Santana want to do?'"[65] The answer came easily and Davis set to work, "We knew half had to be vintage Santana, but that we also had to incorporate all of the current contemporary influences that Carlos was very much feeling. He said to me, 'Can you suggest other musicians that I could work with for the other half of the album that would be a natural extension of what I do?' and I excitedly began the undertaking."[66]

Clive Davis is a legendary figure in the music business and his list of contacts is almost universal. He only signed winners to his Arista label and kept a roster of fewer than thirty acts. Now, he set about pulling strings and making things happen for Santana. But, he also had a personal interest in seeing Carlos rise again in the charts, "I've always had a tremendous regard for Carlos and his music. I love the fact that he's ambitious, hungry and inspired with all kinds of musical ideas. Santana is as relevant today as he was before."[67] When Clive Davis got on the 'phone and started ringing around his contacts to see who wanted to record with Carlos Santana, he found that there was no shortage of takers. As he said, Santana is relevant today and soon the Mexican had a long list of contemporary superstars to pick from: Lauryn Hill, Dave Matthews, Wyclef Jean, Everlast, Eagle-Eye Cherry and Rob Thomas of Matchbox 20. A more commercially potent group of new stars is hard to imagine. On recent albums sales alone, Hill had sold five million, Dave Matthews four million, Everlast two million and Matchbox 20 a staggering eight million! It was good company to be in and Davis quickly realised that he had a major prospect on his hands.

Davis is a very astute business man and it had not escaped his notice that Spanish was already the first language of many American states and that a new teenage Hispanic heartthrob called Ricky Martin had crossed over to the mainstream charts with a smash hit single. Carlos Santana was still a name without peer in the Latin community and Davis knew that if they could target a single at the huge Hispanic audience, sales would soar. To achieve this they recruited producer KC Porter who had worked the mixing desk for Ricky Martin, and Maná, a Mexican rock band who were given the label, "rock en español". Finally, to keep the guitar fans happy they pulled off a last minute coup by getting Eric Clapton to cut a track. There were so many music fans out there who knew the Santana name but had lost touch with his activities, that a little burst of publicity and success would bring them flocking back. For his part, Carlos Santana was ready to get on with it and do whatever was necessary to hit the top again.

Getting on with it meant frantic activity for an entire year. It led even the casual Santana observer to ask why would Carlos Santana, at almost 52 years of age, want to go through all this again – especially after years of being almost totally estranged from the ethos of the music business? It's not that difficult to understand his motivation; once you've had a taste of the top, it's hard to kiss it goodbye. The guitarist himself put it down to passion, "I want to be with passionate people, people who have the necessary vision to place my music back on the radio. Clive only has twenty seven artists and has enough passion to take care of them all."[68] Fired by this desire, the guitar man also stepped into the lights at dates with Lauryn Hill, paving the way for the new disc; it was even rumoured that the feisty Hill had invited the guitarist to join her band! Such arrogance can probably be put down to the rush of success. Hill's fame was enormous and she was as big in 1999 as Santana had been in 1969. Santana was delighted that her audience warmly welcomed him at the Californian dates he played with her, but by April, he was back with his own outfit, introducing his new material to ecstatic crowds at the Fillmore in San Francisco. They had just announced that the new disc was to be called *Supernatural*, which sounded like another homage to Peter Green. The shows were extremely well received, with fans and band alike appearing to be on a new high, as if they all felt they were on the edge of something big. New songs were offered-up for the first time and went down well and there were gasps of recognition for some real old favourites, "Singing Wind, Crying Beasts", "Dance Sister Dance" and "Incident At Neshabur". The rhythm section thundered, the Santana guitar roared and caressed, whilst Chester Thompson continued to reside in an urban Hammond groove that underpinned the entire troupe. The "classic sound" was still alive and well in the live arena.

Just before the album's release in June the marketing campaign for it started with a feature in *Billboard*, the music industry's trade magazine. The first single from the album was slated as "Smooth", a song that was originally written for George Michael by Rob Thomas who was lead singer of US chart champions Matchbox 20. The album would then be supported by a massive US media onslaught. Santana would record a session on *Hard Rock Live* for the grey hair version of MTV, VH-1, when they would be joined by some of the new friends. Then there was going to be a spot on the top-rated *Letterman Show* in June and even some schmoozing on morning talk shows. It was all self-generating hype, the idea being to turn the album's release into a media event. It worked and as the release date drew closer Clive Davis' sense of the growing clamour led him to increase the first pressing of the disc from 125,000 to 210,000 and, finally, 350,000, almost instant gold record status. The main question that remained as the album hit the stores was, would the album's artistic content match the hype or would it be a mere super-guests session?

The answer was a resounding "yes" but mainly because the power of Carlos Santana's guitar playing remains undiminished. Notably, a number of subtle changes had been visited upon the Santana sound and presentation. Santana's commercially awkward lyrics about angels and spirits were replaced with love-songs and some of the key features of the Santana sound had been diluted virtually out of existence, notably Chester Thompson's Hammond organ. Stalwart Santana players like Raul Rekow and even

Thompson himself were absent from entire tracks and singer Tony Lindsay, who had put in years on the road with the band, was almost totally reduced to the role of a backing singer. Clearly, both Santana and Davis realised that if the new Santana album was going to be a hit, it could not be based around the classic Santana sound of guitar, Hammond and Latin percussion. That was OK for the live arena where Santana's loyal band of followers would always turn out to hear it, but as far as the charts were concerned *Milagro* in 1992 had comprehensively proved that the "classic sound" had no commercial potency. The stalwart fans had loved that album because it was "the real Santana" delivered through the "classic sound", but in the world of MTV, it didn't add up to anything. Arista were not about to repeat that kind of marketing mishap.

To some extent *Supernatural* pitches Carlos as the guest guitarist on his own record. This is because Everlast sounds exactly like Everlast, Lauryn Hill sounds exactly like Lauryn Hill and Eagle-Eye Cherry sounds exactly like Eagle-Eye Cherry. These singers hadn't written songs for the Santana sound, they had given songs for Santana to record. There's a big difference. The only track which was a real writing and playing collaboration was "Love Of My Life" with Dave Matthews and, probably for that reason, it's the most effective. A more subtle transformation had occurred on the Latin tracks, which adopted the Puerto Rican pop arrangements and sound which had worked so well for Ricky Martin.

Nevertheless, *Supernatural* opens with a pleasing slice of the familiar Santana sound on "Yaleo", a song the group had played live since 1994. It was originally recorded by an Afro-French pop band, Mama Sez, who Carlos chanced upon on tour in France in the early 1990s. It is a great party tune in the mould of "Oye Como Va" and "Guajira" with small cameos for each of the musicians and some roaring guitar from the star. Next up was the collaboration with the amazingly popular South African singer Dave Matthews and "Love Of My Life" emerges as one of Santana's strongest recordings for years. It is also an interesting piece of Santana archaeology as it recalls the guitarist's early childhood when European classical music resounded in the Santana household as the very pretty and touching guitar part and most of the main melody come directly from the third movement of Brahms' Third Symphony. In the hands of a sensitive conductor this can be amongst the most affecting passages of all classical music, on "Love Of My Life" Carlos Santana expresses it with great grace as pure romance. Dave Matthews contributes a smoky, bar-room vocal as the piece works out to a steamy salsa coda which finds Santana recalling the "talking guitar" of his great Latin solos on "Guajira". The reason for the song's impact is that it emerged from a very emotive period for the guitarist, "When my father passed away I wouldn't listen to music for a week. I was kind of numb. Then I finally turned on the radio and the first thing I heard was Brahms. It just hit me so hard, like a tattoo." It must have been a subconscious reaction as Carlos had used the melody before as the inspiration for part of his film music for *La Bamba*, it was a theme that ran very, very deep through his life.

Of all the collaborations on this album, the session with hip-hop hard-man Everlast must be the most unlikely, but Carlos adds Hendrix-style wah-wah guitar and even some grunge chords to the singer's "Put Your Lights On", a piece that sounded like it could have been Metallica or The Black Crowes. This dark but passionate song had been cut in the Bay Area in February 1999 and probably because it sounded absolutely nothing like Santana, was a good bet for a future hit. "Put Your Lights On" is in contrast to the next section of the disc which goes Latin again with "Africa Bamba" and the first single "Smooth". The former is an adaptation of "Guerrilla", the song by West African stars Touré Kunda which Santana played with them in Paris way back in 1991. It had stuck in his head since then and now he adds his own charming Spanish vocal and a great salsa coda to create five minutes of Afro-Latin pleasure. "Smooth" sounds suspiciously like a faster, rockier version of "Guajira" but has a nagging quality that lodges itself into the listener's mind and even Rob Thomas' clichéd lyrics can be forgiven as they are swept up in the joyous horn-driven cha-cha-cha and Santana's exuberant guitar.

Thomas' band Matchbox 20 are inconceivably popular in the USA which made "Smooth" a good choice for the first single, but on a world-wide level the next guest, Lauryn Hill, is better known. Her close ties with Bob Marley's family give an interesting Kingston tinge to the opening horn charts of "Do You Like The Way", a track that would have fitted comfortably onto her own recent album. The simple chord change is a familiar one for Carlos Santana and it's a pretty harmonic groove over which he adds some expressive guitar passages before the song's third part which is more gospel than hip-hop. This segment is delivered by a forceful Cee-Lo vocal which paves the way for some testifying guitar as the mood becomes Marvin Gaye meets Al Green. The Fugees interlude continues with Wyclef Jean's pretty but modest "Maria, Maria", which again falls foul of clichéd lyrics about Hispanic life and surprisingly includes tributes to Carlos Santana in the chorus.

The updating of the Santana Latin sound proceeds with "Migra", which includes as angry a lyric as Carlos has ever written – it is a verbal assault on the Californian immigration police. Actually, the song by Algerian artist Rachid Taha is another that originated in the Paris Afro-French music scene that Carlos always locks into when he plays there. The venomous lyrics aside, "Migra" is a surprising cocktail of Native American Indian drumming, Mariachi trumpet themes and Hendrix flavour guitar. Less controversial is another mirror-image of "Guajira" on "Corazon Espinado", recorded with Mexican rock favourites Maná. A typically Mexican heartbreak tale of a cold-hearted lover, it is clearly aimed at the Latin market worldwide and would fit perfectly onto mainstream radio in Spain. Santana is on home territory here and responds to singer Pher's exhortations to "echale guitarritos" with more exciting Latin guitar, backed by Karl Perazzo's exultant timbales rolls.

Amongst the most contemporary of the hit material is "Wishing It Was", a dreamy offering from Eagle-Eye Cherry, the son of Don Cherry, a true jazz and world music adventurer. It opens with a Brazilian mood from Santana's acoustic guitar before producers The Dust Brothers conjure up a patchwork quilt of sounds and colours as a backdrop to Cherry's ethereal melody and lyrics. "Wishing It Was" is the last of the collaboration material before the traditional Santana identity takes over for the remainder of the disc. This is signposted by the most emotionally substantial piece on the album, "El Farol", the guitarist's elegy to his late father, which he had played at José Santana's memorial service in 1998. Set in the traditional Santana Latin-ballad arrangement, "El Farol" is a moving but understated performance which highlights again Carlos' inherited Mexican melodic sensibility, some harmonic touches from European classical music and sheer expressive beauty. Here his guitar caresses the audience's emotions with true sentiment. The captivating mood of "El Farol" is suitably complemented by the best Latin track on the disc, "Primavera", an intoxicating piece about rebirth and new life. Producer KC Porter steps out from behind the mixing desk to sing his own pretty composition with aplomb on what could easily be a big hit in the Latin market. It's home ground for Santana's fans – an attractive melody, Latin percussion, a few bursts from Chester Thompson's Hammond organ and one of Carlos' hottest recorded solos for some time.

The track listing indicates that the album closes with a much-hyped guitar duet with English guitar legend Eric Clapton, but those expecting eight minutes of histrionics from the pair on "The Calling" were to be disappointed, this was a meditative affair. The initial segment is from a concert-opening overture Carlos had as early as 1995 and the two "guitar heroes" intertwine like two old masters, not in competition but in graceful exploration. The second half of the track is a blues jam circa San Francisco 1967 updated with a modern drum track ! More of the mainstream Santana musical sensibility also appears on a "secret bonus track" called "Day Of Celebration", a song which has been a staple of the Santana set since 1996. All the classic Santana ingredients are present here: the hybrid conga pattern, Hammond organ, lengthy guitar introduction, esoteric melodies, soul-rock vocals, new age lyrics and unrestrained guitar which fades out just as the Californian indulges in some Sonny Sharrock-style noise.

The surprising thing about *Supernatural* is that for all the contrivance, it works and works well. Its success rests entirely on the personality of Carlos Santana who was probably shocked himself by how well respected he was by the major stars of the day. Everlast for one reported that he would not have given over his song "Put Your Lights On" to anybody else other than Santana and there were very few stars of a 1969 vintage who could pull in a roster of young admirers like the guests on *Supernatural*. His innate love for soul music makes his work with Lauryn Hill, Wyclef and Eagle-Eye Cherry entirely natural and as a testament to the barrier-smashing nature of Carlos Santana as a musician, *Supernatural* is without peer. Clive Davis had done a great service to his old friend, knowing full-well that young music fans who were tempted into the Santana world by the presence of a Matthews or a Thomas, could well be captivated by this unique musical voice. On the down side the album did lack a little emotional depth in places and was certainly no *Caravanserai* or *Welcome*, but it didn't need to be – on its own terms and in its own way, *Supernatural* is a remarkable Santana album.

The critics seemed to agree and the album was showered with positive reviews upon its American release. In the midst of a four-star review, *The San Francisco Chronicle* spotted that, "the ease of performance suggests that Santana is hip to his guest stars... *Supernatural* is Santana's best outing since 1983's *Havana Moon*."[69]. Others went further, "most of *Supernatural* triumphs by combining inspiring guitar solos with '90s coolness. It is also Santana's most Latin-sounding album to date. Not quite the religious experience of 'Incident At Neshabur', but almost there."[70] *Billboard* declared it, "a new landmark in a career filled with them," and *Rolling Stone* was equally enthusiastic, "eclectic, lively and only occasionally goofy, *Supernatural* offers a glossy but winning context of musical fusion that highlights Santana's unique ability to make that guitar of his cry expressively." What reviewers realised was that for all its sophisticated marketing *Supernatural* revealed that the mature Carlos Santana has the same musical personality as the young lion of 1969, he plays from his soul and from his gut, without artifice.

It looked like Carlos was all set for a big hit album and so he was. *Supernatural* entered the *Billboard* chart on 26th June at number nineteen, rising to fifteen on the back of the success of "Smooth" as a single, which made the top 30 by early August. These were Santana's highest chart places on *Billboard* since *Zebop!* in 1981 and "Hold On" in 1982 but there was more to come as the album hit the Top 10 and sold a million by the end of the month. Sales were boosted by the start of another major US tour that seemed to be a celebration of "rock en español", as Carlos and his men took in dates accompanied by Maná and Ozomatli, two of the most popular names in the modern Latin market, which was belatedly being recognised as one of the biggest in the States. The numbers were very big as this tour was playing stadiums to an average 20,000 fans per show. As the Santana name appeared on the cover of *Rolling Stone* for the first time in more than twenty years and the band tackled the TV chat show circuit, it was a certainty that Carlos was about to become a major media superstar again.

As *Supernatural* hit the Top 10 of *Billboard* Santana became one of the very few acts to have had a Top 10 album in the '60s, '70s, '80s and '90s and the success of the album underlines the potency of Carlos Santana. It was the commercial comeback of the decade and a richly deserved one. Few musicians have worked as hard on the road as Carlos Santana and few have so comprehensively laid themselves bare emotionally through their instrument. Thousands and thousands of new listeners were about to become entranced for the first time by that guitar sound that carried with it the essence of generations of Mexican musicians and the spirit of the black masters of blues and jazz. It was an extraordinary new chapter in the remarkable life story of a man who came from origins so humble that most people reading this book could not conceive them. Carlos Santana has never forgotten his roots and, as he surveys the lot of Latin American immigrants in California, he probably realises that a Mexican from Tijuana is probably the single most unlikely American superstar. The Santana band burst into the world as a no compromise multi-racial unit and, through his music, Carlos Santana has celebrated this positive aspect of life around the world. His politics have always been expressed through the music of inclusion and his guitar will always be a celebration of the possible.

☯

As the start of a new millennium beckoned Carlos Santana had good reason to look back with satisfaction on his musical life. *Supernatural* has already reached sales of four million copies, peaking at number 1 on the *Billboard* chart. Santana has also enjoyed his biggest ever hit single "Smooth" which simultaneously reached number 1 on the *Billboard* chart. Doubts would persist about how long he would remain interested in platinum discs and the rest of the trappings of mega-stardom, but for the time being it felt good.

For any musician a great source of satisfaction is gaining respect from his fellow players and a clear manifestation of the regard with which the guitarist is held by his peers came in February 1996 when a concert celebrating his career was held in Los Angeles. The list of musicians who came out to honour Santana was extraordinary and included blues greats John Lee Hooker and Buddy Guy; jazz legends Herbie Hancock and Wayne Shorter; contemporary rock guitarists Kirk Hammett and Vernon Reid; Cuban trumpeter Arturo Sandoval; gospel singer Tramaine Hawkins; Mickey Hart and Bob Weir of the Grateful Dead, plus the current "king" of the conga Giovanni Hidalgo.

Other than obviously being a musician widely respected by his peers, summing up Santana is not easy, but at its very core the single word that best describes the music of Santana and its impact on the listener is "positive". Santana has always played uplifting music and has rarely touched on the darker aspects of life. The music has a sense of forward motion, of making progress, which is a function of Carlos Santana's own extraordinary physical and musical journey from Mexico to San Francisco and the world beyond. Publicly, Santana has tended to distance himself from his Mexican origins, but the truth is that his Mexican roots make him what he is today and provide the foundations for his family-oriented, spiritual world-view that is directly transmitted through his music. Carlos has often been criticised or even ridiculed for his sense of the spiritual and his desire to express it musically, but the reality of music throughout history is that it has its roots in spiritual expression. Many of the greatest emotional experiences available in the world of music are generated as an expression of spiritual belief, not least John Coltrane's *A Love Supreme* or Gustav Mahler's "Resurrection" Symphony. Carlos' belief is absolute and at the core of his being. Santana's true, but somewhat premature epitaph, is that the single factor that has kept people going to Santana concerts and buying their records for thirty years is that, at its best, Santana's music is a glimpse into the power of belief.

Epilogue

In the summer of 1996 I happened to be at the North Sea Jazz Festival, the annual and enormous event which attracts literally hundreds of the world's great jazz musicians. It's held in Den Haag, The Hague, the administrative capital of The Netherlands. Most of the musicians lay up for a couple of days at a hotel no more than a quarter of a mile from the vast venue; it becomes an airport lounge of jazz men and women.

Santana played a brief, hour-and-a-half set on the Saturday afternoon. Before the show, I sat in the luxury pre-fab that was the guitarist's relaxation area, as he quite excitedly played a tape that Gregg Rolie had sent him. It was a home demo of a tune the organist had written with Carlos in mind. It was a reasonable melody, but nothing special. The show beckoned.

An hour and a half is the Santana equivalent of a half set and there was barely time for the "old favourites", a few cameos for the band and a couple of new tunes. These included the strong Afro rhythms of "Day Of Celebration" and a commercial, blues-rock number, "Serpents And Doves". As ever, it was anybody's guess if these songs would make it onto a new Santana album, but they went down well with the crowd. By the time he finished the set with the old salsa favourite, "Oye Como Va", the guitar star was in a very good mood.

The high spirits were partly a result of his walk-on jam the night before with Sly Stone's bass-slapping extrovert, Larry Graham, and now he was looking forward to what the festival had to offer later in the evening. In a matter of hours, he would be watching sax legend and old friend Wayne Shorter, and George Clinton's inter-galactic crew, Funkadelic. His ever-

187

ready tape recorder was primed for action and he was especially keen to hear the drummer who was touring with Shorter at the time – the extremely gifted Rodney Holmes.

Before he headed off to check out old friends, I took a beer with the great guitarist in the hotel bar (not a cheap beer or a big one – hotel beer, hotel prices). I noticed that as well as the fans milling around for a glimpse of the Mexican, Santana seemed to be a magnet for other musicians. From an adjoining table the keyboard maestro Joe Zawinul bellowed, "Santana is wearing *my* hat!", an immense grin cracking his face. Both Zawinul and Santana share a taste in West African headgear. Minutes later and George Benson pulled by to exchange a few words of greeting and, after another couple of expensive sips of Oranjeboom, the exceptional Indian percussionist Trilok Gurtu appeared and suggested that he would love the opportunity to work with Santana.

This was surely rich pleasure for the San Franciscan, especially after he had just enjoyed the roared approval of an eight thousand crowd for his music. I suggested to the man that all this success and obvious respect from his peers must give him great satisfaction. Just then, a guy came by to clear the empty glasses from the table. It set a thought running in Carlos Santana's mind, "I used to mop floors and wash dishes for a living," he told me, "I'd be happy to do that again if I had to. I'd survive."

Footnotes

1   *Billboard,* 7th Dec 1996
2   *Billboard,* 7th Dec 1996
3   *Billboard,* 7th Dec 1996
4   *Guitar Greats,* BBC, 1982
5   *Melody Maker,* November 17th 1973
6   *Melody Maker,* November 17th 1973
7   *Billboard,* 7th Dec 1996
8   *Rolling Stone,* 7th Dec 1972
9   *Guitar Player,* August 1999
10 *Guitarist,* Sept. 1989
11 *Guitar Player,* August 1999
12 *Bay Area Magazine,* Feb. 1978
13 *Rolling Stone,* 7th Dec 1972
14 *A Journey Through America with the Rolling Stones,* Robert Greenfield, Helter Skelter 1997
15 Columbia 485106 2 (1997)
16 *Rolling Stone,* May 6, 1976
17 *Making Music,* September 1992
18 *Guitar Player,* Jan. 1988
19 *Guitar World,* August 1999
20 *Rolling Stone,* 7th Dec 1972
21 *Rolling Stone,* 7th Dec 1972
22 *Rolling Stone,* 7th Dec 1972
23 *Rolling Stone,* 7th Dec 1972
24 *Rolling Stone,* 7th Dec 1972
25 *New Musical Express,* 8th May 1971
26 *Danish Radio Interview,* May 1971
27 *Rolling Stone,* 7th Dec 1972
28 *Musician's Industry,* July 1980
29 *Ascension - John Coltrane and His Quest* Eric Nisenson, Da Capo Press 1995
30 *Zig Zag,* 1977
31 *Melody Maker,* December 2nd, 1972
32 *Melody Maker,* December 2nd, 1972
33 *Melody Maker,* Mar 10 1973
34 *Seconds,* Mar 1995
35 *Guitar Greats,* BBC 1982
36 *Seconds,* Mar 1995
37 *Melody Maker,* Mar 10 1973
38 *Guitar Player,* August 1999
39 *Village Voice,* 14th Mar 1974
40 *Bay Area Magazine,* Feb. 1978
41 *Guitar Greats,* BBC 1982
42 *Circus Weekly,* 12th Dec. 1978
43 *Guitar Player,* August 1999
44 *Bay Area Magazine,* Feb. 1978
45 *Guitar Greats,* BBC 1982
46 *Downbeat,* Jan. 1981
47 *Musician's Industry,* Sept. 1980
48 *Guitar Greats,* BBC 1982
49 *Seconds,* Mar 1995
50 *Seconds,* Mar 1995
51 *Bay Area Magazine,* 7th June 1985
52 *Guitar,* Oct. 1985

53   *Bill Graham Presents*, Robert Greenfield and Bill Graham, Delta 1992
54   *Bill Graham Presents*, Robert Greenfield and Bill Graham, Delta 1992
55   *Latin Beat*, October 1992
56   *San Francisco Chronicle*, June 17th 1988
57   *San Francisco Examiner*, June 17th 1988
58   *San Francisco Chronicle*, 9th Oct 1994
59   *Relix,* 1992
60   *Bassist,* April 1996
61   *Seconds,* Mar 1995
62   Figures from *Guinness Book of Rock Stars*, Guinness 1989
63   Santana remained a major world-wide concert attraction in the 1990s. A concert in Bogota,
     Colombia in 1996 attracted 38,000. Other figures include: 17,000 in Tucson, Arizona ('90);
     30,000 in Lisbon, Portugal ('91); 25,000 in Athens, Greece ('91); 12,000 in Paris, France ('92);
     20,000 in Warsaw, Poland ('94); 8,000 in Casablanca, Morocco ('94); more than 35,000 in
     Lima, Peru ('95); 25,000 in West Palm Beach, Florida ('97) and 25,000 in Pessaro, Italy ('98).
     The were also major stadium concerts in Malaysia, South Korea and the Philippines in 1996
     and the band's Bay Area shows regularly attracted between 10,000 and 30,000.
64   *San Francisco Chronicle*, 9 Oct 1994
65   *Billboard*, May 28th 1999
66   *Billboard*, May 28th 1999
67   *Los Angeles Times*, 9th Sept 1998
68   *Los Angeles Times*, 9th Sept 1998
69   *San Francisco Chronicle*, 13th June 1999
70   *Los Angeles Times* June 1999

APPENDIX 1

SANTANA DISCOGRAPHY

Note: This section covers the main albums and videos released by, or featuring, the Santana Band or Carlos Santana. As Santana is an American band, it gives American catalogue numbers. I have chosen to ignore all but the essential greatest hits packages. It would be an impossible and pointless task to list all the Santana compilations that Columbia have released over the years, there aren't enough trees to go around. Likewise with alternative Japanese releases, which are mostly compilations – any reader who has been tempted by an album called *Santana – Live In Japan* should be aware that it is merely an edited version of the *Lotus* album. In fact, whilst Japanese vinyl pressings of Santana albums are worth seeking for their superior sound quality and photo inserts, only the limited edition *Sacred Fire* CD of any Japanese release includes bonus tracks. It came with a second disc containing "Spirits Dancing In The Flesh" (not the video version), "Wings Of Grace" and "Get It In Your Soul", which makes it one of the more collectible Santana items. The facts regarding the many budget CDs with titles like *Evolution*, *Persuasion* and *Acapulco Sunrise* are as follows: they **are not** outtakes from the *Freeway Jam* album (so, they are **not** the "original album" whatever they may claim), but are outtakes from rehearsals the group held at Pacific Recorders in San Mateo in early 1969. As such, the CDs are reasonably interesting archive material.

SANTANA BAND

Santana (Columbia PC 9781)	October 1969
Abraxas (Columbia JC 30130)	October 1970
Santana III (Columbia PC 30595)	October 1971
Caravanserai (Columbia PC 31610)	November 1972
Welcome (Columbia PC 32445)	November 1973
Greatest Hits (Columbia PC 33050)	August 1974
Borboletta (Columbia PC 33135)	October 1974
Lotus (Columbia 66325)	May 1974
Amigos (Columbia PC 33576)	March 1976
Festivál (Columbia PC 34423)	February 1977
Moonflower (Columbia C2 24914)	September 1977
Inner Secrets (Columbia FC 356000)	October 1978
Marathon (Columbia FC 36154)	September 1979
Zebop! (Columbia FC 37158)	March 1981
Shangó (Columbia FC 31822)	August 1982
Beyond Appearances (Columbia FC 39527)	February 1985
Freedom (Columbia FC 40272)	February 1987
Viva Santana! (Columbia C3X 44344)	October 1988 *
Spirits Dancing In The Flesh (Columbia C 46065)	June 1990
Milagro (Polygram 314 513 192-2)	June 1992
Sacred Fire (Polygram 314 521 082-2)	October 1993
Dance Of The Rainbow Serpent (Columbia C3K 64605)	August 1995 *
Live At The Fillmore '68 (Columbia 485106 2)	March 1997 *
Supernatural (Arista ARI19080)	June 1999

* Contain previously unreleased material

CARLOS SANTANA SOLO

Carlos Santana and Buddy Miles! Live! (Columbia KC 31308)	August 1972
Love Devotion and Surrender (with John McLaughlin)(Columbia KC 32034)	June 1973
Illuminations (with Alice Coltrane)(Columbia PC 32900)	September 1974

Oneness (Columbia JC 35686)	March 1979
The Swing Of Delight (Columbia C2 36590)	August 1980
Havana Moon (Columbia FC 38642)	April 1983
Blues For Salvador (Columbia FC 40875)	October 1987
Brothers (Guts And Grace/Island 314 523 677-2)	September 1994

VARIOUS ARTISTS

Woodstock (Cotillion SD-3-500)	July 1970
Last Days Of The Fillmore (Fillmore Z3X 31390)	June 1972
California Jam II (Columbia 35389)	July 1978

FILM / VIDEO APPEARANCES

Woodstock	1970
Soul To Soul	1971
Last Days Of The Fillmore	1972
La Bamba	1987
Carlos Santana original score	
Viva Santana!	1988
Sesion Latina	1989 *
Tramaine Hawkins Live (Carlos Santana only)	1990
Sacred Fire	1993
Influences	1995
From Afro-Cuban To Rock	1996
Sworn To The Drum *(Carlos Santana and Armando Peraza only)*	1996

* Contains previously unreleased material

APPENDIX II

CARLOS SANTANA GUEST APPEARANCES

The Live Adventures of Mike Bloomfield and Al Kooper (Columbia 66216) 1969 – "Sonny Boy Williamson"

Bark – Jefferson Airplane (GRUNT FTR-1001) 1971 – "Pretty As You Feel"

Papa John Creach – Papa John Creach (GRUNT FTR-1003) 1971 – "Papa John's Down Home Blues" (Doug Rauch appears; Gregg Rolie plays on another track on the LP)

Luis Gasca (For Those Who Chant) – Luis Gasca (BLUE THUMB BTS37) 1971 – "Street Dude", "Spanish Gypsy", "Little Mama" (Neal Schon, Gregg Rolie, Richard Kermode, Mike Shrieve, Victor Pantoja, Mike Carabello, Coke Escovedo, Rico Reyes, Chepito Areas and Hadley Caliman also appear)

Stories To Tell – Flora Purim (MILESTONE M-9058) 1974 – "Silver Sword"

Garden of Love Light – Narada Michael Walden (ATLANTIC K50329) 1977 – "First Love" (Available on 1996 CD *Ecstasy's Dance – The Best Of Narada Michael Walden* (Rhino 8122-72566-2))

Eternity – Alice Coltrane (WARNER BROTHERS BS 2916) 1976 – "Los Caballos", "Morning Worship" (Santana guests on percussion; Armando Peraza also appears.)

Electric Guitarist – John McLaughlin (Columbia 32684) 1978 – "Friendship" (Armando Peraza and Tom Coster also appear)

Tropico – Gato Barbieri (A&M AMLH 64710) 1978 – "Latin Lady" (Armando Peraza and Chepito Areas also appear)

Giants – Giants (MCA MCF3058) 1978 – "Fried Neckbones And Some Home Fries" (This album is a mix of *Santana III* outtakes and a 1972 Michael Carabello solo album *Attitude*)

Awakening – Narada Michael Walden (ATLANTIC SD 19222) 1979 – "The Awakening" (Available on 1996 CD *Ecstasy's Dance – The Best Of Narada Michael Walden* (Rhino 8122-72566-2))

Monster – Herbie Hancock (Columbia 84237) 1980 – "Saturday Nite" (Greg Walker also appears)

Middle Man – Boz Scaggs (Columbia 86094) 1980 – "You Can Have Me Anytime"

Escenas de Amor – José Feliciano (MOWTOWN 6018LL) 1982 – "Samba Pa Ti"

I'll Never Stop Lovin You – Leon Patillo (MYRRH MYR 1123) 1982 – "I'll Never Stop Lovin You", "Saved" (Gaylord Birch also appears.)

Let Me Know You – Stanley Clarke (EPIC EPC 85846) 1982 – "Straight To The Top", "I Just Wanna Be Your Brother"

Looking Out – McCoy Tyner (Columbia FC 38053) 1982 – "Hannibal", "Señor Carlos"

One Man Mission – Jim Capaldi (WEA 251 350-1) 1984 – "Lost Inside Your Love", "Nobody Loves You" (Snowy White plays lead guitar on "Nobody Loves You" to Carlos' rhythm. Orestes Vilató appears on LP.)

Real Live – Bob Dylan (Columbia 26334) 1984 – "Tombstone Blues"

Who's Zoomin Who? – Aretha Franklin (ARISTA 207 202-620) 1985 – "Push" (Armando Peraza, Raul Rekow and Orestes Vilató also appear on the LP)

Gregg Rolie – Gregg Rolie (Columbia 26636) 1985 – "Marianne" (David Margen also appears; LP features Alan Pasqua, Neal Schon and co-composition with Michael Carabello)

This Is This – Weather Report (Columbia 57052) 1986 – "This Is This", "The Man With The Copper Fingers" (An extended 12" mix of "This Is This" was released as a promotional item)

Dance To The Beat of My Drum – Babatunde Olatunji (BLUE HERON BLU 906-1 D) 1986 – "The Beat Of My Drum", "Loyin Loyin", "Ife L'Oju L'Aiye", "Akiwowo", "Se Eni A Fe L'Amo-Kere Kere", "Ilere, Ilere, Ilere" ("Ilere, Ilere, Ilere" only appears on original 1986 CD issue. Set was comprehensively remixed and released in 1989 as *Drums of Passion – The Beat* on Rykodisk (RCD 10107))

La Bamba (Carlos Santana original score) – Various Artists (Columbia Pictures CVT 11285) 1987 – "I Got A Gal Named Sue (That's My Little Suzi)" (Film only; Los Lobos with Santana on guitar)

Gringo – Gregg Rolie (Columbia BFC 40789) 1987 – "Too Late, Too Late", "Fire At Night" (Neal Schon also appears; "Fire At Night" features Santana -Schon guitar duet)

Uptown – Neville Brothers (EMI FA 3255) 1987 – "Forever...For Tonight"

Behind The Sun – Clyde Criner (NOVUS PL83029) 1988 – "Black Manhattan", "Kinesis", "Behind The Sun" (Rodney Holmes also appears)

Real Life Story – Terri Lynne Carrington (VERVE FORECAST 837 697-1) 1989 – "Human Revolution" (Keith Jones and Patrice Rushen also appear)

Old Friends New Friends – Ndugu (MCA MCAD-6302) 1989 – "Ooh Yah Yeh", "Trying Again" (Alphonso Johnson also appears)

The Healer – John Lee Hooker (SILVERTONE ORE LP 508) 1989 – "The Healer" (Entire Santana Band appear)

Save The Children – Bobby Womack (SOLAR SOLLP 3648) 1989 – "Too Close For Comfort", "Tough Job"

Touma – Mory Kante (BARCLAY 843 702.1) 1990 – "Soumba", "Gaden" (Santana's part on "Gaden" did not appear on standard LP release; only released on a promotional item)

Live – Tramaine Hawkins (SPARROW SPD1246) 1990 – "Lift Me Up", "Who Is He" (On video too; Santana's full performance on "Who Is He" only heard on video version)

Alex Acuna and The Unknowns – Alex Acuna and The Unknowns (MAXUS MAXCD 1029) 1990 – "Psalms"

Amen – Salif Keita (MANGO MLPS 1073) 1991 – "Yele N Na", "Nyanafin", "N B'i Fe"

Mr. Lucky – John Lee Hooker (SILVERTONE ORE LP 519) 1991 – "Stripped Me Naked" (Entire Santana Band appear)

Solo Para Ti – Ottmar Liebert + Luna Negra (EPIC 469198 2) 1992 – "Reaching Out To You (Todos Bajo La Misma Luna)", "Samba Pa Ti (Thru Every Step In Life U Find Freedom From Within)"

Mystic Jazz – Paolo Rustichelli (POLYDOR 513 415-2) 1992 – "Full Moon" (CD re-released entitled *Capri* in the same year. "Full Moon" recorded at sessions for *Spirits Dancing In The Flesh* but is a different mix)

Travelers & Thieves/On Tour Forever – Blues Traveler (A&M 75021 5400 2) 1992 – "Mountain Cry" (*Travelers and Thieves* was released in limited quantities with a second promo only CD called *On Tour Forever* which features "Mountain Cry")

Paths To Greatness – Caribbean Allstars (ROKK STEADY 50168 00201) 1992 – "Sette Masagna", "Caught In The Middle", "Ras Clatt Riddm"

Chill Out – John Lee Hooker (VIRGIN VPBLP 22) 1995 – "Chill Out" (Entire Santana Band appear; from same session as "Stripped Me Naked")

Everybody's Getting Some – Junior Wells (TELARC CD 83360) 1995 – "Get Down"

In From The Storm – Various Artists (RCA VICTOR 09026-68233-2) 1995 – "Spanish Castle Magic" (Promo only mix minus orchestra released on JH001)

Sworn To The Drum – A Tribute To Francisco Aguabella 1995 (FLOWER FILMS FF1162) 1995 – "A La Escuela" (On film only – Armando Peraza also appears)

Crossroads II – Eric Clapton (POLYDOR 529 305-2) 1996 – "Eyesight To The Blind/Why Does Love Got To Be So Sad" (Live recording from 1975 US tour; Armando Peraza and Ndugu also appear)

Fifa – Angélique Kidjo (MANGO CIDM 1112 524 203-2) 1996 – "Naima"

Mystic Man – Paolo (GUTS AND GRACE 162-531 065-2) 1996 – "Get On", "Rastafario", "Vers Le Soleil"

Cuando Tú No Estás – El Tri (WEA Mexico 185532) 1997 – "Virgen Morena"

The Miseducation Of Lauryn Hill – Lauryn Hill (Columbia 489843 1) 1998 – "To Zion"

APPENDIX III

SANTANA PLAYERS, OFF-SHOOTS AND VISITORS

Note: This section gives brief biographical and career details of the musicians who have played in Santana and those who have been involved on albums and tours as guests. Where a player was a part of a special project, but has a well-documented career of their own, no discography is included.

Francisco Aguabella: One of the foremost Afro-Cuban percussionists, Aguabella was born in Matanzas, Cuba, immigrating to the USA in 1952. Early work in the States included sessions with Dizzy Gillespie, Tito Puente, Perez Prado, Peggy Lee and famously with the touring company of Katherine Dunham, eventually settling in Los Angeles. Had a brief spell in Santana in the summer of 1976, subsequently appearing on *The Swing Of Delight* and *Spirits Dancing In The Flesh*. Has recorded and released his own albums and can be heard on three Malo albums (*Dos, Evolution* and *Ascension*). In 1985 Les Blank made a short film celebrating the career of Aguabella, this included footage of a special celebration concert in San Francisco at which Carlos Santana and Armando Peraza appeared. The film is now available on video, *Sworn To The Drum*. Discography: *Dance The Latin Way (Fantasy 1962), Hitting Hard (Epsilon 1977), H2O (Olm 1996), Agua De Cuba (Cubop 1999)*

Jose "Chepito" Areas: Born June 25th 1946, Leon, Nicaragua. Expert timbales and conga drummer, he joined Santana in May 1969 and remained until December 1974. Chepito was largely responsible for introducing the Santana Band to true Latin music and for the Latin sound of *Abraxas*. He recorded a fine solo LP in 1974 before joining Bay Area fusion band Cobra. Returned to Santana briefly in 1976-77 for *Festivál* album and tour and again in 1988 when he reappeared half way through the *Blues For Salvador* tour. Remained in the band until midway through the 1989 European tour. He is widely recognised as the greatest of all Santana timbales players. Subsequently a member of The Abraxas Pool, his virtuoso playing can be heard on the 1997 recording of the same name. Has recorded with Elvin Bishop, Cold Blood, Boz Scaggs, Herbie Hancock (*Mwandishi*), Gato Barbieri and John Lee Hooker. *Discography: José Chepito Areas (Columbia 1974), Abraxas Pool (Miramar 1997)*

Azteca: Band led by Coke Escovedo which featured many Santana musicians including Neal Schon, Wendy Haas, Rico Reyes, Paul Jackson, Lenny White, Tom Harrell, Mel Martin, Victor Pantoja, Pete Escovedo, Paul Jackson and Tom Rutley. Made two fine albums in the mid 1970s that were a mixture of Afro-Cuban percussion, jazz and rock with a strong emphasis on powerful horn charts. *Discography: Azteca (Columbia 1973), Pyramid Of The Moon (Columbia 1974)*

Richard Baker: Canadian keyboard player who joined Santana in 1980, remaining until 1982. He was introduced to the band by Graham Lear who played with Baker in Gino Vanelli's band, he later worked with Alex Ligertwood and composed film music.

Gaylord Birch: Drummer who was well known for his work with Graham Central Station and The Pointer Sisters, before playing on the *Festivál* album. He briefly toured with Santana in the spring of 1991 but died in 1997.

Willie Bobo: New York percussionist and band leader (born February 28th 1934), who was an early exponent of Latin-R&B fusion, including the songs "Evil Ways" and "Fried Neckbones" that Santana were to record. Worked only once with Santana at the 1971 *Soul To Soul* concert in Ghana, Africa; continued a solo career prior to his death in 1983.

Tommie Bradford: A previously unknown San Francisco drummer who played live dates with Santana in the early summer of 1994, including the World Cup soccer match appearance at Stanford University. Had worked live with the Wynans and later recorded with Neal Schon.

Jules Broussard: San Francisco based reeds player, featured on *Welcome, Illuminations* and *Borboletta*. Knew Tom Coster from mid 1960s jazz clubs in the Bay Area, also played with Ray Charles, Van Morrison and Dr. Hook. Jules has made three albums under his own name, the last two with help of Tom Coster. *Discography: Jules Broussard (Fleur 1980), Jules Broussard (Headfirst 1989), Love Notes (private release 1996)*

David Brown: Born Houston, Texas, 15th February, 1947. Original Santana bass player from 1967, he played and recorded with the band continuously until 1971. David Brown had played keyboards in local bands before taking up the bass and joining the Santana Blues Band during a jam at Grant Avenue, he had been taught music by his uncle. His approach to the bass was significantly different from the standard 12-bar blues approach of most bass players of the period. His bass line on "Soul Sacrifice" is amongst the most famous in modern music. After the break-up of the "original" Santana Band in 1971, he re-emerged to record on *Borboletta* and *Amigos*, remaining in the touring band until spring 1976. Also recorded with Randall Bramlett, Charlie Daniels, Boz Scaggs and Mistress. Appeared on-stage with Santana in 1996 and still plays club dates in the Bay Area.

Hadley Caliman: Born Idaho 1932. Reeds player who transformed the sound of Santana with his opening sax on *Caravanserai*; also appeared on *Carlos Santana and Buddy Miles ! Live !* Recorded with Malo, Mongo Santamaria and Phoebe Snow plus a series of fine solo jazz dates for the Mainstream label. Continued to work with Bobby Hutcherson and Freddie Hubbard and can be heard on the Leon Thomas/Freddie Hubbard 1980 LP *A Piece Of Cake*. *Discography: Hadley Caliman (Mainstream 1970), Iapetus (Mainstream 1972), Projecting (Catalyst 1975)*

Michael Carabello: Born California 18th November, 1947 of Puerto Rican descent, he was a street conga drummer who knew Carlos Santana from art class. Became an original member of the Santana Blues Band but was fired when Santana went into hospital with TB. After manslaughter charge against Marcus Malone, rejoined Santana in January 1969 and was instrumental in bringing Chepito Areas to the group. Occupying the front of the stage with Areas, Michael Carabello was a key performer in the 1969 Santana Band, his simple style emphasised pure rhythm over flashy content. Left Santana in 1971 after major rift with Carlos Santana but overdubbed a part on *Carlos Santana and Buddy Miles ! Live !* After Santana he started work on a solo album *Attitude* which didn't appear until 1978 under the title *Giants*, an LP which also included *Santana III* outtakes. Carabello played with Santana at the 20th anniversary show in 1986 and at the Rock'n'Roll Hall Of Fame in 1998. His work with Neal Schon in the early 1990s was the spark for the formation of The Abraxas Pool. He played on Gregg Rolie's 1998 *Rough Tracks* CD and in early summer 1999 he emerged in the Bay Area with a new band, Primitive Medicine. *Discography: Giants (MCA 1978), Abraxas Pool (Miramar 1997)*

Ndugu Leon Chancler: Drummer, producer and arranger who had worked with Miles Davis, Weather Report and George Duke before joining Santana in 1974. Worked closely with Tom Coster on *Amigos* and introduced new faces to the group, Greg Walker and Byron Miller. Remained in the band until summer 1976. He recorded with his own band Ndugu and The Chocolate Jam Co and reappeared for the *Blues For Salvador* and Santana-Shorter tours of 1988 and recorded on *The Healer*. Later, he formed The Meeting with Alphonso Johnson and Patrice Rushen. *Discography: Ndugu and The Chocolate Jam Co: Do I Make You Feel Better (Columbia 1980), Spread Of The Future (Epic 1980) Ndugu: Old Friends, New Friends (MCA 1989)*

Stanley Clarke: Jazz bass player who appeared on *Borboletta* as his stint with Return To Forever was nearing its conclusion and a successful solo career beckoned. Santana played on his *Let Me Know You* album. Later in 1995 he participated in the *In From The Storm* session with Carlos and Tony Williams.

Alice Coltrane: Jazz pianist, she is the widow of John Coltrane. Alice Coltrane was a major influence on Carlos Santana in the 1972-1976 period; they collaborated live in 1974 before recording together on the impressive *Illuminations*, Santana later made an unnamed appearance on her *Eternity* LP. Her music has a heavy spiritual sense which permeates Santana's music of the period and her recording *Lord Of Lords* was a strong force on *Welcome* and *Oneness*, particularly her abstract orchestrations and recording of the Afro-American spiritual "Going Home".

Vorriece Cooper: A previously unknown rap singer who joined Santana briefly in 1993 for South American tour and later US tour, he appears on *Sacred Fire*.

Tom Coster: Jazz pianist born August 21, 1941 in Detroit, Michigan. He was gigging with Gabor Szabo when spotted by Carlos Santana in 1972. Formed a remarkable partnership with the guitarist and co-wrote classic "Europa". Coster left the group in 1978 to pursue a solo career but returned for tours in 1983 and 1986 and is heard on *Freedom*. Continued a fine solo career as well as membership of Vital Information, the band led by Journey drummer Stevie Smith which featured many Coster compositions. Most of his solo albums are in a jazz-rock vein and have featured Peraza, Vilató, Johnson, Rekow and Perazzo. *Cause And Effect* and *Where We Come From* find Coster reviving his trademark Hammond Organ and Fender Rhodes sound circa 1973. *Discography: T.C. (Fantasy 1981), Ivory Expedition (Fantasy 1983), Did Ya Miss Me? (JVC 1989), From Me To You (JVC 1990), Gotcha (JVC 1992), Let's Set The Record Straight (JVC 1993), The Forbidden Zone (JVC 1994), From The Street (JVC 1996), The Best Of Tom Coster (JVC 1999), Tom Coster, Larry Coryell and Steve Smith: Cause And Effect (Tone Center 1998) Vital Information: Fiafiaga (Columbia 1988), Vitalive (Verabra 1990), Ray Of Hope (Intuition 1996), Where We Come From (Intuition 1998)*

Sterling Crew: Born San Francisco July 15th, 1958, he played keyboards on the Santana tour of 1985 and appeared on *Freedom* and *Blues For Salvador*. A studio musician, his work includes record dates with the Tubes, David Foster, Earl Slick and Pablo Cruise.

Steve De La Rosa: Bass player who replaced Gus Rodrigues in the Santana Blues Band in 1967.

Devadip Orchestra: This band was Carlos Santana's vehicle for playing his spiritually focused jazz fusion charts of the late 1970s. It was a sub-set of the Santana Band and was the "support act" on the band's 1978 European Tour, playing music from *Oneness* and *The*

Swing Of Delight. It comprised Carlos, Graham Lear, Chris Rhyne, David Margen and Russell Tubbs.

Myron Dove: Bass player who joined Santana in 1992 and remained until 1996. Prior to Santana he played with Clarence Gatemouth Brown, Narada Michael Walden and Kenny Loggins. He was part of Spangalang with Tony Lindsay.

Coke Escovedo: Percussionist, born California in 1941, Coke was a professional musician at an early age in The Escovedo Brothers with his brother Pete. He played percussion with Cal Tjader before joining Santana as a stand-in for Chepito Areas in 1971. Although a "hired hand" Coke had a very strong influence on the group and *Santana III*. After Santana he played an important role on Malo's first album and formed his own group Azteca, a large Latin-Jazz unit that featured Pete Escovedo *(see Azteca).* After Azteca split in 1974, he started a short-lived solo career before almost returning to Santana in 1981. Coke Escovedo died on 13 July 1986. *Discography: Azteca (Columbia 1973), Pyramid Of The Moon (Columbia 1974) Coke Escovedo: Coke (Mercury 1975), Comin' At Ya (Mercury 1976), Disco Fantasy (Mercury 1976)*

Pete Escovedo: Born in Pittsburgh, California on July 13, 1935. Timbalero and band-leader, older brother of Coke Escovedo, he was a professional musician by 1955, opening for Count Basie. Played with Coke as the Escovedo Brothers before sessions with Cal Tjader and brief live stint with Santana in 1971. Pete was a key member of Azteca before joining Santana for just over 18 months in 1977. Continued to an impressive solo career including works with his daughter Sheila E. *Discography: Azteca (Columbia 1973), Pyramid Of The Moon (Columbia 1974) Pete and Sheila Escovedo: Solo Two (Fantasy 1977), Happy Together (Fantasy 1978) Pete Escovedo: The Island (EsGo 1983), Yesterday's Dreams, Tomorrow's Memories (Crossover 1987), Mister E (Crossover 1988), Flying South (Picante 1996), E Street (Concord 1997)*

Fabulous Thunderbirds: Texan blues group which included Jimmie Vaughan (brother of Stevie Ray) and Kim Wilson. Worked closely with Carlos Santana on his *Havana Moon* album, including a live television appearance and a 1987 session in honour of B.B. King.

Tom Frazier: Friend of Gregg Rolie who saw Carlos Santana at a 1966 Fillmore jam. Frazier was instrumental in bringing Rolie and Santana together and went on to play rhythm guitar in the Santana Blues Band before being "fired" in 1967. Little is known of him after this.

Friends Again: A four-piece band comprising Gregg Rolie, Carlos Santana, David Margen and drummer Steve Smith which recorded some demos in 1982 just before the *Shangó* album. A result of the renewed contact between Santana and Rolie, the unit never really got off the ground.

Luis Gasca: Born Houston 3rd March 1940. Trumpeter and flugelhorn player who moved to the San Francisco area after stints with Perez Prado, Stan Kenton, Lionel Hampton, Mongo Santamaria and Janis Joplin. Having recorded his own album *Little Giant* in 1968, he played on *Santana III* and invited nearly all the current 1971 Santana Band to record on his next album which is known as *For Those Who Chant*, an important Latin Jazz album and one that was a strong influence on Carlos Santana and Michael Shrieve. Luis later played on *Carlos Santana and Buddy Miles ! Live !* He became a member of Malo, playing memorably on their first album. He remained in touch with Santana appearing with the group at a 1991 Los Angeles date, but was killed in Hawaii in February 1997.

Alberto Gianquinto: Pianist who worked with Santana on their *Santana* and *Abraxas* albums. He also played live dates with the band. Gianquinto was a strong influence on the group, encouraging them to reduce the length of the solos and to concentrate on firmer arrangements.

Wendy Haas: Singer/pianist who was Michael Shrieve's wife at the time of *Caravanserai* and *Welcome* both of which she played on. Shortly before this she played in Loading Zone with Doug Rauch and Tom Coster; after Santana she joined Azteca, is heard on the *Giants* album, as well as appearing on records by Lee Oskar and Melissa Manchester.

Herbie Hancock: Jazz pianist-composer who has had a remarkable solo career as well as playing an equally legendary role in Miles Davis' 1960s group. Hancock has recorded many classic albums (*Maiden Voyage, Speak Like A Child, Head Hunters etc*) which have shaped the course of jazz. First hooked up with Carlos Santana in 1979 when he invited the guitarist to play on his *Monster* recording, this led to the great *Swing Of Delight* collaboration and live dates throughout 1980 and 1981, including one particularly memorable Tokyo session. Appeared at Santana's 1996 NARAS concert in Los Angeles.

Danny Haro: Friend of Carlos Santana from his earliest days in San Francisco, he was the first drummer that Santana worked with. Little is known of him after he left the Santana Blues Band in 1967.

Rod Harper: Drummer who replaced Danny Haro in the Santana Blues Band in 1967. Little is known of Harper before this or after he was replaced by Bob Livingston.

Tom Harrell: Born Urbana, Illinois in 1946, trumpeter and arranger responsible for the outstanding "Every Step Of The Way" horn arrangement. He has a strong jazz pedigree, working with Stan Kenton, Bill Evans, Lee Konitz and Horace Silver as well as pursuing his own solo career. Harrell also appeared on both Azteca albums.

Carlos Hernandez: Bay Area guitar player who is Carlos Santana's nephew. Recorded on the *Brothers* CD and occasionally appears live with Santana. He leads his own band Chemical.

Horacio "El Negro" Hernandez: Cuban drummer who played in Santana for one year only, 1997. A very well respected master performer who was considered to have revolutionised the use of drums and percussion, El Negro is heard on one track on *Supernatural*.

Rodney Holmes: Drummer who was a Santana player in 1993-94 and later in 1998-99. Plays on *Supernatural*. He is also known for his work with Special EFX and Wayne Shorter and is a member of the Hermanators.

Booker T. Jones: R&B organ legend for his Booker T. and The MGs band, he was an early influence on Carlos Santana in his Tijuana years. Eventually, Santana enlisted Jones to work on his *Havana Moon* LP which looked over his formative musical years. Jones added the classic vocal to the title song and appeared live with Santana in a TV special to promote the LP.

Keith Jones: Fluid Jamaican bass player who toured with Santana in 1983 and 1989, appearing on *Spirits Dancing In The Flesh*. A widely used session musician he has worked with Airto Moreira and Jean Luc Ponty. Keith also appeared on the *R.O.A.R.* album.

Alphonso Johnson: Born February 2nd 1951, a well known bass player when he joined Santana in 1984 for five years. A solo recording artist he had also played in Weather Report and is considered to be one of the great bass players of the present era with a strong melodic style.

Billy Johnson: Drummer who originated from Philadelphia and played live with Santana in 1991 and then 1994 to 1996. Recorded on *Milagro, Brothers* and is heard on one track on *Supernatural*. His main work prior to this was with Frankie Beverley & Maze as well as George Howard and Dianne Reeves.

Ernie Johnson: Bay Area based blues singer who overdubbed a vocal for Santana on "Daughter Of The Night" as it appeared on *Viva Santana!*.

Richard Kermode: Pianist who was a part of Santana in 1972 and 1973 making a significant contribution to *Lotus* and *Welcome*, including his classic composition "Yours Is The Light". His work with Janis Joplin, Luis Gasca and Malo was well known to Carlos Santana who was particularly impressed with Kermode's ability to play authentic Latin piano. He died in 1996.

Saunders King: Born Staple, Louisiana March 13th 1909. Carlos Santana's father-in-law was one of the earliest blues stars. An accomplished singer and guitarist he worked with Billie Holiday as well as having his own solo success with songs like "S. K Blues" and "Empty Bedroom Blues". He has been a strong influence on Santana who wrote a cameo for King on his *Oneness* album, "Sliver Dreams, Golden Smiles". Saunders King appeared live with Santana at a Tokyo concert in 1983.

Graham Lear: English born drummer (July 24th 1949) who moved to Canada as a child. Played with Gino Vanelli before joining Santana in 1976 where he remained until 1987 (missed 1984 tour). An attempt to bring him back to Santana in 1991 didn't bear fruit. Now living in Portland, Oregon he plays with Rev. Gary Small and the Deacons and has backed Paul Anka.

James Mingo Lewis: Conga drummer who joined Santana in autumn 1971 after a chaotic New York gig, Lewis remained until end of 1972 tour but recorded on *Caravanserai*. After Santana he was an in-demand session musician playing with Return To Forever, Billy Joel, Buddy Miles, and Al Di Meola. Released his own solo album in 1976, it's a heavy Latin-jazz fusion LP. *Discography: Flight Never Ending (Columbia 1976)*

Alex Ligertwood: Singer/guitarist born in Glasgow, Scotland (December 18th 1946), he moved to US in 1970s after work with Jeff Beck. Alex played with Brian Auger & the Oblivion Express and David Sancious before joining Santana in 1979 for *Marathon*. Remained on and off until end 1994. Released his own CD in 1997 and regularly appears in and around Los Angeles. *Discography: R.O.A.R: R.O.A.R (Tabu 1985), Metro (Kore 1997)*

Tony Lindsay: Singer originally from New York, Lindsay's first experience of being on the road was when he joined Santana in 1991. He sang on *Milagro, Supernatural* and toured constantly from 1995 to 1999. Tony was part of Spangalang and recorded his own private CD in 1996. *Discography: Different Moods (private release 1996)*

Bob "Doc" Livingston: Bay Area drummer found by Stan Marcum as replacement for Rod Harper in summer 1967, who was a part of Santana when they were signed and first recorded by Columbia Records. Livingston was sacked in February 1969 after the abortive recording session in Los Angeles with David Rubinson since when he has disappeared completely from the music scene. His drumming is heard on *Live At The Fillmore '68* Santana release.

John McLaughlin: Virtuoso English jazz guitarist and composer. He had already played European free-jazz when he moved to New York to work with Miles Davis at the birth of jazz fusion. Formed his own Mahavishnu Orchestra in 1972 before branching out with his Shakti group in which he played Indian music. As a fellow disciple of Sri Chinmoy he played with Carlos Santana at many meditation concerts before they recorded *Love, Devotion, Surrender* and toured together in 1973. McLaughlin's then wife, Mahalakshami (Eve), also occasionally played on these sessions. McLaughlin later appeared on *Welcome* whilst Santana played on his *Electric Guitarist*. The two joined each other on stage at concerts in 1980 (Berkeley Jazz Festival), 1983 (Paris, France), 1985 (Mahavishnu concert, San Francisco) and most recently at the Montreux Jazz Festival in 1993.

Malo: Latin-rock band formed in 1971 by Arcelio Garcia, Jorge Santana and Pablo Tellez, originally called the Malibus. With these three leaders Malo recorded four albums *Malo, Dos, Ascension* and *Evolution* (the last minus Garcia), each giving a different slant to a mix of Afro-Cuban percussion, Latin-rock, jazz horns and pop. Many musicians connected with Santana played in Malo including Luis Gasca, Victor Pantoja, Richard Kermode, Raul Rekow, Hadley Caliman, Francisco Aguabella and Coke Escovedo. The first four albums were produced by David Rubinson, *Dos* is normally felt to be the best of them. In the 1980s and 1990s Arcelio Garcia maintained Malo as a performing unit making irregular recordings of lesser quality; Jorge Santana and Pablo Tellez would occasionally appear live. *Discography: Malo (Warner Brothers 1972), Dos (WB 1972), Ascension (WB 1973), Evolution (WB 1974), Malo 5 (Traq 1981), Coast To Coast (Blue Heron 1987), The Best Of Malo (GRP Crescendo 1991), Señorita (GRP Crescendo 1995)*

Marcus Malone: First conga drummer in Santana to bring in true Afro-Cuban influence and was responsible for introducing song "Jingo" to the group in summer 1967. Malone was found at Aquatic Park conga sessions, remaining in the band until 1969 when he was convicted for manslaughter. Little heard of since except as a fashion designer for rock stage-wear !

David Margen: Berkeley-born bass player who joined Santana as a teenager in 1977 replacing Pablo Tellez. Remained until 1982, since when he has been in demand as a session player including work with Gregg Rolie.

Buddy Miles: Born Omaha, Nebraska 1947. Singer-guitarist-drummer best known for his part in Jimi Hendrix's *Band Of Gypsies* which included his signature song "Them Changes". Live session with Carlos Santana in 1971 led to the poor *Carlos Santana and Buddy Miles ! Live !* album after which Miles continued to pursue his own solo career. Reappeared in Santana in 1986 after a chance encounter with Carlos at a Bay Area recording studio, remaining in Santana until 1987 after participating on *Freedom* album and tour. Continues to record. *Discography: Expressway To Your Skull (Mercury 1968), Electric Church (Mercury 1969), Them Changes (Mercury 1970), A Message To The People (Mercury 1970), Buddy Miles Live (Mercury 1971), Carlos Santana and Buddy Miles ! Live ! (Columbia 1972), Chapter VII (Columbia 1973), Booger Bear (Columbia 1974), All The Faces Of Buddy Miles (Columbia 1974), More Miles Per Gallon (Casablanca 1975), Bicentennial Gathering Of The Tribes (Casablanca 1976), Roadrunner (Ttown 1977), Sneak Attack (Atlantic 1981), Hell And Back (Black Arc 1994), Miles Away From Home (EFA 1997), The Best Of Buddy Miles (Mercury Chronicles 1997)*

Byron Miller: Bass player for one American tour in summer 1976. Brought into group after David Brown's final exit as colleague of Ndugu's from work with George Duke. He worked closely with Ndugu after Santana on albums by Flora Purim and others.

Airto Moreira: Brazilian percussionist who worked on Santana's *Borboletta* LP. Airto has brought the world of indigenous Brazilian percussion to a mass audience with an unparalleled spirit and virtuosity. Latterly, his song "Tombo In 7/4" from the *Fingers* album has found new popularity as a dance club favourite. He continues to entrance audiences around the globe and usually sits in with Santana when the group plays in his home town of Santa Barbara.

Victor Pantoja: New York-born conguero who played a major part in the 1960s and 1970s Bay Area jazz and fusion music scene, playing and touring with Chico Hamilton, Gabor Szabo, Cal Tjader, Willie Bobo, Malo, Azteca and Santana. His mid-Sixties work with Chico Hamilton on *El Chico* (including "Conquistadores") may have been the first time that Carlos Santana heard congas with electric guitars; Pantoja also played on the original Gabor Szabo recording of "Gypsy Queen". His involvement with Santana was limited to a few dates in the autumn of 1971 and a place on *Carlos Santana and Buddy Miles! Live!* Pantoja was also heavily featured on the 1971 Luis Gasca recording on which most of the Santana Band appeared. With Coke Escovedo, he was the central percussionist on Malo's first album and he played on both Azteca albums.

Alan Pasqua: Jazz pianist (had played with Tony Williams) and Santana member from 1979 through to spring 1980, recording *Marathon* and early *Zebop!* sessions. A fine musician he released two solo releases in the 1990s. *Discography: Milagro (Postcards 1994), Dedications (Postcards 1996)*

Leon Patillo: Singer-pianist who joined Santana in 1974 and remained until 1975, returning for the *Festivál* album. He added the Stevie Wonder style electric piano to *Borboletta* and his own Larry Graham inflected vocals. Leon worked with his band Creation before Santana and has continued a solo career making albums solely for the Christian market ever since. Carlos Santana played on Leon's 1982 album *I'll Never Stop Loving You* which included a fine version of "The River". Leon also appeared on Funkadelic's *Standing On The Verge Of Getting It On* LP. *Discography: Creation: Creation (ATCO 1974) Leon Patillo: Dance Children Dance (Myrrh 1979), Don't Give In (Myrrh 1981), I'll Never Stop Loving You (Myrrh 1982), Live Experience (Myrrh 1983), The Sky's The Limit (Myrrh 1984), Love Around The World (Myrrh 1985), A Funny Thing Happened On My Way To Hell (Word 1986), Brand New (Sparrow 1987), Cornerstone (Word 1987), On The Way Up (Ocean 1989), Church Is On The Move (Positive Pop 1993), Soully For Him (Campus 1994), The Classics (Positive Pop 1996), I Can (Positive Pop 1999), Breathe On Me (Positive Pop 1999)*

Armando Peraza: Born Havana, Cuba May 30th 1924, Peraza is one of the most important Latin musicians of the century who, with Tito Puente and Mongo Santamaria, was central to the music's popularisation. A true master of the bongo and conga, Peraza recorded with Machito and Charlie Parker at his first date on arrival in New York from Cuba in 1947 (*Afro-Cuban Jazz Suite*) and was fundamental to introducing Afro-Cuban rhythms to jazz. This centred on the 1950s California-led boom in Latin music, fuelled in no small measure by Peraza's work with pianist George Shearing and vibist Cal Tjader. Peraza was a teacher to both of these figures and contributed many compositions. His links with Tjader resulted in his recording a 1968 solo album on Tjader's Skye label (*Wild Thing*), but he was also involved in an early fusion of rock and Afro-Cuban music on Harvey Mandel's *Cristo Redentor* LP. Peraza was close to Mongo Santamaria and recorded on Santamaria's important album *Mongo* in 1959 and later on *Mongo's Way* and

Mongo At Montreux. He joined Santana in 1972, remaining on and off until 1990, during which time he was one of the most important musicians in the group. He had little opportunity to contribute his songs to Santana, but two of his classic works were recorded, "Gitano" and "Mandela". Other sessions have included Slim Gaillard, George Duke, Victor Feldman, Buddy Collette & Charles Kynard, Randy Weston, Wes Montgomery, New Riders of the Purple Sage, Tom Fogerty, Rick James, Machete Ensemble, Tom Coster and Linda Rondstadt. He was a part of the R.O.A.R. unit in 1985 and now lives in semi-retirement in San Mateo but still appears on record and live dates. Armando Peraza is a true master musician. *Discography: Wild Thing (Skye 1968) R.O.A.R: R.O.A.R (Tabu 1985) with George Shearing: Latin Lace (Capitol 1958), Latin Escapade (Capitol 1958), Latin Affair (Capitol 1959), Mood Latino (Capitol 1961), Love Walked In (Jazzland 1962 – George Shearing and The Montgomery Brothers) with Cal Tjader: Ritmo Caliente (Fantasy 1954), Mas Ritmo Caliente (Fantasy 1957), In A Latin Bag (Verve 1961), Soul Sauce (Verve 1964)*

Karl Perazzo: Local San Francisco percussionist who joined Santana in 1991 and has remained ever since. Prior to Santana he played with Cal Tjader, Malo, Dizzy Gillespie, Sheila E. and Prince. Perazzo is respected by senior musicians like Armando Peraza; his technique is virtuoso and he is the consummate timbalero showman. His partnership with Raul Rekow has formed one of the great Santana percussion teams and the two released a percussion video in 1996 (*From Afro-Cuban To Rock* which included Santana footage) and he has recently released an interesting CD of folkloric duets with Rekow, including some of the Afro-Cuban showcases they have used with Santana in the 1990s. Perazzo also leads his own Bay Area salsa unit Avance. *Discography: Raul Rekow and Karl Perazzo: Just Another Day In The Park (Mona Records 1998) Avance: Adelante (Mona Records 1996), West Coast Latin Groove (Mona Records 1999)*

Flora Purim: Brazilian jazz singer who, along with husband Airto Moreira, was central to the popularisation of Brazilian music in the 1970s mainstream. Recorded on Santana's *Welcome* and *Borboletta* albums and invited Santana to play on her *Stories To Tell*. Flora has recorded many albums of her own and famously with Chick Corea on the first two, great, Return To Forever albums. Until recently she toured with Airto in a unit called Fourth World that brought them a new popularity.

Luther Rabb: Singer with Columbia band Ballin' Jack, before very brief period touring with Santana in the winter of 1976. He had a brief stint in War and released a disco-funk solo album of marginal quality on which he dubbed himself "St. Luther". *Discography: Street Angel (MCA 1979)*

Doug Rauch: Bass player who appeared with the Voices of East Harlem, Loading Zone (with Coster and Haas), Gabor Szabo (with Coster), before joining Santana in 1972, playing on *Caravanserai, Lotus, Love, Devotion, Surrender* and *Welcome*. His funk style was a major influence on the Santana sound of this period. Later he played with Cobra, Billy Cobham, Betty Davis, Buzzy Linhart and Lenny White, his writing can be heard well on Lenny White's *Venusian Summer* album, including some of the funk riffs he brought to the Santana live set in 1972. He died in the late 1970s.

Raul Rekow: Took up the conga drums after seeing Santana Blues Band in 1967 playing in various Bay Area bands like Soul Sacrifice before joining Malo and subsequently Sapo – local competition fuelled these bands. Sapo cut one LP before Rekow joined Santana in the summer of 1976 to record *Festivál*. He remained in the band continuously until 1987 when he joined a project in the Netherlands, Congarilla, that released a solitary limited edition CD *Calling The Gods*. He was the main driving force behind the R.O.A.R project which came about in a lull in Santana activity in 1985. One of the most exciting percussionists in Santana, he returned to the group in autumn 1990 replacing Armando Peraza and has remained with the band since then. His partnership with Peraza and Orestes Vilató from 1980-1987 is one of the greatest of all Latin percussion sections and he has subsequently formed a unique musical relationship with Karl Perazzo which blossomed on the fine 1998 CD of duets. Rekow is a student of Afro-Cuban music and his early explosive style has given way to something more refined over the last few years. *Discography: Malo: Dos (WB 1972) Sapo: Sapo (Bell 1974) R.O.A.R: R.O.A.R (Tabu 1985) Congarilla: Calling The Gods (D&K 1988) Raul Rekow and Karl Perazzo: Just Another Day In The Park (Mona Records 1998)*

Rico Reyes: Bay Area Latin vocalist who played with Santana on *Abraxas*, *Santana III* and *Caravanserai* as well as making occasional live appearances with the band in 1970. After Santana he joined Azteca and Quicksilver Messenger Service before leading his own band San Pacu. Now based in Los Angeles, he is occasionally seen performing in clubs.

Walfredo Reyes: Drummer born in Havana, Cuba his father is legendary Cuban drummer Walfredo Reyes Snr. He joined Santana in 1989 after work with Larry Carlton and Tania Maria, remaining on and off until 1993 when he joined the Traffic reunion tour.

Chris Rhyne: Keyboard player on *Inner Secrets* and *Oneness* who was known to Graham Lear from his Gino Vanelli days. He also recorded and toured with Jean Luc-Ponty and now plays in clubs with unit called Over The Rhyne.

Benny Rietveld: Bass player who worked with Sheila E. along with Karl Perazzo but came to prominence as a part of Miles Davis' 1989 line-up, appearing on Miles' *Live In Paris* video. Benny joined Santana in 1990, remaining until 1992. He reappeared in 1997 and plays on *Supernatural*. He also records with his own band The Outtakes.

R.O.A.R: A Santana off-shoot formed by Raul Rekow during a lull in Santana Band activity in 1985. The group comprised Rekow, Armando Peraza, Orestes Vilató, Alex Ligertwood, Chester Thompson and vocalist Rafael Cornejo. They made one album which included soul, dance, R&B and Latin grooves, showcasing some innovative use of electronic drums. Other ex-Santana players Greg Walker and Keith Jones are also on the disc. *Discography: R.O.A.R: R.O.A.R (Tabu 1985)*

Gus Rodrigues: Friend of Carlos Santana from his earliest days in San Francisco, he was the first bass player that Santana worked with. Little is known of him after he left the Santana Blues Band in 1967.

Doug Rodriguez: Guitarist friend of Doug Rauch from New York who played on *Caravanserai* and *Welcome*. He continued to work with Lenny White, Mandrill and Terry Reid. His funk guitar style and co-writing with Doug Rauch can be heard well on Lenny White's *Venusian Summer* album.

Gregg Rolie: Born Washington 17th June, 1947. Gregg was one of the two central figures in the 1969 Santana Band along with Carlos Santana. They formed a musical partnership in 1967 that lasted until 1972 but which they have rekindled off and on since 1982. Rolie was the main vocalist in Santana from 1966-1971 and his Hammond Organ sound was a major part of the group's definition. He contributed a number of rock flavoured songs but lost interest with jazz direction of *Caravanserai*, leaving the group and music to open a restaurant with his father in Seattle. Eventually he returned to form AOR monsters

Journey with Neal Schon, but left that band in 1981 tired of the constant touring. Rolie worked again with Carlos Santana in 1982 in a casual unit "Friends Again" and contributed to *Shangó* album. He released two solo LPs (also in AOR vein) in 1985 and 1987 both of which feature Santana's guitar and worked with Santana again on *Freedom* and the 1988 *Viva Santana* tour which left him far from satisfied. In the 1990s Rolie again enjoyed chart success with his new group The Storm which included Ross Valory and Steve Smith, again in a rock setting Rolie had cracked *Billboard*. He was instrumental in setting up the Abraxas Pool with Neal Schon in 1984-85 and contributed many Santana style songs and vocals to the CD. Despite press reports of harsh words between Rolie and Santana, they were constantly in touch throughout the 1990s. *Discography: Gregg Rolie (Columbia 1985), Gringo (Columbia 1987), Rough Tracks (1998) Journey: Journey (Columbia 1975), Look Into The Future (Columbia 1976), Next (Columbia 1977), Infinity (Columbia 1978), Evolution (Columbia 1979), Departure (Columbia 1980), Captured (Columbia 1981) The Storm: The Storm (Interscope 1991), Eye Of The Storm (Music For Nations 1996) The Abraxas Pool: The Abraxas Pool (Miramar 1997)*

Patrice Rushen: Jazz pianist, composer-arranger who enjoyed pop cross over success with the single "Forget Me Nots". She was a key player on the 1988 Santana-Shorter tour introducing two compositions "Shh" and "Fireball 2000", the former she recorded with drummer Terri Lynn Carrington. She formed The Meeting with Alphonso Johnson, Ernie Watts and Ndugu Chancler after the tour and continues to be in demand as a performer and arranger.

Tom Rutley: Bass player who knew Michael Shrieve from the College of San Mateo Big Band. Toured with Santana in 1971 as a replacement for David Brown and is featured on *Caravanserai*. Tom also recorded with Azteca, Flip Nuñez, Link Wray and Lorraine Ellison.

Curtis Salgado: Blues harp player and singer, who had worked with Robert Cray and led his own band. Salgado appeared with Santana for one very short tour in the early summer of 1995.

David Sancious: Multi-instrumentalist who was a part of Santana's 1984 stadium band and contributed to *Beyond Appearances*. He was known to singer Alex Ligertwood who had been a member of Sancious' band Tone in the late 1970s.

Jorge Santana: Guitarist and younger brother of Carlos Santana who formed Latin-Rock band Malo with singer Arcelio Garcia and bass player Pablo Tellez in 1971. Recorded four fine albums that originally found Jorge Santana sharing guitar duties with Abel Zarate but after Zarate left Santana's guitar gained prominence. After break up of Malo he made two solo albums on Tomato label before retiring from the music business. His brother encouraged him to join Santana in 1981 but aside from a few dates it didn't happen, Jorge Santana went on to work in music business administration. He started touring with Santana more regularly in 1989-90 culminating in the *Brothers* album. Jorge Santana is seen on the *Sacred Fire* video and toured Europe with the group in 1994. He plays live from time to time with Malo and in 1998 he took up his career again appearing in the Bay Area as a solo artist. *Discography: Jorge Santana (Tomato 1978), It's All About Love (Tomato 1981) Santana Brothers: Brothers (Guts and Grace 1994) Malo: Malo (Warner Brothers 1972), Dos (WB 1972), Ascension (WB 1973), Evolution (WB 1974)*

José Santana: Carlos Santana's father was born 18th January, 1913, in Cuautla in the state of Morelos, Mexico. He was an accomplished violin player who played orchestral as well as traditional music and moulded Carlos to follow in his footsteps as a musician, teaching him the violin. He worked as a Mariachi musician in Tijuana and later San Francisco, the impetus for the Santana family's periods in these cities. José continued to work as a musician throughout his life and appeared on his son's *Havana Moon* LP as well as a beautiful violin cameo on "I'm For Real", a cut from Malo's *Dos* album. José Santana passed away in 1998.

Urmila (Deborah) Santana: Carlos Santana's wife is a trained classical musician who played with the guitarist at Sri Chinmoy meditation concerts in the mid 1970s. She appears on *Oneness*.

Neal Schon: Guitarist born 27th February 1954 who joined Santana in 1971 after sitting-in on some *Abraxas* sessions. Recorded on *Santana III, Carlos Santana and Buddy Miles ! Live !* and *Caravanserai* before his departure in 1972. He formed the Golden Gate Rhythm Section with Rolie joining in June 1973, this became Journey who went on to multi-platinum AOR success. Schon also recorded with Jan Hammer, Bad English, H.A.A.S and Hardline. He released two New Age style CDs in mid to late 1990s and was part of the Abraxas Pool. *Discography: Journey: Journey (Columbia 1975), Look Into The Future (Columbia 1976), Next (Columbia 1977), Infinity (Columbia 1978), Evolution (Columbia 1979), Departure (Columbia 1980), Captured (Columbia 1981), Escape (Columbia 1981), Frontiers (Columbia 1983), Raised On Radio (Columbia 1986) Neal Schon and Jan Hammer: Untold Passion (1981), Here To Stay (1983) Schon, Hagar, Aaronson and Shrieve: Through The Fire (1984) Neal Schon: Beyond The Thunder (1995), Electric World (Higher Octave 1997), Piranha Blues (Shrapnel 1999) The Abraxas Pool: The Abraxas Pool (Miramar 1997)*

Wayne Shorter: Jazz saxophonist who formed the great Santana-Shorter band with Carlos Santana in 1988 for a major tour of the summer European jazz festivals and limited US dates. Shorter also appeared on *The Swing Of Delight* and *Spirits Dancing In The Flesh* and at Santana's 1996 NARAS concert in Los Angeles. Shorter is one of the great figures of jazz, a virtuoso soloist and composer-arranger who has graced many of the great bands of jazz including Miles Davis' legendary 1960s quintet and Art Blakey's Jazz Messengers. He recorded a number of excellent albums for Blue Note in the 1960s (*Juju, Speak No Evil*) before forming Weather Report with Joe Zawinul in 1971, a wonderful band that lasted until 1986 with reducing input from Shorter who always maintained a parallel solo career. This included the classic album *Native Dancer* which showcased the talents of Milton Nascimento and is one of music's great albums. It included Milton's haunting "Ponta De Areia" which has long been a favourite of Carlos Santana's, he has used it for years as the coda to "Europa".

Michael Shrieve: Drummer born San Francisco, July 6th, 1949, Shrieve has maintained a consistent and creative career. He has worked mostly in the field of experimental, new age music with occasional glimpses of a rock style. Mike Shrieve joined Santana early in 1969 and remained until summer 1974; his importance to the group cannot be overstated and he was critical to the band's change of direction in 1972. After Santana he formed Automatic Man and followed this with a collaboration with Steve Winwood and Stomu Yamashta; *Go*. He recorded New Age works with Klaus Schulze and film soundtracks in the late 1980s which also saw him back with Santana for the disappointing *Viva!* tour. He has continued a fine solo career alongside membership of the Abraxas Pool. Always a sensitive, creative drummer, Michael Shrieve has established himself as one of the foremost percussionists of the era leading the field in the use of electronic drums. He is probably resigned to always being remembered for his famous drum solo in the *Woodstock* film. *Discography: Transfer Station Blue (Fortuna 1986), In Suspect Terrain (Relativity 1987), The Leaving Time (RCA 1988), The Big Picture (Fortuna 1989), Stiletto (Novus 1989), Fascination (CPM 1994), Two Doors (CMP 1995) Schon, Hagar, Aaronson and Shrieve: Through The Fire (1984) The Abraxas Pool: The Abraxas Pool (Miramar 1997)*

Chris Solberg: Second guitarist in Santana from 1978 through to 1980, he was a member of Eddie Money's band before joining for *Marathon*. Little heard of after Santana, but he was recently working as guitar technician for Carlos Hernandez.

Pablo Tellez: Bass player who formed Malo in 1971 with Jorge Santana and Arcelio Garcia. He played on the first four Malo albums and joined Santana in 1976 for the *Festivál* album, touring with the band until the spring of 1977. He now lives in San José and occasionally plays live with the current Malo.

Leon Thomas: Jazz vocalist who was well known for his work with Count Basie and Pharoah Sanders before he launched his own solo career in 1969. He developed an extraordinary improvised vocal style which is somewhat akin to yodelling and appeared on the classic Sanders' albums *Karma* (1969) and *Jewels Of Thought* (1970), the former included the classic Thomas-Sanders composition "The Creator Has A Master Plan". He worked with Santana in 1973 before losing his high profile. He re-emerged in the 1990s and toured internationally, a later work with Sanders, *Shukuru*, is worth hearing for Thomas' haunting "Sun Song". Thomas had a unique impact on Santana and has long been a favourite of the guitarist's. In particular his songs "The Creator Has A Master Plan", "One", "Um,Um,Um" and "Malcolm's Gone" have reverberated throughout Santana's career. Leon Thomas passed away in May 1999. *Discography: Spirits Known And Unknown (Flying Dutchman 1969), The Leon Thomas Album (Flying Dutchman 1970), Leon Thomas Live In Berlin (Flying Dutchman 1971), Gold Sunrise On Magic Mountain (Mega 1971), Blues And The Soulful Truth (Flying Dutchman 1972) Facets – The Legend Of Leon Thomas (Flying Dutchman 1973), Full Circle (Flying Dutchman 1973), Thank You Baby (Don King/New Sounds Records 1975 – 7" single), A Piece Of Cake – with Freddie Hubbard (Paloscenico 1980), The Leon Thomas Blues Band – The Leon Thomas Blues Band (Portrait 1988), Leon Thomas Anthology (Soul Brother Records 1998)*

Chester Thompson: Keyboards player born Oklahoma City, March 9 1945 who has been Carlos Santana's main musical partner since 1983 when he joined Santana from Tower Of Power. He left Oklahoma with Rudy Johnson Trio (which was also called The Incorporates) before recording a burning jazz-R&B solo set *Powerhouse* for the New York label Black Jazz in 1971. Having settled in San Francisco in 1969 he joined Tower of Power in 1973 writing some of their best known instrumentals including "Squib Cakes" and "Walking Up Hip Street". These tracks feature his ecstatic Hammond Organ style perfectly. Since 1988 this Hammond trademark has become his Santana signature while his sweeping synthesiser arrangements have generated memorable duets with Carlos, "Wings Of Grace" and "Blues For Salvador". Today Santana is unimaginable without Chester Thompson who brings the essence of church-gospel-soul organ playing to the group's wide live audience. *Discography: Powerhouse (Black Jazz 1971) Tower Of Power: Tower Of Power (WB 1973), Back To Oakland (WB 1974), Urban Renewal (WB 1974), In The Slot (WB 1975), Live And In Living Colour (WB 1976), Ain't Nothing Stopping Us Now*

(Columbia 1976), We Came To Play (Columbia 1978), Back On The Streets (WB 1979) R.O.A.R: R.O.A.R (Tabu 1985)

Chester Thompson (drummer): One time Weather Report (*Black Market*) and Genesis drummer who joined Santana for the European stadium tour of 1984. His drumming is heard on *Beyond Appearances*.

Russell Tubbs: Sax/flute player who was a member of the Devadip Orchestra in 1978. He toured Europe with Santana that year and appeared on *The Swing Of Delight*. A disciple of Sri Chinmoy, Tubbs also played with Carlos Santana at meditation concerts either in duets or as a part of Sri Chinmoy's Rainbow. He also appeared on *Visions Of The Emerald Beyond*, a 1975 recording by the Mahavishnu Orchestra.

Andy Vargas: Vocalist from Watsonville, California who joined Santana in the autumn of 1999. A young singer-songwriter, he played Mariachi music at an early age with his father Javier Vargas and is due to release a solo album early in the year 2000.

Orestes Vilató: Born Camaguey, Cuba May 12 1944, Vilató is one of the greatest timbaleros since Tito Puente, a true innovator on the instrument. In his distinguished career he has played with José Fajarado, Ray Baretto (*Acid* etc), Johnny Pacheco and the Fania All Stars. Orestes joined Santana in 1980 after leading his own band Los Kimbos and remained until 1987. In that time he introduced a number of Afro-Cuban religious elements into Santana's music and was a magnetic live performer. He was a member of R.O.A.R and later recorded a classic Afro-Cuban session with Carlos "Patato" Valdes and trap drummer Changuito. *Discography: Los Kimbos : Hoy Y Mañana (Cotique 1978) The Big Kimbos with Adalberto Santiago (Cotique 1996) Patato, Changuito Y Orestes : Ritmo Y Candela (Redwood 1995) R.O.A.R: R.O.A.R (Tabu 1985)*

Narada Michael Walden: Drummer/producer who replaced Billy Cobham in the Mahavishnu Orchestra in 1974. A disciple of Sri Chinmoy, Walden developed a close musical friendship with Carlos Santana from 1976-1980, playing with the guitarist at meditation concerts, the piece "Guru's Song" is an example of this work. Walden wrote and played on "Song For Devadip" on *Oneness* and Carlos Santana appeared on two of Narada's albums, *Garden Of Love Light* and *Awakening*. Later, as Walden became better known as a producer, he invited Santana to play on Aretha Franklin's 1985 album *Who's Zoomin' Who?*.

Greg Walker: A native of Los Angeles, Walker was introduced to Santana in 1975 by Ndugu Leon Chancler and went on to become one of the most charismatic and popular of Santana vocalists. His main work with Santana was in the period 1975 to 1978 (with a gap at the time of the *Festivál* LP) but re-emerged in 1983 after Carlos Santana had been lobbied by tennis star John McEnroe to bring back the singer. His second spell ran from 1983 to 1985. His session work includes Herbie Hancock, Jeff Lorber, Ronnie Laws and Kazu Matsui and he has released two solo CDs which are strictly in a soul vein. Greg has latterly been touring with the Fifth Dimension and occasionally joins Santana on stage. *Discography: Love You So Good (Taylor Made 1991), Admiration (Wilma's Son's Music 1997)*

Ricky Wellman: Drummer who toured briefly with Santana in the autumn of 1997 and previously best known for his work with Miles Davis at the time of the *Amandla* LP and *Live In Paris* video. He works full-time in the US military.

Tony Williams: Jazz drummer who was a close musical friend of Carlos Santana who was well aware of Williams' 1960s work with Miles Davis and his own ground breaking

Lifetime group that included John McLaughlin, Jack Bruce and Larry Young. The two finally worked together on *The Swing Of Delight* in 1980 and held a session in 1985 with bass player Pat O'Hearn that resulted in the song "Trane" on *Blues For Salvador*. They appeared together live in a special Japanese session with Herbie Hancock in 1981 and again in 1989 at the San Francisco Bammies. Shortly before Williams' death the two recorded on a Jimi Hendrix tribute *In From the Storm* which gave ample evidence of the extraordinary power of Williams' drumming and the empathy between the two players. He died in 1997.

Larry Young: Jazz organist who played with John McLaughlin in Tony Williams' Lifetime group after a series of impressive solo albums for Blue Note including the classic *Unity*. Carlos Santana was considering offering him a place in Santana 1972 but didn't think the organist would be interested. This was a miscalculation, Young was happy to participate on the *Love, Devotion, Surrender* album and tour in 1973, adding his own tune "I'm Aware Of You" to the tour (he later recorded it on his own LP *Space Ball*). He died in 1978.

Index

Titles available from SAF, Firefly and Helter Skelter Publishing

No More Mr Nice Guy: The Inside Story of The Alice Cooper Group
By Michael Bruce and Billy James (reprint due soon)
The dead babies, the drinking, executions and, of course, the rock 'n' roll.

Procol Harum: Beyond The Pale
by Claes Johansen UK Price £12.99 (available early 2000)
Distinctive, ground breaking and enigmatic British band from the 60s.

An American Band: The Story of Grand Funk Railroad
By Billy James UK Price £12.99
One of the biggest grossing US rock 'n' roll acts of the 70s - selling millions of records and playing sold out arenas the world over. Hype, Politics & rock 'n' roll - unbeatable!

Wish The World Away: Mark Eitzel and American Music Club
by Sean Body UK Price £12.99
Sean Body has written a fascinating biography of Eitzel which portrays an artist tortured by demons, yet redeemed by the aching beauty of his songs.

Ginger Geezer: Vivian Stanshall and the Bonzo Dog Band
by Chris Welch and Lucian Randall UK Price £12.99 (available spring 2000)
Stanshall was one of pop music's true eccentrics. An account of his incredible life from playing pranks with The Who's Keith Moon to depression, alcoholism, & sad demise.

Go Ahead John!: The Music of John McLaughlin
by Paul Stump UK Price £12.99
One of the greatest jazz musicians of all time. Includes his work with Miles Davis, Mahavishnu Orchestra, Shakti. Full of insights into all stages of his career.

Lunar Notes: Zoot Horn Rollo's Captain Beefheart Experience
by Bill Harkleroad and Billy James UK Price £11.95
For the first time we get the insider's story of what it was like to record, play and live with an eccentric genius such as Beefheart, written by Bill Harkleroad - Zoot himself!

Meet The Residents: America's Most Eccentric Band
by Ian Shirley UK Price £11.95
An outsider's view of The Residents' operations, exposing a world where nothing is as it seems. It is a fascinating tale of musical anarchy and cartoon wackiness. Reprinted to coincide with the recent world tour.

Digital Gothic: A Critical Discography of Tangerine Dream
by Paul Stump UK Price £9.95
For the very first time German electronic pioneers, Tangerine Dream mammoth output is placed within an ordered perspective.

The One and Only - Homme Fatale: Peter Perrett & The Only Ones
by Nina Antonia UK Price £11.95
An extraordinary journey through crime, punishment and the decadent times of British punk band leader, Peter Perrett of The Only Ones

Plunderphonics, 'Pataphysics and Pop Mechanics
The Leading Exponents of Musique Actuelle
By Andrew Jones UK Price £12.95
Chris Cutler, Fred Frith, Henry Threadgill, John Oswald, John Zorn, etc.

Kraftwerk: Man, Machine and Music
By Pascal Bussy UK Price £11.95
The full story behind one of the most influential bands in the history of rock.

Wrong Movements: A Robert Wyatt History
by Mike King UK Price £14.95
A journey through Wyatt's 30 year career with Soft Machine, Matching Mole & solo artist.

Wire: Everybody Loves A History
by Kevin Eden UK Price £9.95
One of British punk's most endearing and enduring bands combining Art and Attitude

Tape Delay: A Documentary of Industrial Music
by Charles Neal (out of print)
Marc Almond, Cabaret Voltaire, Nick Cave, Chris & Cosey, Coil, Foetus, Neubauten, Non, The Fall, New Order, Psychic TV, Rollins, Sonic Youth, Swans, Test Dept and many more...

Dark Entries: Bauhaus and Beyond
by Ian Shirley UK Price £11.95
The gothic rise & fall of Bauhaus, Love & Rockets, Tones on Tail, Murphy, J, and Ash solo.

Poison Heart: Surviving The Ramones
by Dee Dee Ramone and Veronica KofmanUK Price £11.95
Dee Dee's crushingly honest account of life as junkie and Ramone. A great rock story!

Minstrels In The Gallery: A History Of Jethro Tull
by David Rees UK Price £12.99
At Last! To coincide with their 30th anniversary, a full history of one of the most popular and inventive bands of the past three decades

DANCEMUSICSEXROMANCE: Prince - The First Decade
by Per Nilsen UK Price £12.99
A portrait of Prince's reign as the most exciting black performer to emerge since James Brown and Jimi Hendrix.

Soul Sacrifice: The Santana Story
by Simon Leng UK Price £12.99
In depth study of seventies Latin guitar legend whose career began at Woodstock through to a 1999 number one US album.

Waiting for the Man: The Story of Drugs and Popular Music
by Harry Shapiro UK Price £12.99
Fully revised edition of the classic story of two intertwining billion dollar industries. "Wise and witty." The Guardian

The Sharper Word: A Mod Reader
Edited by Paolo Hewitt (available November 1999) UK price:£12.99
Hugely readable collection of articles documenting one of the most misunderstood cultural movements

Dylan's Daemon Lover: The Tangled Tale of a 450-Year Old Pop Ballad
by Clinton Heylin UK price £12.00
Written as a detective story, Heylin unearths the mystery of why Dylan knew enough to return "The House Carpenter" to its 16th century source.

Get Back: The Beatles' Let It Be Disaster
by Doug Sulpy & Ray Schweighardt UK price £12.99
No-holds barred account of the power struggles, the bickering, and the bitterness that led to the break-up of the greatest band in the history of rock 'n' roll. "One of the most poignant Beatles books ever." Mojo

XTC: Song Stories - The Exclusive and Authorised Story Behind the Music
by XTC and Neville Farmer UK Price £12.99
 "A cheerful celebration of the minutiae surrounding XTC's music with the band's musical passion intact … high in setting-the-record-straight anecdotes. Superbright, funny, commanding." Mojo

Like The Night: Bob Dylan and the Road to the Manchester Free Trade Hall
by CP Lee UK Price £12.00
In 1966 at the height of Dylan's protest-singing popularity he plugged in an electric guitar to the outrage of folk fans who booed and jeered. Finally, in Manchester, fans branded him Judas. "Essential Reading" Uncut

Born in the USA: Bruce Springsteen and the American Tradition

by Jim Cullen UK Price £9.99

"Cullen has written an excellent treatise expressing exactly how and why Springsteen translated his uneducated hicktown American-ness into music and stories that touched hearts and souls around the world." Q****

Back to the Beach: A Brian Wilson and the Beach Boys Reader

Ed Kingsley Abbott UK Price £12.99

"A detailed study and comprehensive overview of the BBs' lives and music, even including a fore-word from Wilson himself by way of validation. Most impressively, Abbott manages to appeal to both die-hard fans and rather less obsessive newcomers." Time Out   "Rivetting!" **** Q "An essential purchase." Mojo

A Journey Through America with the Rolling Stones

by Robert Greenfield UK Price £12.00

This is the definitive account of their legendary '72 tour.

"Filled with finely-rendered detail ... a fascinating tale of times we shall never see again" Mojo

Bob Dylan

by Anthony Scaduto UK Price £12.99

The first and best biography of Dylan. "The best book ever written on Dylan" Record Collector "Now in a welcome reprint it's a real treat to read the still-classic Bobography". Q*****

MAIL ORDER

All Firefly, SAF and Helter Skelter titles are available by mail order from the world famous Helter Skelter bookshop.

You can either phone or fax your order to Helter Skelter on the following numbers:

Telephone: +44 (0)171 836 1151 or Fax: +44 (0)171 240 9880
Office hours: Mon-Fri 10:00am - 7:00pm, Sat: 10:00am - 6:00pm,
Sun: closed..

Postage prices per book worldwide are as follows:

UK & Channel Islands	£1.50
Europe & Eire (air)	£2.95
USA, Canada (air)	£7.50
Australasia, Far East (air)	£9.00
Overseas (surface)	£2.50

You can also write enclosing a cheque, International Money Order, or registered cash. Please include postage. DO NOT send cash. DO NOT send foreign currency, or cheques drawn on an overseas bank. Send to:

Helter Skelter Bookshop,
4 Denmark Street, London, WC2H 8LL, United Kingdom.
If you are in London come and visit us, and browse the titles in person!!

Email: helter@skelter.demon.co.uk
Website: http://www.skelter.demon.co.uk

For the latest on SAF and Firefly titles check the SAF website:
www.saf.mcmail.com